SELF-MASTERY

Mission and Meaning in Modern Life

RAMON G. CORRALES, Ph.D.

CORPORATE MASTERY USA
9001 W. 110th St., Se. 260, Overland Park, KS 66210
PH: (913) 906-9330 **E-mail:** info@masterycenter.com

2\12

Self-Mastery: Mission and Meaning in Modern Life

Copyright 2000, Ramon G. Corrales, Ph.D.

Book cover and interior design by Tim Lynch

Book publishing services by BookWorks Publishing, Marketing, Consulting

Publisher's Cataloging-in-Publication

Corrales, Ramon Garrido.
    Self-mastery : mission and meaning in modern life / Ramon G. Corrales. – 1st ed.
    p. cm.
    Includes bibliographical references and index.
    LCCN: 99-69651
    ISBN: 0-967-7616-0-3

    Self-actualization (Psychology)
    Self-management (Psychology)   I. Title.

BF637.S4C67 2000   158
        QBI99-1909

*Dedicated to Annabel, my wife, my dearest friend,
and my spiritual partner.*

To our children Rachel Corrales Sands and Anna-Lisa Corrales.

*To Adrian Sands, our son-in-law, and newest family member,
Asli Gulcur, our beloved "adopted daughter" from Turkey.*

Acknowledgments

My special thanks go to Cindy and Bart Hastert, friends who share the vision of self-mastery. My appreciation goes to my colleagues, Larry Ro-Trock, Ray Price, Jay Peters, Karen Harrison Speake, Dick Sanderson, and Chuck Rhodes. Larry and I have worked together for twenty-two years doing co-therapy, training, and seminars. Our relationship has been a quiet bedrock of support both in our professional and personal lives. Ray Price and I met twenty-one years ago to capture the work of Virginia Satir on videotape. His belief in my work has been a steady source of support. My thanks also go to the Rev. Bill Murphy, pastor of Rolling Hills Presbyterian Church in Overland Park, Kansas. Bill has opened the boundaries of his church family to me, allowing me to teach there regularly for years. My thanks too to Pola Firestone and her team of consultants at BookWorks, who have been of great help in giving shape to this book. The gratitude I feel toward my counseling and my corporate clients is unspeakably deep. I also hear the not-too-distant drumbeat of the mentors that guided me in the past—the master theorists and therapists who had the gift of teaching and of touching people's lives in profound ways. Above all, I am grateful for God's presence in my life and for the divine gift of finding meaning in my mission.

Contents

Foreword

And who knows, we might, you and I just might, in the upper reaches of the spectrum of consciousness itself, directly intuit the mind of some eternal Spirit—a Spirit that shines forth in every I and every we and every it, a Spirit of which every conversation is the sincerest worship, a Spirit that speaks with your tongue and looks out from your eyes, that touches with these hands and cries out with this voice—and a Spirit that has always whispered lovingly in our ears: Never forget the Good, and never forget the True, and never forget the Beautiful.

–Ken Wilber[1]

We have now entered the new millennium. We have entered a world in great tension, a world that is full of promise and full of confusion. For these reasons, it is important to have a general framework with which to make sense of life and its great questions. I use Ken Wilber's words as an epigraph to this book because they reveal the essential features of a useful framework for approaching modern life. The maps we use to navigate life need to rest on an idea that unites all of us as bodies, as minds, as individuals, and as nations.

That idea is that Spirit lives in everything and in everyone.

When I look at your eyes, I need to see Spirit looking at me. When I feel love for my wife, it is Spirit loving her through me. If I feel frustrated, Spirit is struggling to express something good, true, and beautiful within me. The energy coursing through the redbud tree outside our house is Spirit-as-redbud-tree, the same energy that runs through me, except at a different level of life and consciousness.

It is this oneness of Spirit immanent and evolving in the universe of matter and mind that is the great idea of our time. Whatever uniqueness we bring to our view of life, that view needs to be embedded in this great idea.

I have chosen *self-mastery* as the unifying concept around which to suggest ways to live our mission and to experience a life with meaning.

I think of self-mastery in process terms: mastering or developing aspects of ourselves individually and in relationships. Self-mastery is a guiding vision, not a finished product. It is grounded in a paradigm of discovering what works in our lives, especially in terms of what is productive and joyful. It is not a control paradigm bent on engineering or predicting outcomes. Life is much too rich and too free to be subjected to such control.

I have focused on mastering thinking, feeling, and willing as these internal aspects of consciousness relate to our personal behavior and relationship patterns (structure). Since we cannot escape the impact of culture, these ideas about personal and relationship effectiveness are described in the context of Western and, specifically, American culture.

This first volume of *The Self-Mastery Series* lays out the beginning framework of self-mastery. Later volumes will address areas such as relationships, personal productivity, family life, organizational synergy, and the spiritual quest. May your own quest be fruitful.

[1] Wilber, K. (1997). *The Eye of Spirit*. Boston: Shambhala Publications, Inc.

Chapter 1
THE CONCEPT OF SELF-MASTERY
For Whom and Why This Book?

FOR WHOM?

In writing this book, I asked myself: To whom am I writing? I'm writing to those who wish to make a significant mark on themselves and on their intimate circle of mates, children, extended family, friends, and associates. I hope to reach those with an open mind and heart who are searching for ways to live their own higher wisdom as they walk their unique path. More personally, I find myself writing to my wife, our daughters, our son-in-law, my friends, my corporate and clinical clients, and those who participate in my retreats, seminars, and groups. I'm writing about *the path of self-mastery*, as I call it.

WHY THIS BOOK?

The main reason for writing this book has to do with my intense desire to live a significant life—a life with meaning. Such a life must be lived with conscious intent. Writing is a way of clarifying ideas beyond simply thinking quietly about them. I also want to share these ideas with others and have them benefit as well. I want to continue testing and refining my thoughts—continuing the inevitable "experiment of life" within myself, in my relationships, and in my world. I invite you to be conscious about this experiment, as the spirit in you seeks happiness and creative expression.

How would I know if these ideas were fruitful?

I would find substantial joy and meaning in my life. I would not always feel pleasant feelings, but I would find ways to learn from all emotions as the language of my soul. I would find ways to move from one peaceful plateau to another, allowing for the turbulence of growth in between. I would live my daily life proactively, not passively or reactively. I would be a knowing navigator in a world of events that I do not control. And I would hold myself responsible only for my response.

That sense of responsibility will crystallize in the conscious commitments that I make. Along the way, I would keep my childlike curiosity, bolstered by reasoned knowledge, inspired by my deeper intuitions, as I face the hand of destiny in the events that come to me.

If these ideas were truly useful, I would also see a positive difference in my wife's inner life, making an impact on what she thinks of herself, our children, her profession, and the nature of her relationship with God. Likewise, I would make a substantial contribution to the lives of our two daughters: their self-esteem, their handling of relationships, the successful pursuit of their mission, and their ability to impact their peers. I would know this by observation and by an ongoing, empathic dialogue with all of them. This requires staying in significant contact with them.

The deepest center of my life would come from a personal relationship with Spirit, both as the God within me and as the Goddess that is manifest in the ecology of matter, mind, and society. I would listen to that God within as I live my mission, producing the fruit of the talent that is uniquely mine. I would become a productive member of my community, bringing forth goods and services that would lift the *kosmos*[1] ever so gently. In that productive interaction with my world, I would gain the economic benefits that I deserve, as a byproduct of that labor of love, and become a wise steward of these material resources.

If the concepts of this book do not help to accomplish at least some of these dreams, then the book would be useless and should never have been written, much less read by anyone. But these dreams are the reason for writing this book.

HOW CAN THIS BOOK HELP?

This is Volume I in the *Self-Mastery Series*. The series will be built upon the principles of self-mastery, which are the ideas I have found useful in personal, relational, organizational, and spiritual development. I have organized these principles around six major categories, which I call the Requirements of Self-Mastery:

1. PERSONAL PURPOSE: We each need a clear purpose for being, along with a clear reason for our goals and actions. Our purpose identifies the guiding reason for being—our personal mission. Purpose brings intentionality to our lives.
2. PERSONAL MANAGEMENT: This is the ability to manage our faculties of thinking, feeling, and willing as we act in the service of our mission. Success in this area will nourish our need to be unique individuals. However, our actions are meaningless without a clear purpose.
3. VIABLE RELATIONSHIPS: It is important to have a core of significant relationships that will nurture our need to belong and our courage to be unique. Present relationships continually mirror our thirst for ultimate union with God, as well our thirst for being known uniquely by God.
4. PERSONAL PRODUCTIVITY: This is the effective use of our talents to create tangible and intangible goods (products and services). Productivity is an important way to express our individuality. It is our way of contributing to our community.
5. ORGANIZATIONAL SYNERGY: We must learn to synergize, which means the capacity to participate with others in

3

a way that brings added value to a working group, so that
1 + 1 = 3. Such teaming may happen at home, at work,
or elsewhere.

6. DYNAMIC SPIRITUALITY: This refers to the fabric of meaning
and identity—who we are and why we are. This includes our
personal relationship with the God of the universe. It brings out
our capacity to acknowledge the spiritual fabric that connects the
entire universe of matter, mind, and soul. Spirituality puts our
personal purpose in the context of universal purpose. A natural
byproduct of this universal view of oneness is compassion: an
outpouring of service to humanity and to ecology.

This book deals mainly with an overview of the self-mastery
approach, with a special focus on the first three requirements: personal
purpose, personal management, and viable relationships. Additional
volumes will give greater attention to relationships, family life, personal
productivity, synergistic organizations, and dynamic spirituality.
Although each volume highlights different aspects of self-mastery,
every book incorporates the principles implied by all six requirements.

This volume presents the vision of self-mastery and provides a
guide for managing our thinking, feeling, and willing faculties effectively,
in order to produce actions that bring forth the highest fulfillment
of our mission.

We will learn to think correctly and usefully, so that the fruit of
our actions will be good. The cornerstone of correct thinking is the
way we view cause and effect in a world of multiple causes. Correct
causal thinking is the rational foundation of our ability to be self-
responsible. It is a necessary ingredient of self-mastery.

With good thinking at our command, we will learn to manage our
feelings without repressing them and without being overwhelmed by
them. There is a way to mine the soul jewels contained in our emo-

tions, including the internal explosions (pleasant and unpleasant) that sometimes drive us, instead of us driving them. These internal grenades are one of the primitive languages of the soul that we must learn to read so that we may mine the jewels revealed by them.

The self-mastery approach maintains that it is important to stay in touch with our feelings, to decode the message they carry, and, passing the scrutiny of our reason and intuition, to act on the message, not on the feelings. It is unwise to act on the feeling itself. This would take us back to the prepersonal[2] stage of our development, before we had full use of our cognitive and intuitive faculties.

In this volume we will also highlight the faculty of *will*, a much-neglected aspect of the mind. It is through the act of will that we make decisions and take positions. We—you and I—come through in the act of will, and, in the process of taking a position, we act in this three-dimensional world. When we take a position, we are making a commitment to do something or to take a stand on something. That is the self-responsible act. The self-mastery approach puts the will back on the psychological map, along with the thinking and the feeling faculties of our mind.

Throughout the book, we will see relationship applications of the self-mastery approach. We need the ability to nurture viable relationships if we are to survive and to thrive as individuals. It is important to be able to see relationship dynamics as patterns (the dance) that transcend the behavior of the individual (the dancer). As we look inside ourselves (the dancers), we will get one view of reality—one "angle of the elephant," so to speak. As we look outside and notice the sequence of behaviors among the players of an interaction (the dance), we will get a totally different view of reality. For the moment, just note that the rules that govern our individual-internal world are different from the rules that govern our external world of action (individual) and interaction (collective).

5

To live our personal purpose we need to express our talents and be productive: to produce goods and services. This is the ability to produce through individual effort. We need to get in touch with our creativity, our values, and the external circumstances that call us to action and interaction. Out of that mysterious mix emerges a sense of our calling, our passion (personal mission), expressed uniquely at various stages of life.

Productivity through individual effort is not sufficient to fulfill our mission. We need to learn to produce synergistically through effort. This is inescapable given that we are essentially social beings. Synergy does not apply only in work settings. Every viable relationship requires synergy, where the combination of 1 + 1 leads to a sum of 3 instead of 2 or less. So, whether we are in the role of co-parent, mate, child, sibling, associate, or member of a team in an organization, we need to learn to synergize. This is one of Stephen Covey's habits of highly effective people.[3]

In looking at the spiritual component of self-mastery, the concept of the Higher Mind or Higher Self will be integrated throughout the book. If your religious path has already sensitized you to the presence of a source of wisdom higher than your rational mind, then this concept will be easy for you to apply to the areas discussed. If not, this idea will be a challenge for you to understand and to integrate. This is partly because Western psychology has few orthodox models of the mind higher than the rational-intuitive level. Carl Jung and Roberto Assagioli are exceptions. Many modern writers[4] are making the Higher Self part of their theoretical framework. This is fortunate because the idea of a Higher Self is a crucial ingredient of self-mastery and of spirituality.

Spirituality takes us to the essence of life. It allows us to put our personal mission in the context of universal purpose. It pushes us to raise questions about who we are and why we are. The highest expression of spirituality helps us to see the interconnected universe of matter, life, mind, and spirit—to grasp the mystical view of oneness. This view transforms our personal passion into universal compassion, which naturally flows as loving service for humanity and for our ecology.

WHY ME?

Everyone needs to ask the question: Why are you the author of this book? In other words, what do you bring to the plate, besides being an adult male on the planet?

This book distills my experience as a therapist, a trainer of therapists, an organizational consultant, and a seminar leader for over twenty-seven years. Since I observe therapists through live supervision from behind a one-way mirror, I have been able to observe the therapeutic relationship. The relationship between therapist and client has been a great laboratory for discovering the principles of self-mastery. I am able to describe the patterns that promote the process of change.

One of my specialties has been marriage and family therapy. My research, training, and experience in this area have led me to formulate the functional patterns that build a strong sense of belonging and individuality in relationships. These experiences have likewise alerted me to the dysfunctional patterns that constrain our freedom and weaken our security in those relationships. I have applied these in my self-mastery retreats and in the seminars I offer on relationships, parenting, personal growth, personal creativity, and organizational synergy (team building).

My other specialty has been personal creativity and team building in the business organization. I have been trained in assessing people's instinctive ways[5] of accomplishing things and in coaching them to maximize performance according to their natural stride. The fields of sociology and systems theory have guided my experience in organizational team building. It is now quite easy for me to spot healthy and unhealthy patterns in work and in relationships. I see many parallels between family and business organizations. Going from one system to the other has brought invaluable insights.

For many years now, I have conducted seminars and retreats focused on self-development, with a spiritual dimension guiding the experience. These have been in church/synagogue and secular settings. I also hold ongoing Quest Groups™ for people interested in developing a spiritually oriented life. We meet for half a day once a month to discuss various aspects of self-mastery and spirituality. We dialogue, enjoy moments of contemplation, and we study sages, saints, and mystics of various traditions. The main focus is to help us along a spiritual path that integrates the personal, relational, and occupational aspects of our lives. These experiences have nurtured and tested my ideas.

My role as husband for over thirty years and my role as a parent of two daughters have been priceless. Those experiences have unquestionably influenced my insights and my recommendations about life and relationship. I continue striving to be my real self as a husband and as a father to our grown children. If I couldn't benefit from my own ideas, then I would have a difficult time believing them or communicating them.

Not to be forgotten are the six and a half years I spent as a monk living in a monastic community and teaching children in Catholic schools in the Orient. Those years gave me an appreciation for the inner life of prayer and meditation. I will always treasure those years as a Christian Brother when destiny allowed me to focus on my spiritual development in a life of study, prayer, and communal support. I am convinced that spirituality is necessary on the path of self-mastery.

The ultimate test of the value of these ideas and techniques is the fruit they bring to those who study and apply them. I invite you to test them in your life and to give me feedback[6] about what is helpful and what is not, about what is clear or confusing, and about what I should include or expand upon in later works.

[1] I wish to acknowledge my debt to the writings of Ken Wilber. I became acquainted with his works as I was editing this book. I decided to examine my ideas in the light of Wilber's integral vision. Here, I am borrowing a word he coined, *kosmos*, which includes matter (cosmos), as well as life (biology) and mind (consciousness). With Wilber, I think it is crucial to include all three dimensions when we speak of the universe. See Wilber, K. (1996). *A Brief History of Everything*. Boston: Shambhala Publications, Inc.

[2] Wilber, K. (1995, 1996) makes a very important distinction among the prepersonal, the personal, and the transpersonal levels of development. We may value the lessons of our early years, but it is wise to avoid a romantic regression to those levels of development. We were more immature then.

[3] Covey, S. (1989). *7 Habits of Highly Effective People*. New York: Simon & Schuster. This book is a great companion along the path of self-mastery.

[4] Among those who have long been articulating the idea of a Higher Self are Joan Borysenko, Deepak Chopra, Wayne Dyer, James Hillman, Dan Millman, Thomas Moore, Michael Murphy, Scott Peck, James Redfield, Ken Wilber, and Marianne Williamson. A host of notable theorists in the field of transpersonal psychology are making great strides in researching and articulating higher states of consciousness. Wilber is clearly a leader in this group. See Rothberg, D. and Kelly, S. (Eds.). (1998). *Ken Wilber in Dialogue*. Wheaton, IL: Quest Books.

[5] I am a Kolbe Consultant™ trained in the use of the Kolbe Concept.™ This is a framework and a technology designed by Kathy Kolbe for assessing a person's instinctive ways of doing things. See Kolbe, K. (1993). *Pure Instinct*. New York: Random House.

[6] Write to The Self-Mastery Center, 8301 State Line, Suite 216, Kansas City, MO 64114, or write via e-mail to mastery123@aol.com.

Chapter 2

THE VISION OF SELF-MASTERY

Pathways to Personal Effectiveness

AN INVITATION

You are invited to live a life of self-mastery. This is a vision—a frame of mind—that is aimed at helping us fulfill our personal mission more fully and more effectively. This framework is designed to respect our beliefs, cultural background, religious traditions, and personal goals. The Self-Mastery Approach (TSMA) emphasizes principles and process. Principles are foundational concepts about life, and process refers to how something is achieved.

It is up to us to utilize these concepts and guidelines to live according to our beliefs and to achieve our personal goals. It is important to honor our beliefs, traditions, and personal experiences. Examine every idea I present in light of your own goals and your own assumptions about life. Where there is an easy fit, you will naturally integrate an idea into your own framework. Where there is an uneasy fit, chew on that idea and test it to see if it bears good fruit in your life. If not, shelve it or discard it.

This is a journey that we must take individually. Yet, we don't need to do it alone. However, this approach requires that we learn to operate our own vehicle along the terrain of this journey. The territories through which we navigate are far more complex than land, sea, or air. Yet, we are given marvelous vehicles, tools, and guidelines to achieve our goals.

We not only have a magnificently responsive physical body, we also have our faculties of thinking, feeling, and willing, which enable us to figure things out, feel our way through, and make decisions that flower into action. In addition, we have a higher mind that is a source of divine inspiration and guidance—if we choose to listen. We are not alone.

SELF-MASTERY IN ACTION: A Brief Example

Marsha is a single parent with two sons ages ten and seven. Two years ago, Frank, her ex-husband, divorced her, following the revelation of an affair he had with Judy, whom he has recently married. Marsha called Frank to tell him that his children were hoping to see him the following weekend and that they were sad about not having had contact with him for over a month. Her manner was friendly and her tone of voice was conversational. Frank hung up the phone after yelling at Marsha, calling her a controlling person who used guilt to manipulate people. She felt hurt and unsettled about this event. (Let us assume that Marsha is a student of self-mastery.)

Marsha goes to her room and sits quietly. Tears flow as she feels the hurt, the frustration, and eventually the anger. She welcomes the feelings in her body and mind, realizing that these are her own emotional responses. She is also aware of the thoughts that are connected to these feelings. She welcomes them as well. She sees these thoughts and feelings as communication from her soul. She becomes aware of her need to be respected and to be treated with dignity and kindness. She affirms those needs as good.

Marsha then communes with the presence of God in her, asking for the strength and the vision to realize that she is indeed worthy of respect and kindness, whether or not she is treated so by others. She affirms to herself and to God that she is secure in her dignity and that her dignity does not depend on the way others treat her. She is aware that she is responsible only for her actions, not for anybody else's actions. Having felt and owned the hurt and anger earlier, she develops a level of compassion for Frank, which helps her to understand how someone might lose his cool. This allows her to forgive Frank but without giving what he did power to derail her from carrying on the tasks of the day.

Marsha decided to leave Frank a voice message, telling him that she did not like the way he talked to her. She also wrote him a note: "I have no right to ask you to change your thoughts and feelings about me, for that would be mind control. I do, however, have a right to ask you to change the way you act toward me. I want to be treated respectfully, even if you do not like me. I know I cannot control you, even if I desired to do so. I can only appeal to your love for the children and to their well-being as reasons for your kindness toward me. This weekend I have made plans, which include the children. As soon as you decide that you want some time with them, just let me know. Rest assured that I will support you in your role as father to them in any way I can."

That evening, when the children found out that their father had still taken no steps to spend time with them, Doug, the older boy, expressed his disappointment and said that he wasn't that interested in seeing his father again. Marsha called him aside and asked:

"What are you feeling?"
"Angry. Dad does not really care about us."
"How would you know if your dad cared about you?"
"He would spend more time with us and call us more often."
"Would you be willing to tell him that?"
"He doesn't listen to me. It's not going to do any good."
"I encourage you to tell him. By the way, I disagree with you. He does care about you."
"But why doesn't he call us more often?"
"I don't know, but I agree that he should see you more often."

"I don't really want to anymore."

"I know you feel that way. When he calls, though, please realize that I will expect you to go."

That slice in Marsha's life is self-mastery in action. She was able to make a clear distinction between the external event and her internal response. She listened to her body and to her emotions by staying in touch with the sensations and the feelings. She welcomed them and then listened to the message from her soul—her need for respect and kindness. She affirmed her soul's need and asked for affirmation from God.

Having done her inner work, Marsha then had a clear course of action in relation to Frank and in relation to her children. She was able to differentiate her own issues from those of her children. In so doing, she was able to listen to her son's concerns without inviting him into a coalition with her against his father. Neither did she fall into the trap of vicariously solving her issues with Frank by asking Doug to do the work for her. For instance, she could have asked Doug to tell his dad that he needed to treat his mother in a nicer way. Doug would then be her mouthpiece. Instead, she was able to listen to Doug, to affirm his thoughts and feelings, and still maintain her leadership as mother.

The process of self-mastery doesn't just happen automatically. It takes practice, prayer, meditation, a frame of mind grounded on self-responsibility, and a vision that sees personal purpose in light of an interconnected universe. Marsha had enough of this vision to manage her thinking, feeling, and willing faculties toward actions that were intended to affect everyone involved in a positive way. Marsha had to get to the point of compassion. By staying in touch with her emotional grenades, she developed enough empathy for Frank's outburst. Marsha knew that she, herself, was capable of such an outburst. Also, by recognizing how her actions toward Frank could affect the children, she was able to act more responsibly. Let us examine those assumptions.

ASSUMPTIONS OF THE SELF-MASTERY APPROACH (TSMA)

TSMA makes certain assumptions that are in line with the perennial wisdom of the ages, many of them are derived from principles found in the world's great religions. Here are some of the assumptions of The Self-Mastery Approach.

The Levels of Mind and Our Ultimate Purpose. As humans, we have a conscious mind and we are free to think, feel, and decide. We also have subconscious and unconscious realms of mind, through which the soul communicates by way of images, urges, and instinctive actions. And we have a Higher Mind that is a source of inspirations, aspirations, ethics, and aesthetics.

During our waking state, we are, of course, aware of being conscious. We think, we feel, and we make decisions. It is important to realize that our conscious mind is at the nexus between the Higher Mind and the lower subconscious and unconscious. The Master-in-Training (MIT) needs to learn to read the unconscious mind effectively as it bubbles through the subconscious mind. This bubbling will manifest as spontaneous thoughts, feelings, and actions. We can regard these as messages from the soul.

Awareness of the "higher unconscious" has remained at best implicit in Western thought, including psychology. For this reason, it is especially important to become a practical believer of a God-within-us, not just of a God-out-there. Self-mastery calls us to master not just our body, our emotions, our intellect, and our will, but also those inner inspirations that expand our sense of self beyond our ego boundaries.

The concept of a Higher Mind is contained in the teaching of most of the world's great religions, especially in their mystical traditions. In the Mosaic tradition, we are told that we are created "in the image and likeness of God." In the Jewish mystic tradition known as Kabbalah, three levels of the soul are described. The highest level is called *Neshamah:* the divine spark or individualized expression of the divine. In Christianity, St. Paul exhorts us to "let that Mind be in you which was also in Christ Jesus." In Hinduism, the Higher Self is called *Atman.* In Buddhism, it is often referred to as *Rigpa.* In Sufism, the mystical track of Islam, when the Self is capitalized, it means the individualized presence of God in the human being. The following three-level schemes of the mind are roughly parallel:

spirit	spiritual	superconscious	self (oversoul)
mind	mental	conscious	self
body	physical-emotional	unconscious	soul (lower)

The most common depiction of this triadic scheme is body, mind, and Spirit. Body is the symbol we use for our physical, sensing, and feeling nature. Mind refers more to the thinking or rational side of us, through which we reason things out. Finally, Spirit points to the Higher Self, the God individualized within us, the divine spark anchored within our heart. Also common is the four-level rendition: physical, emotional, mental, and spiritual. In this latter case, body and emotion are differentiated.

The sages and mystics of all religious traditions tell us that we are on a journey back to our Source: a journey to find oneness or unity with God. This, they tell us, is the ultimate purpose of our lives. Along the way, we have specific tasks to perform. As we express our talents in fulfilling our mission, we grow in our sense of individuality. The development of that unique sense of self is necessary in the process of finding unity with God as we take our place in the divine tapestry.

Ken Wilber, the eminent philosopher-mystic who has studied the sages of East and West, describes our journey as the Atman project: the attempt to find Spirit in ways that prevent it and force substitute gratifications. The deepest level of this thirst for Spirit will be quenched only when we become united with the God within us, that is, when we become one with Spirit or Atman. No substitute will do. That law is written right in our heart, and this reality permeates the entire fabric of our being. This is the center of our lives. No lasting grasp of self-mastery will be ours without integrating this into the core of our vision. I am greatly indebted to Ken Wilber for his courage to put this central idea of life into such beautiful language. Try to feel the pulse behind the following words:

> In fact, all things, we might surmise, intuit to one degree or another that their very Ground is Spirit itself. All things are driven, urged, pushed and pulled to manifest this realization. And yet, prior to that divine awakening, all things seek Spirit in a way that actually prevents the realization ... We seek for Spirit in this or that object, shiny and alluring and full of fame or fortune; but Spirit is not an object, and it cannot be seen or grasped in the world of commodities and commotion.[1]

While we seek, we cannot find and that is because what we are looking for is already there: the Higher Self that is already in us. We simply need to realize it. Yet it is part of the plan, I believe, that along the way we find healthy substitutes: love from those who are significant to us. We seek this from our family, our mates, friends, and work associates. This is not destructive as long as we don't fall into idolatry and make gods out of them. We need to love one another as reminders of the love that is always already there. But we tend to forget. And then pain and dissatisfaction result. Wilber again:

[The] entire structure of the manifest universe is driven by the Atman project, a project that continues until we—you and I—awaken to the Spirit whose substitutes we seek in the world of space and time and grasping and despair. The nightmare of history is the nightmare of the Atman project, the fruitless search in time for that which is finally timeless, a search that inherently generates terror and torment, a self ravaged by repression, paralyzed by guilt, beset with the frost and fever of wretched alienation—a torture that is only undone in the radiant Heart when the great search itself uncoils, when the self-contraction relaxes its attempt to find God, real or substitute: the movement in time is undone by the great Unborn, the great Uncreate, the great Emptiness in the Heart of the Kosmos itself.[2]

Self-mastery requires that we learn to listen to the yearnings of our soul, which is engaged in the project to find God. It is our task to introduce the soul to the spirit within us and to tell our soul that she is loved by God and that she has never really left paradise. This is the essence of the path of self-mastery. Self-mastery, therefore, is best achieved in a life where you, the conscious self, listen to your body-soul, on the one realm, and to the prompting of the God-in-you, on the other. We are mediators of this wedding of the soul to the Self.

We Are Social Beings. We are definitely individuals, but we are also inherently social beings. Our individuality cannot develop outside a social field—a field of relationships. Our sense of self, or *I*, is inseparable from a *You*, an *Us*, and a *Them*. Therefore, in addition to the graceful management of self, self-mastery includes skill in the dance of social interaction. In life, we cannot dance alone. There are patterns in this interactive dance, a choreography that can be broadly mapped out but that cannot be unilaterally controlled by any one dancer.

I cannot overemphasize how important it is to be aware of these patterns of interaction. The dance in our family relationships can nurture our individuality, but it can also gobble it up. Yet, we cannot escape defining our selves in relation to our significant others in the family, among our friends, and our associates. Our parents and our culture live "in our heads." We have a choice about how they live in us, not about whether they do. We are atoms in a molecule of which we are a part. And since we have greater awareness than atoms, we are not just structurally parts of our social molecule, we are also culturally embedded through shared meaning.

The structure of this social dance can only be adequately understood if you account for the culture in which it occurs. Culture provides the "filters" through which we interpret actions and interactions. We have internalized these "filters" (beliefs, values, moral codes) through millions of communication loops between self and other, especially with those who served as survival figures when we were young. There are two major concepts that can guide us: structure and culture.

As an example, being adopted at age two represents a radical structural change: a transfer from one family to another. Yet each society will influence the meaning of this experience according to the cultural interpretation of this event. In some societies, it may be coated with shame and tragedy. In a society with an extended family system, it may be defined as fairly normal, or at least noncatastrophic. The structure and culture of the social group will mediate the impact on the person.

The person who is not skilled in handling these relationship patterns will hit bumps that may throw her off course. For instance, if she grew up in the middle of a parental war, constantly invited to side with one parent against the other, she may have been unable to integrate her feelings of split loyalty. If her parents were unable to help her make sense of her feelings and of her confusion, she may begin to

question her own worth, and, perhaps, the very meaning of life itself.
We need to understand the forest, not just the individual tree of
the self. This means having a working grasp of the structure (interaction patterns) and the cultural filters of our society, religious traditions,
ethnic and national heritage, our neighborhood, and our families.
We will see, hear, and feel these forces in our body, soul, and mind.
Hopefully, we will learn to detect spirit at work in those forces, striving
to raise our awareness to higher expressions of love in action.

Self-Responsibility and Causality. Given that we are individuals
within a group and are significantly influenced by it, how then do
we assign responsibility for our actions? The massacre at Columbine
High School in Littleton, Colorado, offered an interesting view of
the tension between individual and social responsibility. Thirteen
adolescents were killed by two of their fellow students. Do we blame
the shooters, or the parents, or even the society? That this is not a
simple question was reflected in the contradictory commentaries in
the various media.

Living a correct view of cause and effect is a fundamental principle
of self-mastery. It is easy enough to say that I am willing to take
responsibility for my actions. But will I also take responsibility for
the impact of those actions? Should I also be accountable for the
other person's response to the impact of my actions? And who is
responsible for the patterns of interaction that emerge between two
people in a relationship? If one person dominates and the other
passively submits, who, then, is responsible for the development,
maintenance, and potential changes in the relationship?

We cannot progress toward higher levels of self-mastery without
a solid grounding in the principle of self-responsibility and of
co-responsibility. These questions address the fundamental rungs
in the ladder of self-development. We will cover these in the next
two chapters. Make sure you learn them well.

Feeling as Language of the Soul. The Self-Mastery Approach regards feelings as coming from the soul. In this book, we define soul as belonging to the realms of our subconscious and unconscious. This usage is similar to the concept of an "inner child" as representative of the soul. Therefore, spontaneous thoughts, feelings, urges, and instinctive striving are viewed as soul-level messages that we need to stay in touch with. We will devote special attention to feelings because they are primitive and nonlogical. They confound our rational approach to life. However, they also offer an experiential coding of our soul's response to events that destiny sends our way.

Just because emotions come from primitive levels of our self-development does not mean that we should repress or ignore them. Emotional grenades are powerful aspects of our human experience, whether these internal explosions are pleasant or unpleasant. If we repress undesirable feelings or view them negatively, we will suffer an instant disconnect between self and soul. There will be war between your members, sending negative ripples throughout the conscious mind and the unconscious levels of the soul, including the body and its physical functions.

Feelings are best regarded as a "language of the soul." We need to be in touch with our feelings and to listen to their soul messages. We need not be "driven by" our feelings, but rather to be informed by them. So, another principle of self-mastery is expressed as follows: "Feelings are informative, not directive." We do not discard feelings as we include reason and intuition in the growing inner family, called the self.

Wilber says that there is a universal pattern to "transcend and include"[3] as we go from one stage of development to the next. As we transcend one level (e.g., emotional functioning), we include it as we go the next level (e.g., rational functioning). We will utilize this guideline (transcend and include) as we move along the path of self-mastery.

The Will and the Power of Position. When we make a decision through an act of will, we transcend our thoughts and feelings. However, it is important to include them as we allow thoughts and feelings to inform us in the process of decision making. If my daughter asks to spend some time with me, I have the capacity to say "yes" or "no." I may say "yes" even if certain thoughts and feelings pull me toward another priority. When I say "yes," I do not ignore those dissenting thoughts and resistant feelings. I include them in my total awareness.

Transcending thoughts and feelings means that no one thought or feeling drives us to act in a certain way—at least not at the higher evels of self-mastery. In the act of will, the self transcends all thoughts, feelings, and decision-making processes. Ideally, when I say "yes" to my daughter, I bring all parts of me together. That is the congruent self.

We will learn to own that act of will as a sacred moment when we come through, in time and space, to take a position, that flowers into action. TSMA will develop in us the ability to take positions and to act on those positions congruently. A position is a stand in relation to something or someone. True personal power emanates from a clear and congruent position, as you say "yes," "no," "I will," or "I won't." This means that we have taken command of all our parts (body, emotions, thoughts, and inspirations) and mobilized them in support of the direction we have chosen at a point in time.

This is the power of position, which transcends the position of power.

An Interconnected Universe. Taking a clear and congruent position through an act of will is the foundation of love. In the courage to take a position, the true self emerges to encounter another self in genuine interaction. We could say that this is the infrastructure of love.

In order to embody love in our positions, we need to recognize that the universe is one interconnected whole. The universe is truly a system: parts that are interconnected in mutual causal ways. This is the mystic's view of the kosmos[4] (the universe of matter, mind, and spirit). Because the kosmos is a system of parts mutually (circularly) affecting each other, whatever we do at any level of our being (thinking, feeling, willing, or acting) will reverberate throughout the kosmos.

Every action is like a pebble thrown into the universal pond. The ripples will radiate in all directions—and back. It is crucial to grasp the idea that causality is circular (two-way), not linear or one-directional. Cause and effect are interchangeable: effect becomes cause and affects the original event. This is the meaning of the biblical saying: "What you sow, you shall reap." TSMA shows us how to absorb this principle of Kosmic Interconnection into every layer of our mind: from superconscious to conscious to subconscious to unconscious.

The self is like a little universe. Congruence within the self means that all parts and levels of the self are working together in the service of our personal purpose. Body, mind, and spirit are working together to fulfill our personal mission. Our spirit, made in the image and likeness of God, comes through the body-mind in order to contribute its individuality to the kosmos.

Congruence with the universe means that we are able to express our individuality as parts of the kosmos of matter, life, and mind—all manifestations of Spirit. This view of the interconnected universe pushes us to expand our identity to include all of creation—to love all life because we are part of it. Self-mastery calls us to transcend (but include) our ego and to embrace one and all. This is the basis of love.

SUFFERING AND THE FALSE SELF

If God is the source and end of our journey, then any attachment that does not enhance our mission and connection with God will somehow manifest an incongruity in our being. You could say that there will be an "error message" at some level of being: physical, emotional, mental, spiritual, or relational. The message itself is friendly, even if the medium is painful. This is the basis of suffering.

The spiritual giants of the past, the saints and mystics of all traditions, tell us in their lives and writings that suffering is universally present on the path of wholeness, or holiness. In some traditions, a number of mystics even went out of their way to heap suffering on themselves. This was known as the ascetic path to holiness. The intent behind that practice was holy. However, it was accompanied by an erroneous duality that separated God from creation, viewing God as good and matter as bad. In any case, looking for suffering is unnecessary. It will naturally descend upon us, without effort.

This is not to convey a pessimistic view of the world. In fact, it is important to see creation as the manifestation of the Creator. Furthermore, we are built to love and, therefore, to experience joy, peace, and productivity.

The reason that suffering comes our way is due to our illusions and attachments. If we live in a power-based world, we live in the illusion that we are alone and that life is meaningless. We, then, operate in either helpless or controlling ways. In either mode, our hope comes from the outside: we seek a benign dictator (parent, spouse, pastor, friend, or boss) who will love us. Or we become the dictator, in order to control our world in a way that will fill our need to belong and to be. To operate this way, we have to build a false sense of self—a false ego.

It is important to know how this false self came to be.

How this false self develops is no mystery. However, few of us want to face this reality because we may have to question our image of self. What is mysterious about the false self is the way the mind maintains this image of the self. This image becomes a "personality within us" that takes on an almost separate being—another self. As infants, we groped for a sense of belonging and love. We did this while trying to discover who we are and what our talents are. Adults inevitably curtailed our explorations, since some of our actions were dangerous or inappropriate.

The grenades of rejection led some of us to placate and overadapt to our environment. We became the white knights of our families. Some of us fought back with aggression in an effort to define our uniqueness and early attempts at independence. We became the black sheep. In order to survive as placators or aggressors, we had to adopt certain images of self to fit our behavior and our perception of self and the world. We became outer-directed in our functioning in order to survive with some level of meaning and belonging.

We lost our innocence and, with it, the accompanying trust in the world around us. We grew up, at least in age, if not always in wisdom and inner stature, with a screen around us—a projected screen of the desired self-image.

This screen is the false ego. Carl Jung called it a kind of *persona*— a subpersonality that dominates the personality. In addition, aspects of the self that we learned to detest and to be ashamed of, we repressed, hid, and eventually split off into the underworld of the unconscious. These discarded aspects of the self became, in Jung's language, the shadow self. The shadow is part of our growing self, which we deny and, in doing so, create a war or duality within our very being. There is a part of us that does not belong. Signs of incongruity will likely emerge as symptoms. These symptoms are the mouthpieces of these alienated parts crying for union with the self.

Both persona and shadow become incorporated into this false image. This false self is equipped with its own set of assumptions about life. The false ego becomes an imposter of the real self. The two paradigms of the self compete for leadership in our life, each attempting to take over the reigns of the will using our natural energy to accomplish their ends.

While it is in charge, the false ego draws energy away from the real self. Through the years, it gains an aura of independence and autonomy within our organism. In fact, we get attached to this image. The experiences of emptiness tend to strip these attachments. As the false ego gets shaken, we experience a fear of losing a grip on ourselves, wondering if there will be any self left. We may clutch for dear life.

Events in our life will continually challenge the assumptions of our position: power-based or love-based. We may choose to see these events as random, without rhyme, reason, or interconnection. This view will throw us into a power-based position. If we choose to see life's events as operating within a pattern of universal laws and principles, we will see the hand of destiny in the pattern that connects everything in the kosmos. Reliance on outside events for the quality of our self-esteem will inevitably lead to suffering, since we do not control those events.

Our experience of life will eventually tear down those power-based perceptions and attachments. Examine the tenets and stories of your faith tradition, and you will see these principles taught in different ways and in various metaphors.

Spiritually oriented psychological paradigms sometimes touch on this reality. Wayne Dyer's book,[5] *Your Sacred Self*, offers many useful ideas about detecting and dealing with the false ego. Dyer points to seven characteristics of the false self. It is *false*, teaches *separateness*, convinces you of your *specialness* or superiority, and is always ready *to be offended*. It is *cowardly*, thrives on *consumption*, and is *insane*. Dyer's book is well worth reading.

*All human violence is a reflection of the
belief in our separateness.*[6]

EMPTINESS: Doorway to the Real Self. The stripping of the
ego through the feeling of emptiness is part of the way we experience
life. Maturing is a gradual, developmental process that goes through
various stages. We start in a state of utter dependence and hope to
achieve a state of interdependence, in which we are able to be an
individual in a state of belonging.

Although our goal is union with God, we cannot achieve this state
outside our circle of intimate relationships. This is the paradox we
spoke about earlier. We are social beings and will need to love and be
loved as we pursue our personal mission. In the process of achieving
interdependence, we will hopefully become loving, self-actualized
beings who are joyful and productive. Along the way suffering is
inevitable. If we are to achieve self-actualization, the false ego must
be transcended and reintegrated. Only then can the real self emerge
in integrity and in union with God.

In 1976, Tom Fogarty, a family psychiatrist, wrote an article "On
Emptiness and Closeness,"[7] which articulates the role of emptiness in
a profound manner. I first read the article about twenty years ago. I
reread it recently as I was completing this book and found that I have
a much more profound appreciation today for what he wrote.

Fogarty talks about the importance of going into a "voluntary
depression," much like diving into your grenades to find the jewels of
the soul. Few people do this voluntarily the first time around, because
it is quite painful. Most of us have to be forced into a depression
through the loss of someone or something precious to us.

If you can learn to survive the pain of emptiness, you become
stronger and more confident about your ability to plunge into it
voluntarily. Change demands this plunge into discomfort. According

to Fogarty, it is the only way to avoid running from feelings. I agree. The mystical literature would agree with him as well. St. John of the Cross is not alone in talking about the dark night of the soul. He certainly would agree.

"Symptoms," Fogarty writes, "come from attempts to avoid being in this feeling state ... After the initial experience of emptiness forced on us by events, *periods of emptiness should be planned for oneself whenever and wherever there is an emotional problem that one is involved in* (italics mine)." If we avoid (repress) these painful feelings, we will be adding to the shadow self, instead of integrating those rejected aspects. We need to retrieve those parts of our soul. Staying in touch with our suffering is one road toward this goal.

Here is Fogarty's take on the false ego:

> Emptiness has a great deal to do with fracturing the image that people put between themselves and the world. This image is a partial, screened projection and is used to hide behind and protect oneself from emotional injury. Once the image becomes consistent, a gap results between what one is and what one purports to be. The emphasis then is on perpetuating the image and protecting real self. In effect, the emphasis is not on self. It is on what one would like to be and what others will think of me ... Getting into emptiness forces a person to get something from himself and to get less from the outside.[8]

These are wise and profound words. Fogarty goes on to say that by going into our emptiness, we can get behind the anger, the hurt, the bitterness (behind the grenades). If they remain untapped for the learning behind them, these feelings turn people off and sour relationships. By allowing these feelings to inform us, we experience a vulnerability that increases the muscles of the self and lets others be more available to us.

There is a bright side to this. On the other side of emptiness is the realization that we do not have to "fake it" or hide our true self, especially from ourselves. This realization emerges from the belief that our being rests on divine mind, a God who knows us through and through. There is no need to hide, only to discover who we are.

The only way I know to get there is through a love-based world view. This is the view of the mystics who were able to see the inter-connectivity of the kosmos. They believed that they were always in the presence of a God who is personally aware of all and in all. This is the framework of self-mastery.

WHAT IS SELF-MASTERY?

When body, mind, and spirit are aligned and working together in the service of our personal purpose, we are on the path of self-mastery. Therefore, we can say that self-mastery is a path of spirituality that aims to bring congruence to our thinking, feeling, willing, and doing, as we pursue our personal mission on the journey back to God.

Self-mastery cannot be ours unless we face the ultimate questions: Who am I? What is my purpose for being? How do I go about fulfilling this purpose? Unless we have clear answers to these questions, we will, as Wilber says of the Atman project, use our talents to seek substitute goals and gratifications. We will be like a well-equipped ship with a rudder, but without a map or a destination.

And remember, in this age of scientific expansion, we have accumulated enormous amounts of knowledge and technological resources. We can get nowhere much faster. Our toys are more varied and more sophisticated. We have an endless capacity to do things without knowing why. The path of self-mastery does not spurn these advances in knowledge and science, for these are also footprints of Spirit at work in us as individuals and as groups. But self-mastery helps us to put all of this in perspective under the umbrella of personal and universal purpose.

28

Mastering a field of knowledge or a skill is not the equivalent of self-mastery. Using a talent is an ingredient of self-mastery, but it does not constitute its essential state. It is important to be in touch with our native talents because they reveal innate qualities of our soul. These talents are expressions of our soul's code, to borrow a phrase from James Hillman.[9] I see them as jewels of our soul. Unique capacities innate to our soul, these talents reveal our natural creative modes[10] of action.

In addition to using them for creative action, these talents can become windows to our personal mission in life. If we believe that each soul has a calling, then it stands to reason that the natural talents of a soul are given to effectively achieve that particular calling. It is important to become familiar with our soul jewels. These jewels are revealed in our responses to events that come our way.

Although we do not control the events we face, we are in charge of the way we respond to them. Our responses, on the other hand, may be congruent or incongruent. Congruent responses give us a sense of harmony and happiness—they indicate responses that affirm our soul qualities. Incongruent responses bring an experience of grinding and suffering. They indicate responses that negate or violate some soul qualities. And as we just saw, suffering can lead us to the shadow aspects of the self that we repressed and that we need to recover and integrate into our real self. This is part of the path of self-mastery.

SO, WHO ARE WE?

Simply put, we are extensions of divine mind—emanations from the essence of God. We are individualized sparks of light (spirit) that descend into the matter spheres as souls, with a mission to embody God on earth. Any psychology that does not include this spiritual dimension of the self lacks the most important ingredient for understanding our nature and what drives us from the deepest part of our being.

29

Self-mastery gently urges us to accept that our main drive in life is twofold: (1) we are on our way home—on a journey toward discovering our oneness with God, and (2) we are driven to fulfill our unique purpose in a way that lifts all humanity and our ecology. Any science, art, or religion that is blind to the action of Spirit in nature and in society will fall short of leading us to our highest potential individually and collectively.[11]

The path of self-mastery implies that we know who we are, what we are about, and that we are using our talents to fulfill our individual purpose as parts of kosmos.

IN A NUTSHELL, WHAT AM I SAYING?

To live a significant life, one with meaning and productivity, we need to master the internal and external aspects of the self, as well as the individual and collective dimensions of our lives. The Self-Mastery Approach helps us to do this by addressing the following areas:

- **Vision and purpose.** We need a clear vision of our personal purpose: to know who and why we are. This vision needs to define our identity at all levels of our being—body, mind, and spirit—and to locate our place in the kosmos.

- **Thinking correctly about cause and effect.** We need an effective way to think correctly about the true nature of cause and effect. This is the conceptual foundation of the principle of self-responsibility. At the relational level (the collective aspect of life), we will find ways to think correctly about co-responsibility (joint responsibility). Who, for instance, is responsible for a dominant-submissive pattern in a relationship? We need to read the pattern, assume responsibility for our part, and then act accordingly to rectify it.

- **Managing our feelings.** Feelings are a language of the soul. Like thoughts, they are informative, not directive. We need to decode feelings and find the jewels (qualities) of our soul. We will learn to mine the jewels in our emotional grenades and integrate them with our thinking and willing faculties in order to act wisely.

- **Harnessing our will.** Informed by our thoughts and feelings (not driven by them), we will learn to take a stand through an act of will. A stand is an intentional position through which the self comes through in the act of will. Taking a position is the pinnacle of self-responsibility and of morality.

- **Nurturing significant relationships.** The capacity to love and to be ourselves with our family, mate, friends, and associates is necessary along the path of self-mastery. We need at least a core of viable relationships in order to make it through the initial stages of our self-development. In the later stages of self-development, we need these relationships less, but, paradoxically, we will have a greater capacity for intimacy.

- **Productivity and synergy.** To fulfill our mission, we need to use our talents in productive ways. If we don't use our talents productively, we will be restless and unfulfilled. Since we are social beings, we also need to learn to produce in synergistic ways: in combination with other people's talents so that $2 + 2 = 5$. This is part of self-mastery. Synergy is that mysterious added value that comes from working with others in various roles: spouse, parent, supervisor, associate, or friend.

- **Spirituality and the Higher Self.** Spirituality means that you see the Spirit or essential reality of everything. Everything comes from Spirit and everything is growing toward higher expressions of Spirit. We have a Higher Self, which is Spirit residing in us. We need to learn to bring down the wisdom of our Higher Mind, which is the source of our higher inspirations, aspirations, ethics, and aesthetics. Since we all share the same essential nature, we are all one. This is the basis of all morality and the foundation of love—essentials along the path of self-mastery.

[1] Wilber, K. (1980, 1996). *The Atman Project*. Wheaton, IL: Quest Books. This quote is from the preface to the new edition.

[2] Ibid.

[3] Wilber, K. (1996). *A Brief History of Everything*. Boston: Shambhala Publications, Inc.

[4] Remember Wilber's use of *kosmos* includes not just matter, but also life and mind. See note 1, Ch. 1.

[5] Dyer, W. (1995). *Your Sacred Self*. New York: Harper Collins.

[6] Ibid., p. 172.

[7] Fogarty, T. (1976). "On Emptiness and Closeness," *The Family*, 3 (1).

[8] Ibid., pp. 76-77.

[9] See Hillman, J. (1996). *The Soul's Code*. New York: Random House.

[10] See Kolbe, K. (1993). *Pure Instinct*. New York: Random House. In this book, Kathy Kolbe lays out a model for understanding and harnessing our natural creativity, which she believes is characterized by instinctive action triggered by the will, fueled by emotion, and moderated by reason.

[11] The student of self-mastery will benefit from a careful reading of Wilber's argument that separating Spirit from nature and society diminishes the quality of our ecology and of our social life. See Wilber, K. (1995). *Sex, Ecology, Spirituality: The Spirit of Evolution*. Boston: Shambhala Publications, Inc.

Chapter 3

THE PEBBLE-RIPPLE CONNECTION

Thinking Correctly About
Self-Responsibility

EVENTS AND RESPONSES

One day, I was shoveling the snow from our driveway, eagerly
loosening the ice so the shining sun could dry up the cement surface.
I was looking forward to a game of basketball a few hours later. The
snow on the grass was not a problem to me. In fact, as it was slowly
melting, the snow was gradually releasing moisture into the soil, allowing for gentle watering to take place. The temperature at the moment
was in the low 30s. And though I felt grateful for the action of the
snow, the ice on the driveway was making me work harder than I
wanted.

The ice had formed on places where our cars had traveled and in
spots where we had walked. As I shoveled the snow from the driveway to the grassy areas of the yard, I felt like I was almost dancing
with the snow. The snow seemed to be saying: "If you step on me, I
will turn to ice. If you dance gracefully with me, I will gently moisten
your plants and your trees. Let the sun do the rest."

Feeling this connection with the snow, the sun, and the trees, I
realized that I had something to do with the hardness of the ice and
the extra work that it required. Earlier, I had driven over the snow
and had stepped on it—and the snow did its thing: it acted according
to its nature. I simply got the natural consequences: snow turning
into ice and sticking to the driveway. The consequences came not
because I was mean-spirited about trampling over it. It was simply

the law of nature. I had an impact on the snow, and as the snow responded according to its nature it, too, had an impact on me. The dance had started. The connection with nature put me in a pensive mood.

A few minutes later, a car stopped at the front of the driveway and I saw the driver waving at me. I approached and recognized the man as one of my counseling clients. I had just started to work with him and his wife on a marital issue. We exchanged pleasantries about the improbability of meeting each other this way since he lived on the other side of town. Two minutes later, he was gone. I thought about the pain this man's wife felt in response to his actions. She was devastated when she discovered that he had paid a woman for a sexual favor.

They both decided to stay together and to heal their wounds. Young children were involved. With honesty, a strong commitment, and a lot of pain, they were enduring the crisis surprisingly well. The more I shoveled, the more I began to sympathize with her, wondering about her wounded heart. I thought: "Poor thing. How will she ever get over this?" Then I heard a voice within me saying: "Your limitations, no matter how understandable, are limitations nevertheless. Events, no matter how terrible, are just events. Only your response will build or destroy you."

I intuitively felt the significance of these words. We are sometimes blessed with the gift of hearing "the still, small voice inside." Shovel in hand, I ran through the garage, opened the door, and asked my daughter to write down the words of that message exactly as I heard them. I then continued to reflect on the voice.

OF EVENTS, RESPONSES, AND LIMITATIONS
Your limitations, no matter how understandable,
are limitations nevertheless.
Events, no matter how terrible, are just events.
Only your RESPONSE will build or destroy you.

The event in this woman's life seemed so tragic and unfair to her that it would be understandable for her to grieve and feel forever wounded. Friends and family members could lovingly support her in believing that she was forever victimized and would never recover from it. I, myself, was beginning to feel these feelings and to think about her as a helpless victim, when the voice awakened me.

OUR RESPONSE IS THE KEY
Terrible events deliver a subtle impact: the more terrible the event, the easier it is for us to put on the mind of the victim. We get engrossed with the power of the event. With ordinary events, it is easier to keep focused on our response, instead of the event.

If a motorist honks and yells at me for my driving, I could say: "Well, it's just one of those things; no need to get upset." I can more easily keep the focus on empowering myself in a run-of-the-mill event, rather than on the power of the event itself. But if I am robbed, raped, or assaulted, I would find it more compelling to focus on the victimizing nature of the event. I might more easily forget that the most important factor is my response.

A three-year-old who is molested by her father for ten years clearly fits our category of someone who has experienced a terrible event. She has been victimized and the difficulty of her recovery is easily understood. But even in this emotionally violent situation, *the event is still an event.* It is her response to this tragedy that matters the most. If she is unable, later on, to develop normal relationships with other adults, this is still a limitation—understandable as this may be.

A good explanation for why one responds negatively does not remove the limitation that comes with that response. If my mother deserted me when I was young and I developed an intense fear of abandonment, that fear may be understandable. But if that fear continues to limit my ability to sustain a relationship with a female, that inability is a limitation nevertheless—no matter how explainable. I'd still be the one saddled with that limitation, even if I am not responsible for the event that triggered my response.

Regardless of the source of a limitation, it is a limitation nevertheless.

EXPLANATION AND RESPONSIBILITY

A good explanation for why one responds negatively does not remove the limitation that comes with that response. It may help to understand my situation. I am the one saddled with that limitation, even if I am not responsible for the event that triggered my response. However, I am still responsible for my response to that event. A limitation is a limitation—no matter how explainable.

Distinguishing between event and response has an optimistic side to it. If our response is the key, then we (you and I) hold the key, not anyone or anything outside us. Part of the key is to understand that our internal universe has its own rules. The outside world is not the only universe. We are ultimately the masters of our ship. *We need not carry the identity of victim, even when victimized.* This is true even though we do not unilaterally control the outside world.

OUR RESPONSE IS THE KEY

If our response is the key, then we hold the key. We need not carry the identity of victim, even when victimized. Part of the key is to understand that our internal universe has its own rules. This is true even though we do not control the outside world.

INSIDE AND OUTSIDE: The Pebble and the Ripple

Let us imagine that we are standing near a pond on a beautiful, sunny day, looking at its calm surface. Quietly, I pick up a pebble and throw it into the middle of the pond. We observe the ripples radiating out in all directions.

Let us use this metaphor to capture the relationship between the outside world and our inside world. This is a useful distinction that many philosophers make: the difference between the objective world outside and our subjective world inside (Wilber, 1996).[1] The pebble represents the world of events outside. The pond represents you and me and any form of sentient life—any being able to respond with some level of awareness. The ripple will represent our internal response.

Our actions (words or gestures) become pebbles that we throw into other ponds in our environment. Events that come to us from the outside are pebbles. Our internal responses in the form of thoughts, feelings, and decisions are the ripples we experience.

To get an early hint about the practical implications of making this distinction, let us ask the following questions: Who or what causes the ripples in the pond? If something happens that hurts us, who or what causes the hurt? In other words, who's responsible for a feeling? Our answers will reveal our ideas about cause and effect. And those ideas will have a significant impact upon our level of self-mastery.

So, let us cinch this distinction between pebble and ripple. Without a clear understanding of the difference, we cannot adequately grasp the concept of self-responsibility. Nor will we understand the true nature of cause and effect.

Pebble: The outside world of facts and events that touch us. These are the external triggers that "hit" the external surface of our pond (the self in the world).

Ripple: Our inside world of responses: our experience in the form of internal images, sounds, concepts, feelings, and decisions, whether conscious or unconscious.

Our actions are external manifestations of our internal ripples. Actions join the world of pebbles: they become events that touch other sentient beings. Our actions emerge from our internal world and ripple out into the outside world. Let us remember that these two worlds—outside and inside—although interconnected, operate differently. More on this later.

PEBBLES: The Hand of "Destiny"

As students of self-mastery, we will do well to see events (pebbles) as the fingerprints of destiny. Let us use the word *destiny* quite simply: as the facts/events that come to us. These are the pebbles that touch us. We do not control events. Let us view them as pebbles allowed by God, the "divine director," to occur and to impact us according to the laws of the universe. This is a spiritual view, which presupposes that everything in the universe is grounded in Spirit and governed by principles inherent in the kosmos itself.

The alternative view is rather stark: a spiritually gutted universe that operates through Darwinian billiard balls accidentally impacting each other. But even in this sad view, we do not control the events that come to us. Our response is still the key. Incidentally, neither view (the spiritual or the gutted universe) can easily be empirically verified. So, if empirical science is our only standard for truth, then we can take our pick: either view will do.

But if we want to make an educated guess about which view fits the facts of the universe better, we could make a strong case for the spiritual view. When it comes to seeing the deeper realities, the empirical view is quite insufficient. We need the eye of contemplation[2] in order to detect the patterns in the higher levels of reality.

In any case, it is more useful to see every event in our lives as meant for us—as something for us to handle. *There are no accidents in a spiritually infused universe.* This holds true even if we ascertain that some events come from evil hands or hearts. The Irish saying "God writes straight with crooked lines" holds an important assumption: that cosmic laws operate in everything—even within negative energies.

To paraphrase Ken Wilber, the outside world is the world of things: the world of simple location that can be measured in some empirical way. The kosmos, however, is a manifestation of spirit as matter, as life, as mind, as soul, and, eventually, as spirit itself.[3] So inside each of us, we find our share of consciousness or awareness. This inside world has no simple location and cannot, therefore, be smelled, tasted, seen, heard, or touched. It is a world known only through our awareness and shared only through dialogue.

EVENTS ARE MEANT FOR US TO HANDLE
Let us be willing to see every event in our lives as meant for us—as something for us to handle. There are no true coincidences.

We are masters of our ship. But our ship will find itself in circumstances not in our direct control: waters, winds, land masses, and living beings. This is the environment of the soul. This is the context or the external system in which we are born and through which we navigate the various stages of our lives. This includes the family, the culture, the nation, the political, and the socioeconomic structure in which the soul is embedded. It is helpful to see God's hand in the web of destiny—the matrix of events we face.

To navigate these territories skillfully, we need to have a clear sense of the principles that govern our dance with destiny. Destiny presents us with the events. Our gift to destiny is our response. We are influenced by destiny, at times even hounded by its persistent pursuit to draw the best out of us. All this, so we may fulfill our calling. Yet, *we are not determined by destiny*. We have a part in influencing the course of destiny. This we do through our responses. We are part of the web of destiny.

OUR DANCE WITH DESTINY

Destiny presents us with the events. Our gift to destiny is our response.
Through our response, we influence the course of destiny itself.
This is our dance with destiny.

This brings us to the question of causality. What is our part in this dance?

OF PEBBLES AND RIPPLES: The Principle of Self-Responsibility

To be on the path of self-mastery, we will need to pay close attention to the idea of causality. If we miss even the subtlest nuances of this concept, we may end up with erroneous views of self-responsibility. We cannot afford this: the principle of self-responsibility is the foundation of self-mastery. At the end of the day, our sense of peace will rest on our sense of self-responsibility. At the end of our life, our sense of wholeness (holiness) will depend on our self-mastery. At the core of self-mastery is the ability take full responsibility for our body, mind, and spirit. Let us study this important subject.

THE METAPHOR: The Pebble and the Pond

Imagine again that we are standing in front of a beautiful pond surrounded by palm trees on a calm, sunny day. We contemplate the shiny surface that mirrors the sky and the trees. I bend down and pick up a smooth, colorful pebble, and throw it into the middle of the pond. As the pebble hits the surface, there's a splash followed by rhythmic ripples radiating out in all directions. As we all watch, I say: "With the help of a tiny pebble, I caused those ripples." Let us keep this event vividly etched in our minds: the pond has many insights to offer us regarding cause and effect.

As we reflect on this event, our senses invite us to believe that I "caused" the ripples. There were no ripples before I threw the pebble. After I threw it, ripples appeared. So, is there anything illogical about concluding that I caused the ripples? According to the prevailing view of physical science (based on Newtonian physics), we would be correct. I, in effect, was the agent that acted upon the water, which was the "passive" receiver of my action. This prevailing view assumes that I caused the water to ripple: it had no choice. I, the pebble-thrower, controlled the situation unilaterally. The water was a passive participant.

However, it is not as simple as it looks. If I were standing on our kitchen floor, which is made of hardwood, and I threw a pebble in the middle of that floor, there would be no ripples visible to the naked eye. Why not? Simple. There is no water. There is no ripple without water, is there? Ripple (response) is in the nature of water (responder), not in the nature of pebble (outside event). This is an especially important point to understand: the outside trigger (the pebble) does not determine our response. Our response is a comment on us—on who we are, not on the nature of the pebble or pebble-thrower. Let us go further on this point.

CAUSE-AS-TRIGGER AND CAUSE-AS-CREATOR

THE DIFFRENCE BETWEEN TRIGGERING AND CREATING

*The ripple is in the nature of water and not in the nature of pebble or pebble-thrower. It is more accurate to see the pebble as a **trigger** rather than the **creator** of the ripples. It is the pond that offers the ripple according to its nature. This view allows the water to be an important participant in this dance, not just a passive receiver of "outside forces."*

The pebble only triggers the response. It does not create it. The ripple is the offering of water—the response of the pond when an object perturbs it. The response (ripple) tells us more about the responder (pond) than about the event (pebble). Let us see how this works in human interaction, when meaning and behavior form an inseparable partnership. Let us keep in mind that meaning is internal and behavior is external.

If I yell (pebble) at my wife and she feels angry (ripple), who caused the anger? This is a significant question. It would sound self-serving for me to say that I only threw the pebble and she "offered the ripples according to her nature." As cold as that sounds, it would be true nevertheless. To hold me responsible for her feelings would open up a Pandora's box of endless arguments. I could, for instance, point to something she did earlier that "made me angry" and "caused me to yell at her" in the first place. She could, in turn, "explain" what she

42

did on the basis of something I said prior to what she did. This could generate an endless cycle of passing the buck, with no one taking responsibility. I think this is all very familiar to most of us.

The path of self-mastery requires that I take responsibility for my yelling and not blame it on something my wife did or said prior to that. That was *my* pebble and *I* threw it. I must also take responsibility for dealing with the consequences of my action. Ideally, I will be there to dialogue, negotiate, and collaborate with her on the resolution of this event. I am part of that process. I need to take responsibility for throwing the best pebbles into the pond of life.

But if I conclude that I "made her feel bad" or that I "made her yell at me," I will begin to see her as powerless and as one who is subject to my control. I will start to see her as a person without choice—as a victim. There is no way around this. Given this frame of mind, I will also assume either a guilty or an all-powerful position. If I can "make her feel bad," then why couldn't I "make her feel good" if I choose to do so? That is the danger of thinking cause-as-creator, which is a deterministic, linear view of causality. Let us be alert to this pattern.

WE DO NOT HAVE TO BUY ANOTHER'S CONCLUSIONS ABOUT US

My wife does not have to buy my conclusions about her. She can view herself with her own lenses. But my conclusions about her will influence the way I treat her, just as her conclusions about me or about herself will influence her response.

There is a difference between cause-as-trigger and cause-as-creator. Cause-as-creator adopts a linear view of causality: A, the cause, "creates" the effect in B, who is viewed as making no contribution to the process. This view gives all the power to A and renders B totally passive and "determined by" A. Let us say your friend tells you that you don't really care much for her because you are clueless about her needs, and that she feels hurt. In this situation, you are A, and she is B. She is saying that you "made her" feel bad—you caused her feelings. If you buy her interpretation, then you have bought the view that you have unilateral power in the relationship. Unilateral means one-sided, implying that the other person has no part in a transaction.

This is a fascinating example because, at one level, your friend is saying she is helpless. But at another level, she is defining (for you) the meaning of the interaction. Defining meaning is a powerful function in a relationship. At this level, she is A (unconsciously) and you are B. The key is to be conscious about this process and empower ourselves to *parti*cipate (take part) in the dynamic flow of *inter*action. This allows us to take responsibility for our contribution to the give-and-take in a relationship. If you retreat from the relationship and hold your friend totally responsible for your action, you would be making the same error in thinking.

There is an interesting story about the young Carl Jung and his father, Paul Jung, who was pastor of a Christian church. Paul had apparently lost his religious convictions early in his pastoral work, yet felt compelled to continue tending to his flock for lack of real options. Carl, on the other hand, felt a spiritual connection with God on the basis of his own experiences. One biographer described their interaction on this matter:

... Whenever Carl tackled him with religious questions the pastor became irritable and defensive: 'You always want to *think*,' he complained. 'One ought not to think, but to *believe*.' The boy reflected inwardly, 'No, one must experience and *know*!' But aloud he said, 'Give me this belief.' Whereupon his father merely shrugged and turned away.⁴

Carl refused to accept his father's negative interpretation of his capacity to think for himself about religious matters. Carl took responsibility for his own thinking and did not let his father determine his reality. I'm sure this contributed to his sanity, despite challenging his father in a somewhat rebellious manner.

The cause-as-creator framework further assumes that the environment is not involved in the matter. In this linear view, the main determinant in the transaction is A's action, and nothing else. It is a purely personal interpretation of cause and effect. The context does not enter into the equation at all. Context includes the circumstances and cultural expectations in which the interaction takes place. The meaning and impact of interactions change when circumstance and culture change. This personal, linear view of causality is quite flawed and inadequate.

On the other hand, the view of cause-as-trigger assumes that B participates and contributes to an ongoing process according to B's nature. A's action triggers a response in B. That response is much more a comment on B than it is on A, the pebble-thrower. Let us apply this line of thinking to the area of relationships and see where it leads us.

A husband is in the habit of lecturing to his wife. Although he intends to be helpful, she experiences his lecturing as disrespectful, rather than caring. In response, she feels hurt and starts avoiding a number of conversations with him, gradually arranging her schedule so that she is either away or busy when he is home. In summary, he lectures (throws a pebble) and she sees his actions as disrespectful and feels hurt (ripples).

If we followed the linear view of cause and effect, we would conclude that he "caused" her hurt. Her response would be seen as a natural consequence of his action, just as the ripples were the natural consequence of throwing a pebble into the pond. She becomes a passive victim of his actions. He would be responsible for her feelings.

Consider this conclusion carefully because it follows the dominant thinking pattern of our society. A well-meaning friend might even tell the husband that "you are driving your wife away through your nagging." Without meaning to do so, that friend is implying that the distancing wife has no choice in her response. The assumption is that the only response to a nagging husband is to withdraw. This response may be understandable, but it is not inevitable. It is a limitation, nevertheless. One limitation lies in believing that her feelings and thoughts were "created" or "determined" by the husband's lecturing. Another limitation has to do with the belief that she has no choice in the way she acts when hurt: to distance or to fight. She becomes either a passive or an aggressive victim.

Take a moment to do the following exercise so you can add experience to this thought.

EXERCISE: For a brief moment, think of yourself as a totally passive receiver of someone's actions. Imagine that this person is significant to you and that he or she is telling you to change an important aspect of your personality. Picture two scenarios: (1) you become angry, yell obscenities, and threaten to end the relationship; (2) you feel depressed and begin to retreat from the relationship. In either scenario, you bear no responsibility for the

---

46

nature of your response because you see yourself as the malleable clay being sculpted according to this person's image. Give this person all the responsibility (credit and blame) for shaping your relationship. *Pay attention to your thoughts, feelings, and wishes, and consider the impact they would have on your future actions. Map out a few of the actions you might take within this frame of mind.*

If we take responsibility for our internal response (ripple) and for the way we decide to act, then we empower ourselves and preserve our ability to shape our lives according to our vision. This is not an easy path. It demands a depth of sincerity that makes us face the good, the bad, and the ugly within us. But then we free ourselves from blaming others or from taking responsibility for their actions, over which we have no control. Let's take it a little further.

From the husband's side, the picture looks quite different. As he notices his wife distancing, he is not likely to think that she is simply exercising her independence. If he sees her actions as attempts to avoid him, he will likely have a different response. He feels angry. From this view, her withdrawing behavior is the pebble and his angry feelings are the ripples. The more she withdraws (pebble), the angrier he feels (ripples). He also feels helpless and unsuccessful. He feels controlled by her and concludes that she has all the power. He now believes that she determines how much closeness they can have and how much happiness he can feel in the relationship. He believes that he is helpless. He feels depressed and takes on the mind of the victim. Try the next exercise:

EXERCISE: Take five minutes to think about an event in your life in which you felt hurt by what someone did. *Assume a* *victim's position.* All you have to do to feel powerless is to see the other person as *totally* responsible for your responses. Remember that the key here is to give this person all the credit (and the blame) for all of your actions and reactions. If you keep this in mind, you will surely succeed in becoming a powerful victim. After five minutes, make sure you get out of your role (in thought and action) and simply reflect on that experience.

LINEAR CAUSALITY

It may be useful to look for other examples in the past when we assumed the role of victim. Let us look at ourselves and boldly take responsibility for all of our thoughts and feelings, as well for all our actions. It might also be helpful to extend this exercise by thinking of times when we took sole credit or blame for the way things happened. For, in either case, that view of causality would be one-directional.

This simple cause-effect view may be useful in mapping out the visible world of matter. If I lift a chair, we could say that I caused the chair to move. The chair had no choice. I was the cause and the movement of the chair was the effect. This is known as *linear causality*. Linear, because the flow from cause to effect is one-directional. It may be diagrammed as follows:

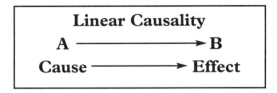

Let us be alert in detecting this type of thinking, especially when it concerns psychological and relationship issues. The linear causal framework is too simple a view to be applied to matters as complex as awareness and relationships. The effect of this kind of thinking is to put us either in a dictatorial position or in the role of victim. Embedded in this paradigm is a control metaphor: either I did it to you or you did it to me.

What is the alternative? Isn't this the cornerstone of our legal and ethical system where we require people to take responsibility for their actions? If we question this, are we not eroding our ability to assign responsibility to those who perpetrate? Can we still secure justice for those who are victimized?

Self-responsibility is indeed important. The difficulty with the linear view and its control metaphor is that it is only partly true and often leads to blaming instead of clearly sorting out *my part* from *your part* of the responsibility. Responsibility remains an important dimension. In the above example, if the husband truly believes that he has no choice and that his wife holds the only key to his happiness and his self-esteem, then his subjective options will be quite limited.

Let us take the example a little further. As the wife feels pursued more intensely, she increases her efforts to protect her boundaries by defending her actions and accusing him of being dependent and controlling. She then amplifies her distancing moves. Getting stuck in this pattern could eventually spell serious trouble for their relationship by disrupting the balance of togetherness and apartness. Their sense of intimacy and independence could be threatened.

If we asked the husband why he nagged so much, he would probably say that he did so because his wife was never there for him. If we asked her why she was distancing herself so much, she would likely say she did so because her husband nagged and complained so much. Those are the frames of mind that float in the heads of couples stuck in this kind of pattern. These ideas themselves are part of what keeps them stuck in those patterns. These ideas are not simply the effect of the couple's actions. They are a part of the entire "causal network."

If the husband says he nags because she avoids him, he is, in essence, giving her all the power to shape him and the relationship. He sees himself as a victim of her actions. In effect, he views himself as "the poor thing who has no choice but to nag every time his wife withdraws." He has other choices. Herein lies one error in his thinking: the assumption that he has only one response to her seeking space–to prod, plead, persecute. This is a subtle error in thinking.

The other error in the husband's thinking lies in assuming that to seek some space is wrong and that the only motive for doing so is negative. If the husband viewed his wife's withdrawing as healthy independence, he may feel differently about her actions. This thought could put a different spin on his awareness, which could, in turn, have a positive impact on his reactions toward her. Since it is he who holds that thought, again *he* holds the key to his response.

When the wife says she withdraws *because* her husband nags, she, too, gives him all the power for shaping her and the relationship. Like him, she makes herself a victim, powerless to do anything but withdraw and emotionally distance herself when he nags. She believes that she has no choice but to run. She sees him holding the key to the solution: "If he would stop nagging, give me space, and trust my decisions, these problems would not exist."

These are potentially devastating conclusions, especially if these thought patterns are pervasive in the relationship. Again, her ideas are a causal part of the pattern. She, too, assumes that she only has one possible response to his nagging pursuit. Furthermore, if she could view his pursuit as a loving, caring attempt to get close, instead of a desire to control her, then her own thoughts, feelings, and actions would be different. She, too, holds the key to her responses.

CIRCULAR CAUSALITY

There is a more useful way of understanding cause and effect patterns in our personal and social world. We call it *circular causality*. In this view, cause and effect interact and are viewed as interchangeable, each becoming part cause and part effect of the other. In the chain of interaction, this concept views causes as triggers rather than as creators of responses. The relationship between cause and effect is no longer one-directional. It is at least circular. Using a 3-D metaphor, we would call it *spherical*: a spherical network of mutual influences. That causal network of causes and effects includes the physical and cultural environment (context). Where, how, and who are important aspects of an event.

We may diagram the circular framework as follows:

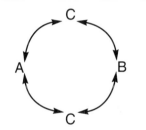

Circular Causality

A and B represent the components (people or things) in the system being analyzed. C represents the context or the environment (physical and cultural).

In the previous example, the circular framework would interpret the nagging and the withdrawing as both cause and effect: the nagging and withdrawing are "triggers" of each other. However, the husband and wife must be held fully responsible for each of their actions and reactions. The question "Who started it?" is a childish one that is not only difficult to sort out, but, more importantly, is not a fruitful question to ask.

The question "Who started it?" has two erroneous assumptions. First, it assumes that the one who started it is the one responsible for the whole process. Second, it assumes that the reactions of the other participants have nothing to do with the resulting process—only the initiator's actions count. It assumes that the one who starts has control of everything that follows. You will now recognize both of these assumptions as having a linear causal frame. Once the interaction process starts, it is erroneous to conclude that only one element has a determining influence on the rest of the interaction process.

We may never be able to answer the question "Which came first, the chicken or the egg?" However, it is important to note that they are vitally related. Both chicken and egg are crucial elements in the equation. It is also important to understand how to assign personal responsibility for actions while adopting a systemic or circular view of causality. It is accurate and useful to see yourself as the creator of your actions and the trigger of someone else's reactions to you.

THE BOTTOM LINE

We are responsible for our actions and for the impact of those actions; others are responsible for their reactions and for the impacts of those reactions.

If I yell in anger at my wife, I am responsible for the yelling and for the negative impact of the yelling. In other words, I trigger an event in the environment that she has to deal with. Although she has a choice about how to deal with that event, she is affected by the nature of the trigger. Nevertheless, her response will be her own creation. As we saw earlier, that response will be more a reflection of her than of the trigger. With me, she becomes co-responsible for the rest of the interaction—even if I started it with an attack.

IN A NUTSHELL

The scriptures of many faith traditions propose a proactive view. The Christian injunctions to "Love your enemy" and to "Do good to those who hate and persecute you" are based on the principle of self-responsibility. I encourage you to examine the scriptures from your own faith tradition and find some passage that embodies this idea of proactivity, as opposed to reactivity. Meditate on it because, in the context of worldly views of power and advancement, the difference between proactivity and reactivity becomes illusive. It is easy enough to love those who are kind and generous to us at the moment. It is more difficult to live according to our principles when we do not get the response we like.

If we believe that yelling is not a good way to talk to people, then we need to talk respectfully even if the other person is not being gracious and kind. This is not a formula for being a victim; it is a formula for living according to our principles. To love someone ultimately means that we are treating that person according to our beliefs about how people should be treated. This is the basis of the golden rule. Acting on principle means being true to ourselves. It has nothing to do with acting like a doormat. Stephen Covey[5] has provided our culture a magnificent service by clearly articulating the desirability and the advantages of living a principle-centered life. The first of Covey's seven habits is to Be Proactive.

The correct view of causality is foundational along the path of self-mastery. We have barely begun to plumb the depths of this concept. But it is a start. In the next few days, let us keep seeing the image of the pebble being thrown into the pond. Let that visualization remind us of these ideas and spur us to own every thought, feeling, decision, and action we experience.

Here are some of the essential points we covered.

1. Our limitations, no matter how understandable, are limitations nevertheless.

2. Events are just events. Only our response will build or destroy us.

3. If our response is the key, then we hold the key.

4. It is useful to see every event in our life as meant for us and as something for us to handle. There are no coincidences.

5. Destiny presents us with the events. Our gift to destiny is our response. Through our response, we influence the course of destiny itself. This is our dance with destiny.

6. The Principle of Self-Responsibility: I am responsible for all of my actions, not for another person's reactions—only for my response. My response is a comment on me.

7. The linear causal view violates the Principle of Self-Responsibility: It assumes that one person (the cause) unilaterally determines the effect on another. The linear causal framework is too simple to be applied to matters as complex as awareness and relationships. This kind of thinking puts us either in a position of dictator or victim. Embedded in this paradigm is a control metaphor: I did it to you or you did it to me.

8. The circular causal view: Cause and effect interact and are viewed as interchangeable, each becoming part cause and part effect of the other. In the chain of interaction, this concept regards causes as triggers rather than as creators of responses.

9. The pebble and the ripple: The pebble is the outside event that triggers a response (ripple). The response is a comment on the nature of the self (the pond)—it reveals, rather than determines, aspects of the self as it interacts with the outside events.

10. The bottom line: We are responsible for our actions and for the impact of those actions; others (spouse, child colleague, friend ...) are responsible for their reactions and for the impacts of those reactions. This is being proactive.

[1] Wilber, K. (1996). *A Brief History of Everything.* Boston: Shambhala Publications, Inc.

[2] For a good discussion on the relationship between science and religion, see Wilber, K. (1998). *The Marriage of Sense and Soul.* New York: Random House. Wilber makes a strong case for distinguishing among three ways of knowing: empirical (eye of flesh), rational (eye of mind), and contemplative (eye of spirit).

[3] Remember that for Wilber, the term *kosmos* includes the entire universe, internal and external: matter, life, and mind. He sees Spirit as immanent in all levels of the kosmos: physical, biological, emotional, mental, and, of course, spiritual.

[4] Stevens, A. (1994). *Jung.* Oxford: Oxford University Press. Included in Storr, A. and Stevens, A. (1998). *Freud and Jung.* New York: Barnes and Noble Books, p. 6.

[5] Covey, S. (1989). *The 7 Habits of Highly Effective People.* New York: Simon and Schuster.

Chapter 4

OF PEBBLES AND GRENADES

Mastering Feelings (1)

FEELINGS CAN GUIDE OR DRIVE US

One day as I was driving out of the parking lot of a busy shopping center, I encountered a car driven by a woman with three active, young kids in the back seat. Because of construction work going on, the lane from which I was coming out was too narrow for two cars. Since she had to wait for me to get out, she lost her patience and started to honk and yell at me.

As I was turning into the exit lane, I felt a sharp feeling of anger shoot through the pit of my stomach and began to hear unkind words in my head that I felt like saying to the other driver. When I got on the main road I started some deep breathing, allowing myself to feel the depth of that anger. Soon the feeling became hurt which, in turn, triggered thoughts about being treated unfairly and disrespectfully. I said to myself "It's okay; just feel it." I stayed with whatever feelings came. There were many branches and hues to the feelings that came, but, primarily, they were feelings of anger and hurt.

Early on, I had to resist the temptation to focus on the event that took place and especially the woman's behavior. That focus triggered many thoughts on the "rightness" of my position in the matter. I took my attention back to my feelings, just staying in touch with these feelings, and breathing deeply into them. I then reflected on my anger and hurt, asking these feelings to tell me what I needed at that moment. The message was that I needed to be treated respectfully and fairly. I started to feel the muscles in my face relaxing and beginning to form a mild smile. "What a beautiful message," I heard myself say quietly. The insight was a familiar tale in my life, a theme that ran through many of my past experiences as a child, friend, worker, spouse, and father.

I decided to give myself what I needed. I thought about some of the aspects of me that I like and told myself that I was a good, worthwhile human being who contributed many positive things to people around me and in the work that I did. At that point, I had no more negative ties to the woman in the other car. She had become irrelevant to my issue. In fact, it was now possible for me to feel compassion for her and her situation. I sent a prayer for her and the little ones who, I assume, were her children.

I was happy that I allowed my feelings to guide instead of drive me. This little triumph gave me a taste of what the saints do. Even they are not spared those moments of pained anguish when the soul struggles to define, protect, connect, and express herself along the road back to God. Sainthood cannot be separated from the path of mastering those little challenges in our daily experience.

Self-mastery is the chemistry of sainthood.

FEELINGS: The Language of the Soul

The emotional part of the mind is the vehicle of our "feeling body." It offers us the richness of feelings, which provide us with a personal experience of reality. When we feel, we are involved: we are in our bodies, experiencing something from inside out. At that moment, we are part of the dance, not spectators or bystanders.

Feelings are a natural part of our experience. They are naturally good, not evil. They simply are—as natural as breathing air, seeing with our eyes, or hearing with our ears. We experience feelings along the continuum of pleasant to unpleasant, not along the continuum of morally good to bad. When speaking of feelings as positive or negative, let us be clear that we are referring to the pleasure-pain dimension, not the moral one.

In addition to providing us with an in-depth, involved experience of reality, feelings are a form of communication from the soul. They are packed with jewels: important messages for us to decode and to apply. The feelings of anger and hurt I experienced in the parking lot unveiled some important needs I had. These needs are messages about certain soul qualities that are important for me to discover, nurture, and express.

Feelings contain messages that point to what is of value to us. It is wise to act on the message of the feeling, not on the feeling itself. The advice to "go with your feeling" is not precise enough. It is more correct to say "go with the meaning within the feeling."

We will do well to shed all negative connotations attached to feelings as such, especially those attached to painful feelings. Let us regard feelings as teachers. *Every feeling has an offering for us.* This is true no matter how intense or mild, pleasant or unpleasant, a feeling is. We need to pay attention.

FEELINGS ARE INFORMATIVE, NOT DIRECTIVE

As language from the soul, feelings are informative, not directive.
They contain messages that point to what is of value to us.
It is wise to act on the message of the feeling, not on the feeling itself.
Let feelings guide, not drive us.

Mining the jewels within our feelings is easier said than done. This path requires a solid commitment to reverse the programming we got from early childhood and to rethink the belief systems we absorbed from the culture of the power-based world around us.

MANAGING FEELINGS

The emotional system is the part of the mind that is closest to our physical system. Feelings are registered in our bodies. The body-mind connection is obvious. For example, a feeling of fear or excitement will be evident in our breathing, pulse rate, skin color, and facial muscle tone—to mention a few indicators that link body and emotions. Let us learn to experience, to read, and to apply the messages our feelings give us.

DORI'S TALE: A Story with Feeling

Dori is a thirty-six-year-old woman, married, and a mother of two boys, age nine and fourteen. She had been happily married to Andrew for sixteen years when she realized that she had become intensely infatuated with Roger, her tennis instructor, an attractive thirty-nine-year-old single man who had never been married. Dori was extremely confused and emotionally troubled about her situation. She entertained the fantasy of having a romantic connection with Roger and even went out several times to dinner with him. It was clear that Roger wanted to sexualize the affair. It was up to Dori to give the go or stop signal.

She decided to tell Andrew about her turmoil to see if this might help her get over the feelings. Although hurt and concerned, Andrew took an understanding position on the matter. He listened and gave her some room to experience her feelings without much judgment. But he also told her that this relationship could not continue if he were to remain her husband. Since it was winter, he encouraged Dori to take two weeks to visit a friend who lived in California. Before she left, she made an appointment to see me for therapy.

When she got back, Dori was as torn as ever. She felt a strong compulsion to see Roger, to spend time with him, and to write to him daily. She came in by herself for the first session, with strong support from her husband. She told me her story. I learned that Dori was the fifth-born of six children, three boys and three girls. She had a younger brother, two older sisters, and two older brothers.

Her parents, now in their late sixties, had a stable marriage characterized by distance and separate spheres of influence, including separating out their income and bank accounts. Only in the last five years had her parents shown signs of marital closeness. Irene, the older sister closest in age to Dori, was known in the family as "the pretty one" as well as "the naughty one." By contrast, Dori was "the athletic, tomboyish one" and "the responsible one" who made sure never to offend her parents.

Irene received most of the positive comments about feminine beauty and much of the negative attention around her rebellious behavior. The mother, in particular, was heavily involved in an ongoing power struggle with Irene. The father officially supported the mother but thought she was too harsh in her approach toward Irene. There was, in essence, an emotional coalition between the father and Irene against the mother.

Dori was a bystander in this emotional triangle of two against one. She was chubby as a young girl and rarely got compliments about her physical appearance. However, she excelled in athletics and in her academic work. Dori said that she felt hurt about the lack of attention she received from her family and jealous about the focused attention given to Irene.

I asked her if she knew how her attraction toward Roger developed. She thought there were two main components: First, Roger's position as a skilled instructor evoked respect from her, allowing her to "look up to him." Second, Roger complimented her often about her physical beauty and her athletic ability. "It was the first time," she said, "that someone had seen me as feminine *and* athletic. To him, I was not just athletic but also attractive." Roger would say, "You've got great legs ... and you can run too."

Roger's words were like pebbles that triggered grenade-strength responses from Dori both pleasant and unpleasant. On the one hand, she felt liked and esteemed for qualities she considered important for her self-worth. On the other hand, she felt disloyal to her husband and to her family of origin. Her family praised her for her athleticism and her sense of loyalty and responsibility. Here she was being irresponsible and getting praise for something unfamiliar.

After several sessions, Dori and Andrew decided to work on healing their marriage and to find ways to help Dori get past her obsession over Roger. I then suggested that I see Dori alone. I wanted to listen to the depth of her feelings and to help her listen to the messages from her soul. Since her obsession over Roger was so intense and consuming, I assumed that Dori's soul was struggling to reach her in a special way.

I asked her to allow herself to feel what she was feeling at the moment and explicitly to give herself permission to let those feelings arise so that she could feel them as intensely as possible. In between sobs, she revealed feeling confused, guilty, and torn apart. She felt an intense pull toward Roger. She also felt an equally intense push to stay put and not do anything foolish. Thinking herself to be trapped and immobilized, she then felt helpless and lost about what to do.

"If the feelings could speak," I asked, "what might they say you need at this moment?" She said she needed guidance and reassurance about her course of action (that she was doing the right thing). She also needed to feel *whole* again inside the marriage. Her head clearly said, "Stay in the marriage," but her gut was split in two directions: one toward Andrew, her husband, and one toward Roger.

I reminded Dori that she already had laid out some good clues

61

for how to get through her dilemma. Earlier, she had said that Roger's compliments hit the spot for her: he praised her for *both* her athleticism and her femininity. Moreover, the compliments came from "someone she looked up to," someone she respected. I encouraged her to keep those elements in mind as we explored the deeper levels of this experience.

I asked her to remember a moment in her childhood when she experienced feelings and needs like these.

Dori: I remember lying on my bed crying because I could hear my parents fighting about Irene. I was thirteen and Irene was almost sixteen years old. She wanted to date a twenty-two-year-old man who had a reputation for being a womanizer. My mother was adamant about not letting her go out with this man at all. My father was saying that she should get a chance to meet this man so she could discover for herself what kind of person he was. I could hear their arguing, loud and clear.

[Dori is crying intensely as she recounts this event.]

Ramon: I would like you to watch the thirteen-year-old Dori with compassion and assume that her experience makes sense given the circumstances in which she finds herself. Look at her lying on the bed crying. What is the little girl thinking and feeling?

Dori: She feels angry at Irene for causing this kind of trouble for my parents. She feels hurt that so much attention is given to Irene and not enough to her. She feels she has worked hard to be a good daughter. Things don't seem fair to her. She feels terrible about herself because she's chubby. Her friends say cruel things to her at times.

[Tears come and go.]

Ramon: Based on your understanding of her feelings, what do you think she needs right now?

Dori: She needs to feel better about herself. She needs to be *reassured* and *praised*. She needs to be told that she is *liked* by someone.

Ramon: Do you think little Dori feels responsible for fixing things between her parents?

Dori: Yes. But she doesn't know what to do.

Ramon: That's all right. Let's see if you can help her. Do you think she needs to be *relieved* of the responsibility for fixing her parents' problems?

Dori: I don't know what you mean. She really can't change her parents.

Ramon: But she's trying to, isn't she?

Dori: Yes.

Ramon: That's what I mean by "feeling the burden of responsibility." She's carrying a lot of weight. Do you think she wants that burden lifted?

Dori: Yes, definitely. She's been feeling that weight for a long time. She feels trapped and wishes her parents would get their act together and deal with Irene.

Ramon: You are right, by the way, that she cannot change her parents. Perhaps you can help her. Look at her now as she lies on the bed and make sure you view her without judgment but with open eyes and ears. Quietly tell her that you are here and *reassure* her that you will listen to her and that you will not abandon her. Tell her this even if she doesn't believe you. Tell her that you recognize her goodness and her beauty and that you love her unconditionally. [Pause.]

63

Dori: She's listening and I think she likes what I'm telling her, but I don't think she's buying it.

Ramon: Do you mean that she doesn't believe you or that she doesn't think she's good, beautiful, and lovable?

Dori: Both.

Ramon: That's all right. Tell her it's O.K. to feel that way about you and about herself. [Pause. Dori nods.] If you don't mind, you might apologize to her for all the times in the past when you shut her out and the times you criticized her for feeling the way she feels.

Dori: I think I know how I shut her out at times, but I don't know how I criticize her.

Ramon: Do you ever hear voices in your head questioning why you feel this way or that way?

Dori: Yes.

Ramon: When you do that, you are criticizing this little girl for having feelings. That hurts her. The message is "don't feel." Your soul is trying to communicate some messages through those feelings. Telling her not to feel is a form of condemnation. Does that make sense?

Dori: Yes, yes. I know what you mean. I do that a lot.

Ramon: You mean you have thoughts and feelings about having feelings, so that you, for instance, feel bad that you feel bad?

Dori: Yes, exactly.

Ramon: It'll be good for you to be aware of that because when that happens, you insult your soul and give her a negative message about herself. It often has the effect of shutting her down, at least temporarily. Go ahead now and apologize to her for all the times you have been critical. [Pause ... Dori nods.]

Dori: She still looks sad.

Ramon: Good. She's doing her work—she is in touch with her feelings and making those available to you. Thank her ... Now, tell her that you have heard the messages behind the feelings and that *you, not the little girl, are responsible for applying those messages.* Relieve her of the responsibility of applying these messages in your current life—in your relationships. [Pause.]

Dori: O.K. She seems much more relaxed right now.

Ramon: Good. You've been a good parent to her, Dori. Take her into your arms, embrace her, and hold her until she gently becomes one with you ... Imagine her being inside you, ready to give you the gift of feelings and the messages they carry ... Now, Dori, I would like for you to think about how you can apply these messages in your current situation. The feelings told you that you need *reassurance, praise,* and the experience of being *liked* by someone important.

We went on to discuss how Dori could take risks with Andrew by asking him for reassurance and praise, as well as telling her now and then how much he enjoys being with her. Andrew is a gentle and good-natured man who genuinely likes being with Dori. With Andrew, the risk of distancing from Dori was more likely than that of outright rejection or confrontation. More significant than Andrew's response would be Dori's actions—asking for reassurance and praise. After all, that is all she can control. If Andrew responds positively to Dori's request for support, that would be a bonus.

Even more important than asking Andrew for reassurance would be Dori's prior internal work: to be in touch with her feelings and to reassure her soul (the little girl in her). Being in touch with her feelings is already a way of listening and connecting with her soul. Without that inner connection between self and soul (conscious to unconscious mind), Andrew's praise and reassurance will sound hollow to Dori.

I also encouraged her to practice giving reassurance and praise·to her friends, to Andrew, and to their children. This is a creative way to apply the golden rule in areas that are truly meaningful and relevant at the moment. Since Dori needed to reassure and praise the little girl in her (the soul), practicing to "do this unto others" can be an effective way to learn to do this to herself.

Dori became kinder to herself and learned to mine the jewels within her feelings. Instead of acting on her feelings, she acted on the message these feelings contained. However, before taking action in the outer world, I coached her always to give that gift to the little girl first. This new process and awareness became the foundation for an important breakthrough in her marriage. There is a key in Dori's experience that we can learn to harness for our own well-being in our personal, relational, and spiritual functioning. That key lies in the mining of the jewels within our feelings.

A GUIDE FOR MANAGING FEELINGS

MINING THE JEWELS

Managing feelings is among the first skills that a person needs in the repertoire of consciously available tools for self-mastery. Feelings are a personal, subjective part of our experience. Language, in fact, is an inadequate vehicle for communicating our feelings. Feelings belong to the world of primary experience, in contrast to conscious thoughts, which are interpretations based on experiences. Our sensing faculties (seeing, hearing, touching, tasting, and smelling) present material for our thinking, feeling, and willing. Of those three, feelings are the most primary and experiential, as well as the least subject to our direct, conscious control.

As little children, we lived so closely with our feelings that they easily became the barometers of the quality of our lives. As we grow in maturity, we add other indicators of progress: our intentions, the quality of our actions, and the consequences of those actions. But no matter how much we grow, feelings will be there to energize and instruct us.

It is important to have a guide for dealing with feelings and for mining the jewels within those feelings. These jewels are messages from our soul—lessons that we need to apply to various aspects of our lives. Some feelings are so intense that we forget to listen to their message and find ourselves acting on the feeling instead of acting upon the message. This is true whether those feelings are pleasant or painful. This is a significant step on the ladder of personal growth.

By staying in touch with our feelings and mining the messages within them, we will be taking crucial steps in integrating body, mind, and spirit. When we welcome our feelings, we are saying hello to our soul as she communicates through our bodies. This is a psychosomatic (mind-body) connection. If we curse or repress our feelings, we are telling our soul to "shut up" or to "go away." We will unwittingly be reinforcing the duality between body and mind, thus delaying their integration with spirit.

At some point in our growth, provided we continue to integrate body, mind, and spirit, we may hope that our thoughts, feelings, and decisions will no longer be incongruent with our spiritual intuitions. In other words, the wisdom of our Higher Mind will be available to our conscious and unconscious mind in a working partnership. Imagine that our sensations, feelings, thoughts, and intentions are organized around the inspirations of our Higher Mind. Our actions then proceed out of this integrated sense of self. This dynamic way of living is the fruit of self-mastery.

Much of Carl Jung's work was inspired by this same vision. He was aware early in life that he had two personalities, which he called No. 1 and No. 2. Later, he used the terms ego and the self. Jung wrote: "In my life, No. 2 has been of prime importance, and I have always tried to make room for anything that wanted to come from within."[1] Roberto Assagioli proposed a similar framework, which he called *psychosynthesis*[2]—the reconstruction of the personality around its true center, the Higher Self (one's true self). Assagioli emphasized the importance of getting to know one's true self and to organize one's personality around this highest center of our being.

More recently, Ken Wilber,[3] philosopher and transpersonal theorist, has become the primary spokesperson for the approach of integrating the Higher Self into our thinking. In Wilber's model of personal growth, one level of development is called the *Centaur:* half human, half animal. He uses this mythic figure to depict the integration of body and mind.

My hope is that the Model for Managing Feelings will help us attain this crucial stage of growth. This model is a necessary building block along the path of self-mastery. If, every time we experience a strong feeling, we immediately welcome it, listen to its message, and allow our Higher Self to affirm the soul's needs, then we would be exercising our capacity for wholeness. This is holiness in action.

THE SIGNIFICANCE OF THE JEWELS
WITHIN OUR FEELINGS

It is important to know how to mine the jewels in our feelings. These are messages from our soul that we need to apply to various aspects of our lives. Not to do so would be to neglect the prompting of our soul and to lose the very richness of her gift to us.

A REVERENCE FOR FEELINGS

To begin with, it is necessary to have an attitude of reverence toward our feelings. Viewing feelings as communication from our soul is one aspect of that reverence. Monitoring the voices in our heads is another area for cultivating that reverence, making sure we do not insult the soul by criticizing the existence of certain feelings. These voices are so subtle that you may not even hear them. They may be whispers about how "I shouldn't have felt or thought this or that." They may even be curses directed at self or others. If we direct these curses at others, we will be cursing the hand of destiny for "allowing" these incidents to occur. Since we do not control the flow of events that come to us, we need to face them willingly.

There are two forms of the Model for Managing Feelings: the short version and the in-depth version. Dori's tale involves an application of the in-depth version, which includes an excursion into the world of your Inner Child (IC). The IC is the mouthpiece for the evolving soul. The expressions of the IC embody the inherent qualities of our soul consciousness, along with the themes and patterns accumulated through our experiences from conception to the present.

The short version incorporates the essential pieces of the process for managing feelings and mining the jewels within those feelings. This model is deceivingly simple, consisting of three parts: feeling the feeling, listening to it, and acting on the message (not on the feeling itself). See page 70 for an outline.

A MODEL FOR MANAGING FEELINGS
The Short Version

I. **FEEL IT:** Welcome the feeling. Breathe into it and let body and soul inform you.

II. **LISTEN TO IT:** Ask yourself: What is the need behind this feeling? Probe until you get to the core message your soul is offering you.

III. **ACT ON THE MESSAGE** *(not on the feeling):* What could you do in order to meet that need?

(1) Give the message to yourself first, inviting your Higher Mind to affirm those needs.

(2) Ask yourself what you could do in relation to the event that triggered the feeling.

Let us remember the pebble-ripple connection. If someone does something that triggers an emotional grenade within us, we are still responsible for managing those feelings. For example, if I am ignored by someone I care about and I feel hurt, I need to feel that pain. I then listen to that feeling and ask it what I need. If the feeling says that I need to be heard, then I need to act on that message. But first, I tell my soul (the little boy within me) that I am listening carefully and that I will be more attentive to the thoughts and feelings I receive in the future. Second, I think about whether or not to talk to the person involved in this matter. If the decision is yes, then I go ahead and talk that person.

Notice that after the pebble is thrown, this entire process is internal, until I begin to talk to the other person involved. Talking was the action taken. Only in the action was the process externalized. This model prepares us internally for the actions we are to take after experiencing an emotional grenade. Let us now take each step in greater depth.

70

I. **FEEL IT.** The first thing to do when we feel a strong emotion is to welcome it—give ourselves permission to let that feeling reverberate throughout our entire being. This is a good way to connect with our soul and to develop rapport with her. Our body usually registers the feeling in some tangible way. We need to honor the body's way of informing us of the presence of that feeling in this three-dimensional world. Doing this helps to integrate body and emotion.

In situations where we can take a moment of quiet, we focus our attention, close our eyes if it helps to focus, and welcome the feeling as we consciously feel its reverberation within us. We may want to remind ourselves that we have a Higher Mind and that, through that mind, we are always in the presence of God. Doing this helps to integrate the conscious self (ego) with the Higher Self (Atman, in Wilber's language).

Remember the incident when I was driving out of the parking lot and the driver of another car yelled and honked furiously at me. I felt a rush of anger within me. As I got on the main road, I allowed myself to feel that anger as I whispered to myself, "It's okay. Just feel it." I welcomed that feeling for a minute or two without ever losing concentration on the task of driving. Paying attention to the feeling helps the body to relax. Repressing it disconnects the body from the self, lowering the chances of influencing the feeling.

The more permission we give ourselves to feel our feelings, the less likely those feelings are to govern us. There is a beautiful paradox here. The logical mind concludes that the more we allow our feeling to emerge, the more overwhelming the feeling will become and, therefore, the greater the danger of being swallowed by it. However, by explicitly "allowing" or "encouraging" our feeling to come to the fore, we have subtly dis-identified the self from the feeling. By giving permission to a part (the feeling), we are commanding that part of the self to go full throttle. The implicit message is that there is someone else in charge, even while the feeling is taking center stage. Denying feelings often leads to increasing their intensity. This is a paradox that defies the logical mind.

A BEAUTIFUL PARADOX

The more permission we give ourselves to feel our feelings, the less likely the feelings are to govern us. This move also promotes the integration of body and mind.

II. LISTEN TO IT. The most effective way I know for mining the jewel within the feeling is to ask the question, "What is the feeling telling me that I need?" Listen quietly, letting the soul reveal the message. Trust the form in which the soul delivers the message. Quiet the voices of doubt and criticism, reminding them that you are not acting on the feeling, that you are in charge, and that *you* will decide how to act on the message.

In the driving example, when I asked the anger and the hurt what I needed, the message was for some reassurance of my self-esteem. I knew then that the little boy in me had felt scolded by an adult and was feeling shamed and somewhat unworthy. I needed to feel okay as a human being and I deserved to be treated with kindness and respect—whether or not I had erred in that situation. I was grateful for the message.

In developing and practicing this method for managing feelings, I found this step to be the most puzzling one because it involves listening to our unconscious mind, expecting some kind of logical response. When asking our feelings what we need, sometimes we get a complete thought—words, sentence and all. More often, the message is not that clear at all. It may just be a sense of something, an intuition, or an image or feeling that needs to be interpreted. Through trial and error and much practice, we will learn to trust our intuitive knack for interpreting the messages from our soul via the language of feelings. Feelings are the raw data. We—you and I—are the interpreters of the data.

This is a crucial step in our personal development, including the interpretation. If we want to be self-actualized, we need to communicate with our lower unconscious and superconscious mind. Intuition is a form of communication from our Higher Mind, which operates in the realm of our higher unconscious—the realm of our inspirations and lofty aspirations. Self-mastery requires that we develop the capacity to let our conscious self become the nexus of the "figure eight" flow between our Higher Self and our soul. The self is the meeting place of self and soul. This may be diagrammed as seen in the figure to the right.

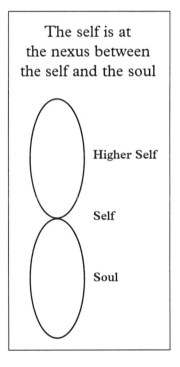

The self is at the nexus between the self and the soul

Higher Self

Self

Soul

The soul's yearnings are vast and infinitely varied, so it takes training and practice to read them. These yearnings are usually revealed to us first as needs, which are the messages from our soul. In the next chapter, we will explore deeper how to read these needs. For the moment, it is helpful to stay in close touch with the feeling itself. If I feel angry, I ask myself what I'm angry about and what in me was violated by the event. It is also helpful to listen to the related thoughts and interpretations that come with the feeling.

If I sense being excluded by a friend who invited a group to his lake house for a weekend of fishing, my anger may reveal a need to be included. That need to be included remains a valid need even if, after thinking the solution through, I realize that I had no business being included in that particular gathering. That feeling is still valid to me and I will benefit by paying attention to it and mining the jewel within it.

So, one clue for soul reading is to think of need. Other examples of needs include the need to be heard, to be independent, to be useful, to be respected, to be trusted, or to express freely. Our feelings are usually revealing, if we pay attention to them. In the early phase of practicing this step, stay very close to the experience of the feeling itself. It is helpful not to complicate the reading of the need with too many questions. By staying close to the "raw data" of the feeling itself, we will get to the need more directly.

If a friend is late for a lunch appointment and you feel irritated, you may discover a need to be important in someone's eyes. That becomes a chance to affirm your own importance to yourself and to the spirit within you. If your daughter raises her voice and you feel hurt, the feeling may reveal your need to be appreciated by her. Your ability to attend to this need within you will help you in your parental role by preventing your personal needs from compromising your decisions as a parent. Otherwise, you may unconsciously demand that your daughter take care of your need to be appreciated. This repressed need could be acted out through a fight with your daughter.

III. ACT ON THE MESSAGE *(not on the feeling)*. There are two parts to this step: (1) self-affirmation and (2) action. The difference between the two parts is significant, partly because the first is internal and the second is external.

First, we need to give that message to ourselves. The message is, of course, the need revealed by the feeling. In the driving example, I told myself that I deserved to be treated kindly and with respect. This self-affirmation is crucial in the process. It bridges you to the soul. It provides the true healing that brings wholeness. It is the essential piece in this model. Without it, no amount of external feedback from loved ones will be effective. Without this affirmation from the self and from the Higher Self, the soul will not believe the support received from the outside.

Second, we ask ourselves how we can apply the message to the situation in which the feeling occurred in the first place. We can decide what to do in response to that event. We may visualize ourselves carrying out a particular action and its potential consequences in order to see if, in fact, that is what we wish to do. By this point, most people report a sense of peace following this process—an inner peace that helps them do their work or have fun even before the action on the message takes place. We don't have to wait for the entire action to occur in order to be whole and integrated.

Let me illustrate this further with the driving example. I told myself that I was a child of God who was worthy of kindness, respect, and patience. Like other human beings, I also deserved to meet my driving needs in a legitimate manner, including the need to drive on that particular lane. I resolved to ritualize this belief later in the day by asking someone I trusted to do me a favor. I started to feel quite at peace. I sent an inner blessing to the driver of the car. That was the self-affirmation part of this step.

When I got home, I asked my wife to listen to me as I recounted some of the day's events. I even asked her to tell me that she liked me. Although I knew (head knowledge) that my wife liked me, I needed to hear it and to feel it. I found, in my world, a resource that confirmed my self-affirmation. The external affirmation, when we can find it, becomes a bonus to this process of self-transformation.

APPLICATION OF THE MODEL TO RELATIONSHIPS

This short version helped one of my clients deal with a situation that, in the past, would have sent him pouting and retreating from his wife for several days. Jack, a professional in his 50s, called his wife, Sandy, who was in another state attending to something important. During the conversation, Jack asked Sandy if he could accept a dinner invitation from friends for the two of them sometime in the following week.

Sandy, who was engulfed with business tasks, said that deciding on a dinner invitation was not a significant priority for her at the moment and that she couldn't deal with it right then. The conversation didn't last much longer. Jack felt deeply wounded as he hung the phone up. The pebble that he felt in his pond triggered a grenade, which reverberated with intense feelings of being discounted by Sandy and of being relegated to the trivial and the unimportant. The grenade gave him painful feelings of rejection along with the belief that his efforts to revitalize their marriage were notched at the bottom of her totem pole. He felt lonely.

Jack, who had just learned the short version for managing feelings, decided to utilize it. He felt the feelings of hurt and rejection, giving himself full permission to feel those feelings, no matter how unpleasant. He became aware of his standard mechanism: to blame Sandy for the whole matter and use the resulting anger to retreat from her. He would first focus on the pebble (Sandy's actions) and his interpretation of the event. Then he would become busy at work. This way, he would disconnect from the pain he was feeling. In other words, he went from pebble to grenade, immediately refocused on the pebble, and proceed to act on that basis—without discovering and appreciating his jewels.

This time, Jack handled the matter quite differently, however.

Being spiritually sensitive, he was able to accept the thought that feelings come from the soul. He owned the experience as part of his destiny and was, therefore, able to view it as something he was meant to face. He had to overcome the inertia of going through the old familiar pattern. He gave up blaming Sandy for his emotional pain. He resisted this temptation to store the matter in his head for evidence in some future argument about how selfish and emotional she was.

He asked the feelings what they were saying he needed. He realized that he needed Sandy's love and friendship. His soul yearned for closeness with her. The little boy in him wanted to be liked by her. Jack recognized that the foundation of this yearning for closeness is the homing instinct we have for union with God.[4] He accepted that need at the levels of the human and the divine. He meditated on God's presence within him and recognized that presence as his own Higher Self who accepted him unconditionally.

He thanked the little boy for the feelings and for the message within those feelings. He assured little Jack that he (the self) loved him (soul) and would remain his best friend, always endeavoring to listen to his thoughts and feelings. Jack liked the little boy and told him so. Jack assured the little boy (his soul) that God loved him and supported him in his efforts to express himself.

The first line of application is always the soul,
even before the application to the outer world.

Jack also decided to do several things: (1) to keep alive the possibility of going to dinner with Sandy and their friends, (2) to let Sandy know about his thoughts and feelings regarding this incident without judging her motives, and (3) to give her a supportive ear with regard to the difficult tasks she was facing during her trip. The issue of the event was worked out two days later in their next phone contact. The rest of the actions were carried out when Sandy arrived home a week later. However, Jack reported feeling at peace even before he took those actions.

THE IN-DEPTH VERSION OF THE MODEL FOR MANAGING FEELINGS

The short, three-step version of managing feelings is the one I recommend for most situations. When we experience intense feelings, we know that the pebble from the outer world has triggered a grenade from our world within. We would do well to set aside some special time to dig deeper into this gold mine of learning and meaning. The following in-depth version can be a useful guide.

RECOMMENDED "SOP": STANDARD OPERATING PROCEDURE
Before digging deep into our psyche, it is a good idea to ask our Higher Self to guide our exploration and to inspire us with accurate and useful interpretations about what we discover.

The main difference between the short and the in-depth version involves venturing into the past—into the world of the Inner Child. This is a way to recover some aspects of the soul that have been repressed or split off from our awareness. By doing this kind of personal work, we are able to shed light upon our shadow side, as Carl Jung would put it. The shadow refers to alienated aspects of the self. It is important to reclaim or retrieve these parts of the self that we rejected in the past; if we don't, they will tend to have grenade-level power over the self.

The key to the power that the shadow aspects have over us lies in our tendency to project those parts of ourselves onto others who display similar characteristics. In his first book, *The Spectrum of Consciousness*, Ken Wilber built upon the work of Freud (repression) and Jung (persona and shadow) by giving us a framework for understanding repression and projection as these defense mechanisms relate to one kind of duality[5] we experience in life. He refers to a duality by which the ego is split into persona and shadow. Ego is used synonymously with our use of the word *self*, as does Wilber himself.

Persona refers to a distorted and impoverished self-image that does not accurately represent the total self. Wilber writes, "In an attempt to make his self-image acceptable, the person renders it inaccurate." The persona is practically identical to what many authors call the false self, as discussed in the second chapter of this book. *Shadow*, on the other hand, refers to "the disowned, alienated, and projected facets of the ego which now appear to be external. Thus ..., man imposes a *dualism* or split upon his own ego, *represses* the underlying unity of all his egoic tendencies, and *projects* them as the persona vs. the shadow."[6]

As the major source of this duality, Wilber points to our being subjected to contradictory communication by our significant others. Since we are capable of communicating at different levels, it is possible to have "tangled" communication, where one level (what is said) contradicts another level (how it is said). How we say something contains "instructions" about how to interpret what is said in the first place. If I say to a friend, "Hey, dummy, come over and play basketball with me," the meaning will depend partly on my tone of voice and partly on the context (words exchanged between friends in a culture common to both). If I say it laughingly, it will be taken as a playful jest and a friendly challenge to a game of one-on-one. But communication with significant others is not always so clear.

Wilber cites Gregory Bateson's classic work[7] on double-binding communication as a good description of what happens when loved ones, parents, for instance, repeatedly give us contradictory messages. The mother who asks a child for a hug and then stiffens as the child hugs her has given the child two contradictory messages: The content of the message (what) calls for a hug. The process (how) communicates the nonverbal message to "get away." The process level of communication is called a "metacommunication" or a "metamessage" because it is a message about a message. Both content and process are present in every communication. If I ask my wife to do an errand for me, she could see my gesture as metacommunicating that I am the boss or that I am dependent on her.

All of us have to contend with metacommunications, trying to sort them out either on our own or by asking others what they mean. Bateson was emphatic about the negative impact of repeated double binds involving survival figures (e.g., parents), especially when people did not feel free to ask questions to clarify confusing messages. He believed that double binding communication was an ingredient in the development of schizophrenia. These are the communication tangles that lead to the duality between persona and shadow.

Most of us try to manage the persona or false ego in an effort to preserve an image of the self that we like, despite the distortions it contains. The shadow, however, contains the disowned aspects of the self that we tend to project to the outside world of people and events. Projection is the process of seeing, in the outside world, an emotion or quality we possess but have unconsciously disowned. These emotions or qualities may be positive or negative. In summarizing the research on this subject, Wilber notes that projected excitement is felt as anxiety, projected desire is felt as pressure, and projected aggression is felt as fear.

These ideas give us a good basis for looking to our feelings for keys about what we need in order to become more whole. This search for wholeness is, after all, what drives us. If we take Wilber's framework of duality→repression→projection, we can reverse the projection to discover the qualities we need to reclaim as ours, including the shadow aspects of the self. By reversing the repression, we take steps toward bridging the duality that severed the wholeness of the self. This is true personal transformation. Here is an especially important point Wilber makes:

> Projection ... is very easily identified: if a person or thing in the environment *informs* us, we probably aren't projecting; on the other hand, if it *affects* us, chances are that we are a victim of our own projection. For instance, Jill might very well have been a prude, but was that any reason for Betty to hate her? ... Betty was not just *informed* that Jill was a prude, she was violently *affected* by Jill's prudishness, which is a sure sign that Betty's hatred of Jill was only projected or extroverted self-contempt. Similarly, when Jack was debating whether or not to clean the garage, and his wife inquired how he was doing, Jack overreacted ... he snapped back at her ... Jack projected his own desire and then experienced it as pressure, so that his wife's innocent inquiry did not just *inform* Jack, it strongly *affected* Jack: he felt unduly pressured.[8]

Wilber's prescription to reverse the pattern of duality→projection→repression in our experience is an almost exact description of the model to mine the jewels within our grenades. The idea of being affected by something is precisely what I mean by an emotional grenade, not just an ordinary ripple on the surface of the pond (self). The surface ripple is my metaphor for simply being informed by an outside event. But when a pebble is transformed into a grenade that explodes within us, we are truly affected.

So, by getting in touch with the grenade and then looking within instead of without, we are in essence reversing the projection by owning these grenades as the negative aspects of our shadow. And when we mine the jewels as ours, we are further reversing the projection by owning these jewels as the positive aspects of our shadow. When we accept the grenades and jewels as part of the total self, we are reversing the repression and healing the duality triggered by our web of tangled communication. We are then ready to act congruently in the world outside.

As we add the in-depth version by going to our past hurts and repressions, we go even further in our effort to reverse the repressions and to develop a congruent self.

In the in-depth version, the extra mile involves going deep into our past, contacting the soul in the form of the Inner Child, and then guiding the IC to go through the steps of managing the feelings in the context of the past. This adds to the healing power at deeper levels of our emotional system. When we experience an intense, grenade-level feeling, it means that an important theme from the past has been triggered. The grenade signals the need to honor the jewel within the feeling. It also means that we need more effective ways to manifest that jewel in our current world.

THE MODEL FOR MANAGING FEELINGS
In-Depth Version

I. **FEEL IT:** Welcome the feelings and stay in good touch with them.

II. **LISTEN TO IT:**

(1) "What do the feelings say I need?" (Jewels).

(2) Inner Child exploration: "Do I remember feelings/needs like these before?" If yes, have the child express the feelings and the needs in the situation. Exit this portion by assuring

the child that you (the self) will take it from here. This establishes your leadership in the inner organization.

III. ACT ON THE MESSAGE *(not on the feeling)*.

(1) Give yourself the message by affirming the needs/qualities within you.

(2) Develop an action plan.

I. FEEL IT: remains essentially the same in the in-depth version. The grenade—that which severely affects us—is always a good starting point for reversing the projection. This we do, as before, by embracing and welcoming the feeling as a form of communication from soul to self. In the driving example at the parking lot, it was the anger and the hurt that gripped me. So I decided to feel it, breathe into it, thereby contacting my soul through the feeling connection.

II. LISTEN TO IT: of the in-depth version starts in the same way as in the short version. We ask the feelings, "What do I need?" When I asked my anger and hurt what I needed as I was driving away, I received the message that I needed to be treated respectfully and that I needed to be liked. To take it further, it now helps to ask, "Have I experienced a feeling like this in the past? Do I remember having these needs before?"

When I asked these questions about the driving incident, I remembered a childhood incident that was significant to me. I was eight years old, the fourth of six children growing up in a metropolitan area in the Philippines in an upper-middle class Spanish household within an oriental culture where the language of education and the media was English. My friend and I decided we wanted to try smoking a cigarette. In the wake of that experiment, we accidentally started a little fire in a closet of the guestroom. My friend disappeared before my mother got home.

When my mother arrived, our maids informed her of what I had done. I still remember sitting on our sofa with short pants looking at my mother. With an angry look on her face, she came up to me and, with open hand, struck my upper leg. I wished then that I had been wearing long pants. The pain I felt was more emotional than physical. I had not thought about this event for many years. I can't say that I didn't remember it, because if the topic ever came up in my family, I'm sure I could have recounted it. But I had not thought about it in probably two decades.

I visualized sitting beside the eight-year-old boy, put an arm around him, and told him to feel whatever he felt. I then asked him what he was feeling: he felt very hurt that his mother did not even talk to him about what happened. The anger on his mother's face and the voice of disgust that she used as she struck him gave him the feeling that she did not like him at all. That was probably the greatest source of his pain. I told him to feel all the pain and any other feelings that came. He now also felt a lot of anger and resentment for the way his mother treated him. I told him it was okay to feel all those feelings. The rapport with this part of me was almost immediate.

I asked the boy what he needed most at this moment. The message I got was that he needed most of all to be liked. I then told him that I not only loved him but that I really liked him; period. But I also liked many things about him: his love of basketball, the way he played with the son of the family gardener, his love of God, and the way he loved to fly kites, among many other things. I then apologized for the many times that I had listened to him in the past by denying my feelings, especially hurt and anger. I promised to be more attentive from now on. I told him I needed him to communicate with me even more than ever, and never to hesitate telling about anything no matter how terrible.

I then told him that he did his job well. *It was now up to me decide what to do* about these needs. This was my way of telling my soul that I, the self, would provide the leadership required—the decision making and the actions that follow. It was important for me to relieve him of the burden of decision making, in the same way that children in families need to be heard but not given responsibilities beyond their ability. It was also a way of saying that I would not be driven by feelings or needs. *I* would drive them.

That is essentially the additional step of the in-depth version. Sometimes memories like those come up spontaneously while we experience grenades. More often than not, it will require some search on our part. Occasionally, a dream may trigger feelings that mirror emotional grenades we have recently felt. Those would also be useful areas to "visit" in our imagination. That too would be a way of going deep into the unconscious and reverse certain repressions by mining the jewels those grenades.

III. ACT ON THE MESSAGE *(not on the feeling)*: is the same as in the short version. The hope is that the in-depth process would have given us a deeper appreciation for the jewel and the importance of affirming these qualities in ourselves. In the affirmation part of Step III, we have the added advantage of being able to "present the little child" to God or to our Higher Self. This can be a powerful moment when the Higher Self, the conscious self, and the soul are all connected and working together to find a effective solutions for issues in the world of pebbles.

ANOTHER EXAMPLE

A LESSON IN BALANCING EVENT AND RESPONSE

A few years ago, my daughter Anna-Lisa called me when she was a sophomore in college. She was angry about how a friend of hers had treated one of her things. After I listened to the details of the event, I asked her to allow herself to feel the feelings she was having. As she told me about her anger, I noticed how quickly she again got focused on the external event, talking about how the other person had violated her property and how a terrible injustice had been done.

I waited a moment and asked her again to refocus her awareness on her inner experience, especially her feelings. I sensed her struggle to stay focused on her inner experience, rather than on the external event itself. My question was premature.

OVERFOCUSING ON THE EVENT
A CRITICAL, EARLY-STAGE ERROR IN
MANAGING FEELINGS

Staying overly focused on the external event before mining the inner jewels is a common error in managing feelings. It gives the event undue weight in that all-important balance between event and response.

Trying to deal with the external pebbles in your life while internal grenades are exploding is an exercise in futility.

I asked Anna-Lisa to probe deeper into the anger to find out more about what her soul was groaning. She got in touch with several facets of her anger. It was partly about the lack of respect her friend showed toward her things and partly about her own attachment to those things. As we probed deeper, Anna-Lisa realized that the event also gave her the impression that her friend showed a lack of respect for *her*, not just her things. She felt discounted as a person and as a friend. This hurt her intensely. I asked her to welcome that feeling and to let that feeling *inform* her. She stayed with it a while, but once again got focused on the event, saying that it should not have happened at all.

Let us learn from Anna-Lisa's tendency to focus on the event. This is a defense mechanism on her part, perhaps as a way for her soul to blunt the pain of emotional hurt and the discomfort of letting go of some attachment. Some people have a greater tendency to focus on the external and to blame the agent of the event. Others have a tendency to blame self and water down the responsibility of the external agent. Either tendency leads to an imbalance: one manifests as persecution (external blaming) and the other as victimization (blaming self).

At this point, I asked my daughter if she was willing to accept the event as part of her destiny. She said she was not yet ready to do so. She felt that to accept it now would not fit with the intensity of her feelings, or with her belief that to see the event as part of destiny would be condoning her friend's actions. I praised her for her honesty with me and especially with herself. I reminded her that although events in our lives are allowed by God as part of our destiny, her difficulty in accepting it was part of the process of learning and listening to herself.

She was not yet done with the task of managing her feelings, as evidenced by her resistance to accept her destiny. The resistance she felt was another communication from her soul. I told her to spend some more time with Steps I and II: to feel those feelings and to listen to the thoughts they triggered. We decided to resume the conversation a day or two later.

Anna-Lisa was much calmer when we continued the dialogue. First she revealed that she had talked to her friend before doing the inner work. The conversation had become heated and ended without any resolution. In the meantime, she had decided to do what I recommended.

I noticed that she was more focused on her response and less on the event itself. She had discovered a few more messages. Two themes emerged from her listening to her soul. First was the hurt she felt about the lack of respect her friend displayed toward her. The second theme involved the disappointment she felt in herself for the way she reacted and handled the event.

What were the needs behind Anna-Lisa's feelings of hurt and disappointment? The need to be respected and to be counted as important was clear. The need behind the disappointment with herself was not as clear because there was an implicit assumption that "I shouldn't falter, nor should I feel angry, nor should I act on that anger." It was a perfectionist frame of mind. It would be useful for her to do two things with this: to give herself permission to feel whatever feelings came to her and to allow for "mistakes" or unexpected pathways in her actions. This will allow her to recover and own more of her shadow aspects—the positive and the negative.

"FEEL" AND "SHOULD FEEL"

There is no such thing as "should feel." We feel what we feel.
The instant we introduce the "should feel" idea into our minds, we introduce the notion that "some feelings are good and others are bad." The soul feels judged and begins to exist in a hostile environment.
There is a rent in the fabric of our being.

With regard to mistakes in one's actions, Anna-Lisa would do well to drop the perfectionist frame of mind and to view mistakes as learning experiences. This view allows for learning by doing. It implies that life proceeds along a spiral-developmental path, rather than along a series of linear steps without waves or detours.

After discussing these ideas, I asked Anna-Lisa to talk to her Inner Child and to give her permission to feel whatever she feels. She was also to affirm the child as someone important to her and as a source of significant messages. Only then would she be ready to go back to the realm of pebbles and to deal with the realities of her current world. It would be important for Anna-Lisa, even before dealing with the trigger event, to look for resources in her life that might serve to support her self-esteem and to reinforce the belief that she does not have to be perfect in order to be lovable.

Let us look for resources in our life that might support our self-esteem and reinforce the belief that we do not have to be perfect in order to be lovable.

This search for resources could involve several aspects of life. We could search our past, our beliefs, and our relationships for clues that we are a part of God's universe, that we are worthy of respect. We might also decide to spend time with a friend or family member who trusts us and with whom we have a sense of emotional safety, so that while in that person's presence we are free to act natural and to be spontaneous.

Going through these steps would make Anna-Lisa more ready to deal with the trigger event. She would be in a better position to deal with her friend in ways about which she could feel good—regardless of how her friend responds. She would be living the Principle of Self-Responsibility: *we are responsible only for our actions, not for another person's reactions.*

89

APPLYING THE GOLDEN RULE

In the process of acting on the message behind the feeling, we can apply the golden rule to do unto others as we would have them do unto us. If we do not apply these lessons in relating to others, it is difficult for us to recognize their value.

In the process of acting on the message behind the feeling, it is important to apply the golden rule. In this story, it means that Anna-Lisa would treat her friend with respect and would view her through compassionate lenses, not through a set of perfectionist standards. If she does not apply the lessons in her relationship with others, she would find it difficult to recognize these truths within herself.

SELF-MASTERY AT THE CENTER OF OUR LIVES

If these principles are correct, we will notice how persistent God is in placing self-mastery at the center of our lives. Everything reverts back to how we view things, how we do things, and how we respond to the events in our lives. At the core of self-mastery is the Principle of Self-Responsibility: We are responsible only for our actions, not for another person's reactions.

The things that happen to us are relevant only as messengers of opportunity, not as definers of our dignity.

SOME THORNY MATTERS

A PARADOX: What If We Don't Feel Like Feeling It?

The Greeks, who have a wonderful philosophical tradition, use a prefix that has happily found its way into the English language. It is

90

meta. It means beyond, above, or about. So when we see the word *metaphysics*, we think of the study of that which is beyond or above the physical. We encountered this in the word *metacommunication.* In communication theory, metacommunication refers to the message beyond or behind the communication. In this sense, the metamessage often refers to the meanings that come from the nonverbal aspects of the communication. Sometimes, the word *metacommunication* refers to "talking about how we talk." A daughter might make a comment to her father about a pattern in their relationship: "Dad, when I share difficult feelings with you, you often give me advice." It is a communication about *how* they communicate.

In a similar vein, we can have *metafeelings* or feelings about feelings. Feeling bad about feeling angry is a form of metafeeling. If someone asks how we feel about feeling sad, the person is asking about a metafeeling. We might even feel glad about being in touch with the sadness and with the meaning of a particular loss. A mother once told me that she felt bad that she felt more positive about one daughter than another.

When the voices in our heads join in, things become even more complicated. We may hear things like, "You shouldn't feel bad about that," or "There you again, wallowing in self-pity." Guilt and shame may become metafeelings to those feelings you experienced in the first place. This kind of layering of feeling upon feeling and voice upon feeling can make the task of *Feeling It* (Step I) difficult.

This is particularly true when we don't feel like feeling it. This is a feeling about the original feeling. It is helpful to own our feeling and the metafeeling as a comment on us—not just a comment on the event. We need to feel the metafeeling—the feeling that we do not like feeling a particular feeling, like fear, anger, or hurt. It may be helpful to go through the three-step model with the metafeeling as the focus before using it for the original feelings triggered by the event.

If a friend or family member does or says something that triggers deep hurt, along with a feeling of self-pity, we may find ourselves immediately distancing ourselves from that person. The self-pity may be a metafeeling: a feeling about feeling hurt. By distancing from that person, we are probably acting on the self-pity. That metafeeling is now directing us. Acting on the feeling is another form of repression because we become focused on the external world and out of touch with the feeling itself. When we act on a metafeeling, we are yet another step removed from the original experience, much less available to deal with it. Let us be mindful of this.

GIVING THE INNER CHILD POWER

If we act on the feeling of self-pity, we have, in essence, given the inner child power and responsibility for handling the event. This is not helpful to the soul. It violates roles and boundaries. The self is the leader, the decision-maker, despite the soul's role in impacting us through feelings and their messages. As decision-makers, we direct the soul through the faculty of will.

The soul is freer to communicate feelings directly when the self in charge.

More often than not, the hurt or angry child will operate from a power base instead of a love base. Acting from the heart means that the will is directing a force that is an integration of feeling, thought, and instinct. This is the state of grace that mystics talk about—when all parts of the self are integrated and congruently support an act. Then we are open to inspiration: the breath of Spirit that comes through our higher mind.

Acting from a power base means that the will is directing a force fueled by feelings that are disconnected from the other parts of the self. This is the opposite of the state of grace. This internal disconnection can lead to relationship imbalance in our external world.

Patterns of relationship enmeshment or cutoff become evident. Being engulfed in or disengaged from an important relationship leads to lack of true relatedness. The feedback one gets from the relationship further confirms the lack of wholeness from within. This is a circular process that can lead to a downward spiral eventually manifesting in depression or aggression.

ACTING ON POWER INSTEAD OF LOVE

Power operates from the level of the solar plexus. Love operates from the level of the heart. Acting from the heart means that the will is directing a force that is an integration of feeling, thought, and instinct. Only then are we subject to higher inspiration (the holy breath of Spirit). Acting from a power base means that the will is directing a force fueled by feelings that are disconnected from the other parts of the self. Our higher inspiration cannot get through. Our Higher Self must wait patiently and lovingly for the lessons of suffering to wake us up.

The person who feels hurt and begins to experience self-pity may have learned as a child that distancing or pouting was rewarded by a parent's pursuing and humoring behavior. The adult will be tempted to let this grenade-level hurt direct her towards self-pitying, distancing behavior designed, consciously or unconsciously, to bring the offending party to his knees. The Inner Child fantasizes that the loved one will (or at least should) shower her with tender, remorseful acts of reconciliation. These grenade-level yearnings are difficult to resist. They are the Inner Child's attempts at a clean and rapid resolution—a sort of soul-level "quick fix." But they are power-based moves founded on the control metaphor.

WHAT TO DO WHEN YOU DO NOT FEEL LIKE FEELING IT

The best advice in a situation when we don't feel like feeling it is first to "hang in there." When the feelings are exploding with intensity, it is not the time for action but for inner attending and contemplating. If we are not ready to deal with the full implications of these feelings, the next best course is to *just feel it!* Let time allow the soul to settle down. Let yourself *be* for a while. Your conscious mind will not be able to make sense of this mode of being. Logic will not cut it. If you try to think it through, it may get worse.

The family psychiatrist Carl Whitaker, one of my mentors, was fond of saying, "Let things cook for a while." Whitaker was a great believer in giving the right brain (seat of the unconscious) a good deal of simmering time, without prematurely pushing those experiences into left brain categories. I think this is good advice. Let us trust our higher unconscious to guide us about when it's time to act, while we sit with the soul levels of the unconscious mind.

Let us not bypass Step I in this process of managing our feelings. We need to experience those feelings. Let us be with the soul in the same way that we would want a friend or spouse to be with us when we are down. Our soul will give us signals about how much depth and time we need to experience our response adequately.

The "emotional body" looks strange to our "intellectual body." Thoughts and feelings are interlocking, complementary levels of awareness, but strange-looking creatures in the mirror of the other. At a moment like this, if we hang in there, we will eventually have a clear experience of the will—directing that will to hold back before pointing toward a direction for action. If we do this graciously and genuinely, the energy field created by the emotions will lighten up and will eventually rise to the level of the heart where we connect with the message behind the feelings.

In testing these ideas, let us remember the paradox: the time we feel the grenade is probably the moment when we least feel like using this process. It is a metafeeling—an unpleasant feeling about an unpleasant feeling. This is one point when teaching has to give way to experience. The only way to learn this is to do it. Then we can develop some conscious conclusions about the techniques and their merit.

Meditation on the concept of destiny, divine providence, and our oneness with God and the universe can give us the courage and the perspective to stay the course. This is the time to take destiny seriously: to absorb the conviction that events that are "allowed" to come our way are meant, by God, for our purification, training, and edification. This is such a nonlogical proposition that few people can buy it beyond a superficial nod.

The emotional mind does not and cannot stand alone. We need the faith that expands our view of ourselves as part of a large, interconnected web of relationships. Our anxiety will kick into high gear if we believe that our lives are meaningless and that we are alone and nobody cares. That is why we need periodically to renew our belief in a faith-filled, systemic-holistic view of life: that we have a soul connected with a Higher Self that is always in direct communion with Divine Mind manifesting as matter, life, mind, and spirit. Through our Higher Mind, we are involved in every aspect of life itself. There are no coincidences; there is no solely random activity. The universe is our spiritual family.

This conviction is necessary for the kind of long-term, emotional stability that is required on the rocky path of self-mastery. It requires honest connection with the Inner Child, but it is not child's play. This is the modern path of sainthood. Dancing with destiny demands the honesty of listening to the soul and the integrity (inner congruence) to respond naturally to the events that come our way.

IN A NUTSHELL

A MODEL FOR MANAGING FEELINGS
Combining the Short and the In-Depth Version

I. FEEL IT

Probe deeply into the different layers and nuances of the major feelings triggered by the event. Get to the core of these feelings. Feel and welcome them.

II. LISTEN TO IT

A. The Message: What are the *needs* behind each of the major feelings experienced? Listen carefully to the pulse within each feeling. This pulsation will lead you to the soul's striving and yearning. The key question is "What is the *need* behind each feeling?"

B. The Inner Child: Ask yourself if there were events in your past (the earlier, the better, especially in your childhood) that remind you of these feelings or these needs. Watch the event as you remember it (or simply watch yourself in the setting) with compassion and without judgment. If no specific event comes to mind, just select an age in your childhood that feels special to you and picture this little child, in some favorite place of yours, going through similar feelings. Then do the following steps in the context of that event:

    1. Feel It: Ask the child how she feels. Then probe deeply into the layers and nuances of her major feelings. Give the child full permission to feel exactly as she feels. There is no such thing as "should feel."

    2. Listen to it: Ask the child what she *needs* at this moment in time. Listen carefully and probe until you get to the core of her needs. These needs are the messages (the jewels) within the feelings.

3. Provide Leadership: Relieve the child of any responsibility for doing anything about these needs. Her part is *to feel* and *to provide those feelings* to you. It is your job to decode the needs and to decide how you will meet them. This division of labor is crucial. Your role is like that of a parent toward a child. Listen carefully but provide the decision-making leadership until the child is able to function well again. This is profoundly relieving to the Inner Child.

III. ACT ON THE MESSAGE *(not on the feeling)*.

A. Love Self:

1. Always give the Inner Child what she needs first. If she needs to feel valued, give her that sense as best as you can. This application to the child within is crucial. If you do not listen to yourself, it is difficult to hear others. If you do not love yourself, it is hard to receive love from others.

2. Examine your relationship world and see where you might find resources to meet these needs. Perhaps some friends and family members are already sending you important messages that you are not recognizing. You may need to ask for support.

B. Dealing with the Pebble:

1. The Event: Now you are ready to deal with the event that triggered the grenade. Think it through carefully and decide what you will do and how you will handle the matter. This is an individual thing. You are now in a much better position to listen to the inspiration of your Higher Self.

2. Apply the Golden Rule: Make sure that you give to others that which you yourself need. If you need to be understood, then practice understanding others. This is now possible.

[1] Jung, C. (1963). *Memories, Dreams, Reflections.* London: Routledge & Kegan Paul.

[2] Assagioli, R. (1971). *Psychosynthesis.* New York: Penguin Books.

[3] Wilber, K. (1980, 1996). *The Atman Project.* Wheaton, IL: Quest Books. (New edition in 1996).

[4] This is a manifestation of the "Atman Project," as Ken Wilber would put it: our attempts to find union with Spirit in ways that prevent it, particularly when we try to find our God outside only. In using the model, Jack is starting to make better progress in finding Spirit.

[5] Ken Wilber identifies four kinds of duality: the observer and that which is observed (or inside/outside); life and death; body and mind; and, finally, the duality of the ego as persona and shadow. Wilber discusses these dualities at great length in his first book, *The Spectrum of Consciousness.* It is a challenging book to read, but well worth the time and effort. The discussion of all four dualities will take us away from our main point for the moment.

[6] Wilber, K. (1977). *The Spectrum of Consciousness.* Wheaton, IL: Quest Books, p. 130 (italics by Wilber).

[7] Bateson, G. (1972). *Steps to an Ecology of Mind.* New York: Ballantine.

[8] Wilber, K. (1977). *The Spectrum of Consciousness.* Wheaton, IL: Quest Books, p. 201.

Chapter 5
FROM GRENADES TO JEWELS
Mastering Feelings (2)

THE PEBBLE-GRENADE-JEWEL CONNECTION

Feelings are indeed the language of the soul. We have learned to honor and value our feelings as communication from deep within us. We will take a further step in the process of mining the jewels within our feelings. If we get in touch with our grenades, we will develop natural empathy for those who experience a similar kind of pain or joy. Besides, our feelings will open the treasure chest of our inner jewels. And if we honor the jewels within our grenades, we will deepen our capacity to love and to produce.

By staying in good touch with our jewels (our soul qualities), we deepen our capacity to appreciate other people's talents and accomplishments, strengthening our ability to offer praise and recognition where it is due. This prevents envy and promotes relationship, which is the best foundation for the teamwork that leads to synergy.

TESSIE'S STORY: Reading the Jewel within the Grenade

Tessie was in a relationship with Tim for ten years when she came to my office.

She loved him deeply but she was feeling hurt and lost in the relationship. Tim had promised to marry her right after he was through paying child support to his first wife. By now, eight years had passed since his last payment, and they were still not married. Tim had significant involvement with his children, especially around some business ventures and leisure activities. His weekends were usually divided between Tessie and his children. The two worlds did not often mix.

Tessie spoke of a painful event between her and Tim. He told her that she had become a wet blanket in his life and the lives of his children and grandchildren. Their meticulously organized house was uninviting to his children. He was not happy with the situation. Tim's words were like daggers ripping Tessie's guts apart. Tears flowed amid sobs that interrupted her words. Between the lines, she heard Tim saying that he did not value what she brought to their relationship. Although Tessie did not bring much money into their partnership, she offered warmth, love, a solid commitment, and a knack for design and organized living. These were expressions of her jewels. During that conversation, she saw Tim throw those jewels out the window.

I asked Tessie to honor her feelings by going deep into them. As the feelings got stronger, I asked her to note the meanings connected to those feelings. She was feeling *empty* and *lonely*. Tim *rejected* her. He did not *appreciate* what she *brought* into the relationship. He had *discounted* and *discarded* her contributions. She was lost and confused about where she *fit* in Tim's life. There was *no use* for her presence there. (Notice the italicized words. They are windows allowing the jewels to shine through.)

With compassion and faith, I was able to be present, remain calm, and still maintain a sense of wonder about the sparks from the jewels that were coming through the grenades. I could detect those rays of light between the lines of her face and her words. The italicized words above were specific sparks of light shining through. Her soul reflected the belonging need more than the individuality need. I asked Tessie what the grenade was saying that she needed. She said that she needed to be appreciated for what she brought to the relationship. That was a wide open door to the jewel.

I suggested that she repeat the following sentence, imagining that she was saying it to Tim. "I need to be appreciated for my contributions as your partner." As she said it, there were more tears flowing, but there was also more conviction in her voice. Next she said, "I need to be recognized as a full and useful partner in this relationship." It was clear that we were touching the core of her soul. The qualities of the grenade had led us to the specific glow that characterized her jewel. Listening to the grenade is a form of soul reading. With prayer and meditation, this kind of soul reading is one of the surest ways to grow psychologically and spiritually. I spoke to Tessie:

Let me tell you something, Tessie. I could feel your soul yearning and groaning. Before I share what I heard, I want you to imagine a diamond as big as the earth with billions and billions of facets or cuts. That is a picture of God. Imagine further that this Great Diamond shines a different glow in each of the two hemispheres. One side reflects the oneness of all creation the interconnectedness of God that is the source of our need to belong and our quest for contact. The other half radiates the uniqueness that is created—the infinite diversity of God that is the source of our need to be individuals and our quest for unique accomplishments. You are a facet cut out of God's essence and given a physical form. *You are a spirit taken directly out of God's essence.*

Now, let me tell you what I heard and saw within your grenade. You are a soul plucked out of the Belonging Side of God. Keep that in mind. Your grenades normally reveal jewels that glow with a *need to connect* in some way. But that need also reveals a deep *capacity* to connect. I suspect that the core of your jewel radiates this strong *ability to bond* with another human being. I also saw some more *specific qualities* of your *gift to connect*. This jewel has an intense glow to be *useful*—to *contribute* in positive ways to those in relationship with you. There is no shame in recognizing that you *need to be appreciated for your contributions.*

Above all, you need to recognize your own jewel by appreciating your useful contributions to this relationship—even if Tim does not express his gratitude. I also urge you to bring those contributions to God in your meditation and renew your belief that God appreciates your jewels. This is the first step to healing yourself. It's also the best way to prepare yourself for communicating and negotiating with Tim.

Though tears were still flowing, they now seemed to have a different meaning to Tessie. There truly was a glow on her face. "So, I am not crazy after all, she commented." "Far from it," I said. "Not only are you not crazy, but you have the ability to spot from a mile away a person who feels rejected or unrecognized for her contribution." She agreed. "Tessie, let your empathy remind you of your great capacity to be useful to someone."

ELEMENTS OF THE FRAMEWORK
FOR PERSONAL TRANSFORMATION

THE THREE ASPECTS OF A JEWEL

Tessie's story contains the ingredients of the framework for personal transformation. Using Chapter 3 as a foundation, this framework will take us several steps further in reading the specific qualities of our jewels. It is helpful to have an accurate reading of our jewel in order to be able to nurture it more effectively. Therefore, it is crucial to get a deeper understanding of the pebble, grenade, and jewel connection.

The pebble is the hand of destiny in the form of facts and events that we face. Grenades, our internal emotional responses, alert us to the important information that the soul wants us to consider. These intense feelings of pain or joy signal perceived violations or celebrations of the jewels within us.

All grenades provide footprints for reading the specific qualities of the jewels in us.

When a grenade is painful, it will reveal a need that the soul demands to be met. A joyful grenade can reveal a need within that has been affirmed. If there is a need, then there also is a desire for that resource. There can be no desire without a capacity to receive it. A desire for food implies the capacity to eat. Tessie's need to be useful in the relationship means that she has a desire to be useful. That desire means she has the capacity to contribute something useful in that relationship. Therefore, the need will reveal a quality of the jewel as a capacity—the ability to do something useful. In Tessie's case, the need for connection reveals the capacity to connect with someone.

NEED REVEALS A CAPACITY

All grenades provide footprints for reading the specific qualities of the jewels in us. The jewel reveals its glow first as a need. Need, which implies desire, reveals a capacity. It is crucial to make the connection between need and capacity.

Need, which implies a desire, reveals a capacity for something. This is a crucial connection to make. If Tessie is unable to see that behind the grenade is a need to contribute usefully to the relationship, she will be unable to mine the jewel within the grenade. She will, therefore, not be able to affirm that capacity or quality within her. When a person is not able to affirm a quality of soul, she will be much more dependent on external recognition and much more vulnerable to pebbles of rejection.

After feeling the grenade and detecting the need revealed by it, it is crucial to connect need to capacity.

The *need to be heard* means the *capacity to be heard.*
The *need to be independent* means the *capacity to act independently.*
The *need to contribute* means the *capacity to contribute.*
The *need to be respected* means the *capacity to give and to receive respect.*
The *need for security* means the *capacity to be secure.*
The *need to be included* means the *capacity to become part of something.*
The *need for open expression* means the *capacity to express openly.*
The *need to be valued* means the *capacity to be valued by someone.*
The *need for partnership* means the *capacity to be a partner.*
There are now two ways to detect the jewel: the jewel as *need,* and the jewel as *capacity.* These are two aspects of a jewel. But there is a third aspect. To get there, we make another important connection.

AFFIRMING GRENADE AND JEWEL LEADS TO EMPATHY

When we are in touch with both the grenade and the jewel, we will naturally experience empathy for those with similar grenades or jewels. Recognizing the need and affirming the capacity naturally leads to empathy for those states of mind. Let us say that Tessie truly stays in touch with her pain of being discounted and discovers her need to contribute usefully to someone in a relationship. At this point, she would have increased her empathic ability to sense another person's pain, especially somebody who experiences similar grenades.

Let us also say that Tessie recognizes and affirms her capacity to be useful in that relationship, even inviting God to affirm that quality in her soul. By then, she will have deepened her empathy to include the ability to appreciate other people's joys and successes. Giving praise to those who deserve it becomes more natural and genuine.

Empathy for pain and for success is a third aspect of a jewel.

Lack of empathy for another's pain is a sign that we are not in touch with our grenades or the need behind them. Lack of empathy for another's success (envy) is a sign that we are not recognizing and affirming an important capacity (soul quality) that we possess.

We can now connect *need* to *capacity* to *empathy*. These are the three aspects of a jewel. And the grenade always presents us with an open door to discover these aspects of our jewels. This is the pathway to personal transformation: the journey from pebble to grenade to jewel. *We will not find it if we go from pebble to grenade and back to the world of pebbles (the external world).* After we mine the jewels within our grenades, we are ready to go back to the world of pebbles.

Personal transformation then is the process of mining the jewels within our grenades before going back to the world of pebbles. The process of personal transformation can be summarized in the following steps:

1. We recognize the pebble as something coming from *outside* and accept it as the hand of destiny. The pebble is not under our control—just our response.

2. We welcome the emotional grenade and feel it fully as something *inside* us. We embrace the grenade as communication from our soul, allowing it to inform, not direct us. The grenade is mostly a comment on us, not on the pebble. We

own the grenade as yours, taking responsibility for our response.

3. We mine the jewel within the grenade, first as need, then as capacity, and third, as empathy. We own the sparks of our jewel as aspects of our soul.

4. We take full responsibility for affirming and nurturing our jewels. It is a good practice to ask God to bless and affirm these qualities in our soul.

5. We determine whether or not we need to deal with the pebble: the outside event or circumstance that triggered it in the first place. If so, we proceed with confidence that we have done the personal transformation work that has prepared us to handle the situation effectively. So now, it's time to go *outside* again— back to the world of pebbles.

All grenades provide footprints for reading the specific qualities of the jewel in us.

That, in a nutshell, is the Framework for Personal Transformation. Let's take a further look at the concept of pebble, grenade, and jewel. We see that this framework is simply a reworking of the model for managing feelings. But it is important to know that, in practicing this model, we are doing personal transformation work.

PEBBLE, GRENADE, AND JEWEL
A Closer Look

THE PEBBLE: The Hand of Destiny

Let us put the concept of pebble in perspective. The term refers to the facts and the events that we meet on the journey of life. These are the events that we see, hear, touch, taste, and smell. *Pebble* then includes the context or the circumstances in which we find ourselves. Since we do not control these circumstances, we conclude that this is the arena of destiny. Destiny is the outside or empirical environment of the soul. It is the context for drawing out the jewel and for cutting, grinding, and polishing it. How well that happens depends on our response. But the pebble is the trigger.

One pathway to self-mastery is the belief that events manifest the hand of destiny.

Self-mastery demands that we take on this attitude in relation to the events that visit us. An attitude is a position in relation to something. Since these events are not in our direct control, we assume that they happen either on a random basis or in patterned ways. The position or attitude we take in relation to the events that come to us influences our response to these events (pebbles). A random view puts us in a universe in which we have to fend for ourselves, either defensively or aggressively. We find ourselves in a power-based world, often driven by fear and anger.

In contrast, the path of self-mastery requires that we view events as coming from the hand of the Pattern Maker. This is the most useful position to take in relation to the events that confront us. That is, we accept whatever comes our way as something for us to handle. We will hopefully learn from these events and respond creatively to them. If we see every pebble in our life as coming from the hand of God, then chances are greater that we will live in a love-based universe. We will assume that the universe is governed by patterns and principles, not run by accidental or arbitrary forces.

Not long ago, a friend called in tears because she had found out that her husband was having an affair. This was not the first time. This couple had spent the last few years rebuilding the trust that was previously broken. I could hear the terrible anguish in her voice and in her tears. "I kicked him out yesterday," she said. "But I am so torn. I love him and I like what we had together. And there are our two young boys. I don't know what to do."

How does one assess that stroke of destiny? It is a terrible event. She said she remembered my teaching about event and response. At that moment, there was little consolation from that piece of logic. I asked her what she needed most right then. She needed a companion. "But I can't have it now," she blurted. I reminded her that the need was still in her soul, even if the means of having it fulfilled seemed out of reach at the moment. She felt so lonely. She needed someone to love and someone to connect with. We finally got to her jewel: the need and the capacity to connect through love.

It is impossible to evaluate the ultimate effect of events in our lives. We live by moral codes and ethical standards—and these are good and necessary. Yet, in response to a specific event, we ought not to be moralistic. Though I consider an affair an immoral act, I must assume that destiny allowed it in my friend's life for some purpose. What that might be, I do not know.

My friend will now have to dance with this piece of destiny in a way that is life giving, if she is to benefit from its ripples and the ensuing grenades. The ripples within us are not givens; they are variables. It was nevertheless important for her to be in touch with her need and capacity to connect lovingly with someone, despite the momentary absence of someone in the empirical world of pebbles. The world of pebbles may not always be kind, but the soul, the self, and the Higher Mind can still work the inner transformation. This is the alchemy of spirit.

GRENADE: The Violation or Affirmation of the Jewel

The grenade is one of the most troublesome parts of the framework. As a concept, most people see emotional pain not just as unpleasant, but as a bad sign. Our society treats it like a headache. Take a couple of aspirins and suppress it. The way we view grenades must change radically. If we see grenades as signs of being "bad" or "mad," we will disconnect from our soul. We will lose rapport with our soul and will surely misinterpret the meaning of her communication with us. This rapport is essential if we are to receive the fullness of the message. We require the richness of the feelings in order to read the specific nuances of the jewel that shines within the grenade.

We require the richness of the feelings in order to read the specific nuances of the jewel that shines within the grenade. For this, we need strong rapport with the soul.

Grenades are troublesome for yet another reason. They are often so painful and unpleasant that we either jump back to the world of pebbles to find a quick fix, or we get mired in the emotional intensity of the moment. These are the two main errors I have detected in response to painful grenades. Let me highlight them.

1. The Quick Fix

This involves the movement from pebble to grenade and immediately back to the world of pebbles (i.e., we focus back on the events outside). We seek to explain the grenade on the basis of the kind of pebble that was thrown. This is futile and ineffective. The logic of events is different from the emotionality of the response. These are two different worlds. We may hear people say, "The reason I feel this way is *because* you did this." It is not incorrect to link the pebble as a trigger of the grenade. However, it is an error to link it as the primary causal agent of the emotional intensity. The pebble is important. It triggers an opportunity for discovery and for learning. But it is not an adequate explanation of our response. This view violates the principle of self-responsibility that we discussed in Chapter 2. It is an incorrect way to think.

When we go back to the world of pebbles before mining the jewel, we will not be ready to negotiate that world wisely and skillfully. We will tend to blame others for our plight or to cling dependently for comfort. Disappointment often comes from depending too much on the outside world for our "salvation."

2. Mired in the Emotional Intensity

The grenade can be so intense that the pain overwhelms us. We may feel hopeless and helpless, sliding into a pit of depression, or we may feel a burning rage that consumes us inside, causing us to withdraw from the world outside. Our retreat from the world may show the face of individuality by distancing from people. We could even display bursts of independence, and protest that we do not need anyone. Our retreat could also be a way to hide the need to belong. But a good "reader of grenades" is able to detect the unconscious hope that our loved ones would rescue us. We need to be the best reader of our own grenades.

The best way to understand a grenade is to see it as a response to a perceived violation (or celebration) of a facet of our jewel.
The pebble is important. It triggers an opportunity for discovery and for learning. But it is not an adequate explanation of our response.

Though painful, it is helpful to realize that the grenade says more about us than about the nature of the pebble. This framework suggests that we always start with the premise: the grenade is telling us something about us. It tells us about the way we interpret the event and about the nature of our soul sensitivity. The grenade may also tell us about the oversensitivities we have developed through past experiences.

We could define a grenade as an oversensitivity that reveals our points of soul sensitivity.

An empowering aspect of this concept is that feelings are viewed as our friends and allies, not our enemies. Furthermore, this understanding of grenades gives a better explanation of the nature of our feelings. The reason these grenades are so powerful is that they are violations or affirmations of something most precious to us: our jewel.

JEWEL: A Facet of the Soul

In talking to Tessie, I described an aspect of my creation myth, which involves the use of a metaphor that means much to me. I see God as the Great Diamond with an infinite number of facets or angles. Imagine a diamond as big as planet earth. Each of us is a facet—a unique cut of that Diamond.

We—you and I—are spirit, emanated from God, entering the material universe as a soul. The spirit is synonymous with the Higher Self. The soul, in my creation myth, is a projection of spirit into the matter universe. Our souls also reflect our unique angle of God. Only we can radiate the particular qualities (jewels) of our soul. It is our dance with destiny that reveals our special glow and the various tints of soul sensitivity. The environment is the arena in which we discover and develop our inherent qualities. This is an empowering meditation and visualization.

I define jewel as a precious stone within your soul. Jewels reflect pockets of soul sensitivity. Most religions portray a creation myth that depicts the soul as an emanation from the essence of God. Just as the soul is a facet of God, the Great Diamond, so a jewel is a facet of the soul.

I offer this metaphor as a useful set of images that help to convey inner realities that are difficult to touch, to see, or to hear. We are all free to develop our own unique set of images. Regardless of the metaphor, there is one principle that is important to honor: *We are unique. Our soul carries a specific blueprint that will be revealed by destiny, not created by the events and experiences of our lives.* In other words, we are not just the product of environmental forces, but neither are we in charge of the environment.

Hillman (1996) makes an important point about the debate surrounding nature and nurture. The field of psychology has been dominated by the debate about what influences behavior and personality more: genetics (nature) or environment (nurture). Lost in the debate, Hillman points out, is the person—the being that comes into this earth with unique qualities and a specific calling. Hillman writes:

> So this book wants to repair some of that damage by showing what else was there, is there, in your nature. It wants to resurrect the unaccountable twists that turned your boat around in the eddies and shallows of meaninglessness, bringing you back to feelings of destiny. For that is what is lost in so many lives, and what must be recovered: a sense of personal calling, that there is a reason I am alive ... But it [the book] does speak to the feelings that there is a reason my unique person is here and that there are things I must attend to beyond the daily round and that give the daily round its

reason, feelings that the world somehow wants me to be here, that I am answerable to an innate image, which I am filling out in my biography.[1]

We must respect the circumstances and the events in our life precisely because they are manifestations of the Divine Hand. How brightly the jewels of our soul shine depends on our response to destiny. Understanding the nature of our soul sensitivities (jewels) is vital in living our mission effectively.

We are unique.
Our soul carries a specific blueprint that is revealed
by destiny, not created by the events and experiences of life.
We are not simply the product of environmental forces.

SPECIAL FEATURES OF THE FRAMEWORK FOR PERSONAL TRANSFORMATION

GRENADE AS SOUL OVERSENSITIVITY

In the previous chapter, we learned that the first thing to do when we feel a grenade is to welcome it. It is a good way to acknowledge our soul. We thank the soul for sending us a message. This is the time to use the three-step Model for Managing Feelings given in Chapter 4:

I. Feel it.

II. Listen to it.

III. Act on the Message (not on the feeling).

This Framework for Personal Transformation is simply another description of the Model for Managing Feelings. The title reveals the model for what it really is: a process for promoting our personal transformation. We will now take each of these steps into greater depth and towards an even clearer focus, especially the second and third steps. Step I is the time to get in touch with the intensity and nuances of the grenade.

Step II, however, is the part that takes much practice if we are to become skillful in decoding the meanings and the feelings within the grenade.

Mike, for instance, felt irritated when his wife would fire off a list of questions about whether he had accomplished certain things around the house. He was a patient man. But when his wife, Carol, got to "question number 27," Mike would feel annoyed. He might then blurt out a loud "WHAT?" This outburst would lead to a conflict between them. Carol, for her part, was intent on being efficient about certain tasks that needed to be done. In her persistence and focus on the tasks, she would lose sight of the communication process she was using. Mike knew this, logically, but the pebble still triggered a grenade of anger. Yet, if Mike focused on blaming Carol's actions and motives, he could easily get stuck in the world of pebbles.

When I asked Mike to feel the feelings of irritation, other thoughts and feelings emerged. He felt frustrated and angry that his wife did not believe that those requests were already accomplished. "She doesn't trust me. She reminds me of my father. I never measured up to his expectations. Every day, I had to prove myself all over again. Carol's questions bring out that feeling in me." Mike's jewel became available. It spoke loudly: "I need to be trusted." It was an individuality jewel—a soul quality emphasizing his uniqueness.

It is interesting to note that while Carol was focused on teamwork, a belonging jewel, Mike was responding with an individuality jewel. His anger was saying, "Leave me alone!," but his jewel was saying, "Just trust me to get it done." (This is a common pattern in all relationships: one is the spokesperson for individuality, while the other is defending the need to belong.)

114

When we get in touch with the grenade, we also get a network of meanings: our interpretations of the pebble. These meanings are as revealing as the associated feelings themselves as they point to aspects of the jewel. Often, these grenades remind us of past incidents, especially in our family of origin. These memories are important clues. They reveal our oversensitivities, which, in turn, shed light on our soul qualities. This is a good time to examine these memories and see if they reveal needs and ways that these needs were thwarted or fulfilled.

So, a key feature in our exploration of our grenades is the connection between the feelings and the needs that they reveal. There are three main dimensions to look for when going from grenade to jewel: need, capacity, and empathy.

JEWEL AS SOUL SENSITIVITY: Need, Capacity, and Empathy

Need

Jewels reveal themselves first as needs. These are soul demands. Let us not confuse needs with being needy. A need is a yearning for a certain quality of the soul to be expressed in some way and, therefore, reveals a soul quality. When we become adept at reading grenades, the connection between the oversensitivity of the grenade and the sensitivity of the jewel becomes obvious.

When we ask the feeling (mouthpiece of the soul), "What do you need?," we often get a description of a process about how to meet that need. For example, when I asked my friend what she needed in response to her husband's affair, she said, "I need a companion." That is an example of a method or condition for getting the need met. So I asked, "What would having a companion do for you?" Her only reply was, "It would give me security, safety, and love. I would feel connected with someone." Notice that the thrust of the need was towards connecting. Hers was a belonging jewel. Security and safety were facets of her belonging jewel. But the stronger hue was the need to love and to be loved. She wanted a companionship that allowed the couple to have a personal, loving connection.

The desired method to fulfill the need becomes for that person an indicator for determining whether or not the need is being honored. These indicators are usually externally driven. The outside world of pebbles is seen as the main source of change. We may hear statements like these: "If only she would show me more affection, I wouldn't be so angry at her"… "If you would stop criticizing me, I wouldn't feel so bad about myself." These are ways of bypassing the grenades and the jewels.

On the path of self-mastery, it is essential that we first go inside to give ourselves what the soul needs. It is helpful to ask, "How do I know if I am growing?" Therefore, the concept of indicator of change is an important one. But if the indicators of need fulfillment are mostly outside us, then we give the world of pebbles control over us. More exactly, our interpretation of those events controls our responses. Useful indicators of progress can be about our patterns of thinking, how we are managing our feelings, our decision-making strategies, and the actions we take. Only the actions are external.

Capacity

The need naturally points to a capacity. It is impossible to experience a need without the corresponding desire for it. Desire cannot be there without the capacity for realizing it. This is the great paradox about grenades and jewels. *The greater the intensity of the pain or euphoria, the greater the capacity of the soul to realize the gift that was violated or celebrated.* The capacity is the gift at the very heart of the jewel. Here are a few examples.

Richard recently decided to break up with his girlfriend, Cynthia. It was a difficult decision. Richard's jewel first revealed itself as the need to be believed implicitly for his good motives. His jewel was affirmed in the way Cynthia admired his love for his children and the honorable manner he treated them and their mother. On the other hand, she would go into periodic rages of jealousy during which she accused him of being unfaithful to her. There was a cycle of affirming the jewel and then violating it. These rages were sometimes quite dramatic. Richard's grenades became so intense that he crossed the threshold of indecision and ended the relationship.

As I talked to him, I became quite aware about how important it was for him to be believed for his good motives. He did not mind negotiating ways of spending time with Cynthia or ways of communicating with her. As long as she believed in his goodness, he was content and flexible. He was, in fact, a generous man. Richard had a deep need to be seen as a man with a good heart, especially as a father and as a mate. He felt defensive about being labeled a male chauvinist or an uncaring father. He was proud of the way that he stayed involved in his children's lives.

Richard's intense need to be seen as a good man and a caring father revealed his capacity to believe in his motives and in his goodness. That is the core of his jewel. His oversensitivity and defensiveness, at the level of grenade, show that he had some doubts about his own motives and his own goodness. He probably repressed aspects of himself that were sometimes unreliable and deceitful. This repression was the basis of his projection.

It was affirming for Richard to hear that I saw him as having a tremendous capacity for trusting his motives. In fact, he relaxed enough to acknowledge that there were times when he lied to Cynthia to "avoid her wrath." Some light was cast on the shadow. I told him that I saw his jewel in his grenade—his painful response to Cynthia's questioning of his integrity. I asked him to see his need to be trusted as a window into his capacity to trust and to be trusted. Connecting the need with the capacity is extremely comforting to people. People on the path of self-mastery must learn to do this themselves.

Empathy

When we are in touch with our grenades and our jewels, we develop a profound sense of empathy for those with similar jewels. When these jewels are violated in others, we understand the nature of their pain. If we are in a position to support them, we will naturally touch them in meaningful ways. If their jewels are affirmed, we are also able to empathize with their joy and are able to join them in their celebration of their gifts. Being in touch with our grenades and jewels allows us to offer support and recognition.

However, when we are out of touch with our grenades and jewels, a cloud of density covers our ability to empathize. If people with similar jewels feel violated, we either deny their pain or become overly sympathetic. It would be difficult for us to be present to them. Our focus turns to our own pain, to a denial of that pain, or even to projecting our shadow side on those struggling with those same issues. On the other hand, if those people are praised for their gifts, we may feel envious of their accomplishments. Thus, their achievements can become a pebble that triggers a grenade about our inability to recognize our own jewels. We become fertile soil for sprouting projections.

Our empathy or lack of it likewise sheds light on the capacities of our jewel. The capacities are always there. The question is whether or not we listen to our grenades and honor our jewels. Pain and joy are both feelings, equally ripe for the mining of jewels. This view is another way of detecting what Ken Wilber describes as the Atman project: the derailment of our relentless search for unity with God by our use of substitutes along the way. And yet, the endless thirst remains within us. We keep on going despite the frustrations of our misguided attempts. Every grenade is a reminder of the Atman project. The master-in-training makes good use of every grenade.

The core of the jewel is the capacity: that native talent or innate quality we possess. That jewel will shine through needs that we can sometimes perceive directly or through our grenades. *All of our feelings reveal facets of our jewel,* even those that are not intense enough to be considered grenades.

> *A pathway to self-mastery is to take the message*
> *of every feeling*
> *and make it available to the will as grist for*
> *decision making.*

The qualities of our jewel also shine through our empathy, sympathy, and antipathy. We can utilize all of these states for jewel mining. Every human activity can be a lens into the soul. The master-in-training becomes an alchemist who is able to transform the lead of grenades into the gold of our soul capacities.

APPLICATION OF THE FRAMEWORK
The Outline of a Story

Without much background or detail, I will outline a pattern of Mark's pebble-grenade-jewel connection. Mark is married to Teresa. They have four children, all under the age of ten. His main source of pain and concern is his marriage.

PEBBLE

Teresa complains about Mark's lack of commitment to their marriage. She sees him as cold and uncaring. When Mark talks about his feelings and his view of the relationship, Teresa gets defensive, angry, and shuts down the conversation. Mark distances. After a few days, there is some warmth and friendliness between them, including some sexual contact. However, Mark does not feel safe to share his deepest thoughts and feelings. Teresa senses his distance and coldness. The cycle is repeated.

Like all couples, Teresa and Mark are mutual sources of pebbles in each other's lives. Each person's action is a pebble in the other person's pond. Teresa's action response is part of Mark's destiny and Mark's actions are part of Teresa's destiny. It helps to be mindful that our actions become part of destiny. They are pebbles triggering ripples throughout the universe.

GRENADE

Mark feels *frustrated about not being understood* by Teresa. His reaction to her anger is to shut down. *He believes that he will never feel free to talk* about his innermost thoughts and feelings. Any time he speaks his mind about something in the relationship that bothers him, Teresa "dumps her anger on him." As I listened to Mark, the part that hurt him the most was not her expression of anger. Rather, it was her cutting him off from the dialogue. Mark would cry intensely at moments when he was in touch with this realization. I could almost hear his soul groaning with frustration. He wanted so intensely *to be heard, to be understood, and to be accepted* for who he was.

For Mark, the indicator for the violation of his jewel came when he believed that he would never be free to express himself to Teresa. He thought that she would refuse to listen to him and acknowledge him for the person he is. He tried very hard to find that freedom in the relationship. He was convinced that Teresa held the key to his self-worth.

Mark's overcompensation would come through distancing and through editing his language and his actions. He thought that by doing that he could prevent a further show of anger. He hoped that by calming the relationship down, he might have the chance to express himself more freely. He was repeatedly disappointed.

JEWEL

Need. Mark had a need to be profoundly *understood* and *accepted.*
He also needed to *express* himself freely and not to be judged for the
differences in their views or for having expressed negative thoughts
and feelings about Teresa and about their relationship.

Capacity. Mark had the *capacity to share himself profoundly* and *to
be understood* deeply. By inference, he also had the *capacity to understand and accept himself* significantly. As indicated by his intense need
to *express himself freely,* Mark also had the capacity to allow freedom of
expression.

Empathy. Mark was in touch with his grenades. He felt his feelings intensely. In therapy, he was able to express these grenades in
both verbal and nonverbal ways. This indicated that Mark has the
ability to empathize with those who feel grenades similar to his own.
He would know what they are experiencing. Since Mark is not greatly
in touch with his own jewel, he may overidentify with those who are
hurting and even become too sympathetic. I have detected Mark's
ability to empathize. His sympathetic tendency is revealed in his reactivity to Teresa's anger. He gives her anger too much power over him.
He then feels that he cannot possibly go on talking because he views
her as too fragile. As Mark begins to honor his own jewel, I predict
that he will be able to listen more carefully and become less anxious
about honestly expressing himself and less protective of Teresa. Such
a step could start a benevolent cycle in their marriage. As Mark listens more carefully to his soul, he will be able to provide a greater
depth of empathy and honesty to Teresa. How Teresa responds to
Mark's openness in the relationship we do not know. Mark will have
to discover this.

Recommendations. Mark needs to recognize that Teresa's responses are more a comment on her nature than on Mark's personhood. He would be wise to go from grenade to jewel rather from grenade to pebble. Every grenade could lead him to a facet of the jewel. He may need to go back to his early experiences in the family of origin. There he could contact the little boy to find out about the early expressions of his jewel, either through past grenades or through some of his accomplishments. Getting in touch with moments of joy would also reveal the facets of his jewel. He needs to give the little boy in him permission to feel his grenades. He could then help the boy realize the sparks of the jewel behind these grenades. He will need to affirm this boy often as a way to ritualize his trust and acceptance of his soul.

Mark's trust and acceptance of himself will be the single most healing aspect of this journey of the soul. This will require that he present the little boy to God during meditation so that the soul can feel God's love and acceptance as well.

At this point, Mark will be ready to go back to the world of pebbles. He will be more able to listen carefully to Teresa. The golden rule is a good guide at this stage. He will need to understand that Teresa's grenades reveal a belonging jewel. Therefore, she will need to be reassured about his commitment, dedication, and connectedness with her. He will be wise to reassure her that his disagreements with her do not mean that he is rejecting her as a partner. Expressing his differences has more to do with his need to be understood, and less with discounting their relationship. He could also emphasize that his need to express himself freely will most likely lead to greater commitment and intimacy in their relationship.

GRIEF: FEELINGS IN STRONG RELIEF

Grief is a very natural emotion; it is really a God-given gift that allows us to come to grips with any loss in life.   –Elizabeth Kubler-Ross

GRIEF AND GRIEF WORK

We find this quotation in the opening paragraph of an article by Elizabeth Kubler-Ross on grief entitled, "Unfinished Business."[2] The concept of grief as a natural emotion goes along with the idea that feelings come from the soul and from God. They may be painful, but feelings are not bad. This emotional faculty of the soul will bring about the healing we need from any loss, if we let it take its natural course.

Kubler-Ross makes a distinction between *grief* and *grief work*. She claims that it is not necessary to work with grief. Grief involves shedding tears, sharing, and talking, but it will heal. She writes: "Grief work, in contrast, is shame, guilt, and fear ('Oh, my God, if I had only done this or that!')." The real grief work should be done before tragedy strikes.

If we feel sad, hurt, or lonely about a loss, and allow ourselves to have those feelings without repressing them or projecting them on somebody else, the grief we feel will activate the natural healing powers of the soul. We will, in time, adjust and integrate the lessons of the event. We will become whole again. This presupposes the love-based position of the soul as a child under the wings of divine providence, able to stay in touch with the inspiration of the Higher Self.

The feelings of shame, guilt, fear, and anger give the soul feedback about a power-based position in which we blame self, God, or somebody else for the loss. If we do not own those feelings and listen to their messages, we tend to control or be controlled by the events in our life. We will become reactive in our approach to life either as a victim or as an aggressor.

"My big hope is that we raise a generation of children who learn about their natural emotions in such a way that they have no grief work."
–Elizabeth Kubler-Ross

This notion about the natural course of our emotions is important to understand with our heart, not just our head. This is not a soapy, sentimental approach to life and its sometimes tragic aspects, such as losing a child. In fact, dying children teach us important lessons about the natural process of grieving and dying.

I would like to present the account that Kubler-Ross gives of an experience she had with a dying nine-year-old boy named Jeffrey. There's nothing like a good story to get the point across.

JEFFREY AND ELIZABETH KUBLER-ROSS

Shortly before he died, I visited him in the hospital where he had spent most of his life. When I walked into Jeffrey's room, I heard a young eager beaver physician who had just taken over the ward say to Jeffrey's parents, "We're going to try another experimental chemotherapy." He said this very casually, as if it were nothing. If he had looked at Jeffrey, he would have seen the child's face pale and his eyes tear up. He was so fragile, I blurted out, "Did anybody ask Jeffrey?" They shook their heads as if to say you do not ask a 9-year-old child if he wants more treatment. I said, "Yes, you do." He knows what he needs, not from his head, but from his heart.

Those who are not afraid of the answer always ask the patient. Jeffrey's parents loved him unconditionally enough to allow me to ask him in front of them and the doctor what he wanted. Jeffrey looked at me and said, "I don't understand you grown-ups that you have to make us kids so sick to get well." It was very clear, to me at least, that this child knew it was useless to start another experimental chemotherapy. While the grown-ups debated, this little guy who could barely stand said very loud and clear, "No, thank you!" The parents were able to hear it, which is the highest form of love. They said, "O.K., in that case, we will take him home."

I said goodbye to Jeffrey, and he said very matter of factly, "No, you come home with me." I thought about all the patients I had to see; before I said a word he said, "Don't worry. It only takes 10 minutes." They know and respect limits, and they answer unasked questions. Total connectedness is the wisdom of these children. So, I thought, "10 minutes, I can be with any child." We hopped in the car and drove to typical suburbia.

As we drove into the garage, Jeffrey said to his father, very brief, unsentimental, and to the point, "Take my bicycle down off the wall." There was a bicycle hanging on the wall that his father had bought for him years earlier. He said that the only thing in life that he had not done and wanted to do once in his lifetime was to ride around the block on his beloved bicycle. He had never been able to do it because of his illness. So he asked his father to take that bicycle down and with tears in his eyes—that is humility—he said, "Put the training wheels on."

With tears in his eyes the father put the training wheels on. Then Jeffrey looked at me with a big smirk (dying patients have more humor than grown-ups and healthy people) and said, "You're here to hold my mom back." That was not a joke; he was dead serious. He knew his mother wanted to lift him onto the bicycle, and she would have held him there and run around the block with him.

So, I held his mother back, and his father held me back. The three of us had to hold onto each other to overcome that urge to be overprotective. This little guy was like a drunk man; with absolutely his last ounce of energy, he climbed on that bicycle with training wheels. The only thing we did was to give a little push. It was the longest wait we had until he came around the block. He was grinning as if he had won a gold medal in the Olympics. The triumph—I mean ... that his biggest wish had been fulfilled. Then, he became again, a typical 9-year-old. He asked his father to take the training wheels off and carry the bicycle upstairs to his bedroom.

Then he looked at me and said, "You can go now." I like that lack of sentimentality. These children do what they need to do. That was the last time I saw Jeffrey. Later that day, Jeff called his brother to his bedroom and told him that he wanted to give him the bicycle now for a birthday present, that he would not be around on his birthday, but that he wanted the pleasure of giving it to his brother himself.

These parents have no grief work, although they have a great deal of grief over the loss of a 9-year-old boy. They would have a fantastic amount of grief work if, because of their own needs, because of their own inability to let go, because of their own lack of unconditional love, they had insisted on another experimental chemotherapy. Jeffrey would have died, probably in an intensive care unit, sick and nauseated, bald and miserable, without having fulfilled his greatest wish.[3]

This is a beautiful account of the painful but natural response that a young boy showed in facing his destiny.

GRIEF WORK BEFORE TRAGEDY STRIKES

"The real grief work should be done before tragedy strikes," wrote Dr. Kubler-Ross. Since loss is universal and pervasive, we can do our grief work on a daily basis if we stay in touch with our feelings. If feelings are from our soul, we can regard our dealing with them as learning and practice sessions in preparation for responding to destiny.

We encounter loss in many different ways from the time we were born: the loss of mother's milk and touch, a toy, a game, an opportunity, a friendship, and, of course, the loss of a loved one through death.

Loss triggers that ancient, core anxiety of being separated from God, our source of security and identity. Every loss, therefore, is a chance to get in touch with our primary mission in life: to find our true identity on the way back to God. Even getting stuck in a power-based position of trying angrily to control a given situation will remind us of the futility and hollowness of our power-based victories. Our efforts to control the outer world are void of the inner connectedness with life, the universe, and God. These attempts are substitutes for God's true healing energies. Power-based control moves divide us, distancing us from fulfilling the need to become more and more a part of one another. Personal transformation that leads to viable relationships is the path to true healing and happiness.

Grief brings out, in strong relief, the life-giving, soul-elevating capacities of our feeling nature, if we allow it to touch us, inform us, but not to direct us. We, in concert with our Higher Selves, must provide the leadership.

IN A NUTSHELL

- We learned to honor and value our feelings as communication from deep within our soul. We took a further step in the process of mining the jewels within our feelings by getting a deeper understanding of the pebble, grenade, and jewel connection.

- We reviewed the idea of pebble as the hand of destiny appearing in the form of facts and events that we face. Grenades, our internal emotional responses, alert us to the important information that the soul wants us to consider. These intense feelings of pain or joy signal perceived violations or celebrations of the jewels within us. We described the model for managing feelings as a process for Personal Transformation.

- We saw how we can connect need to capacity to empathy. These are the three aspects of a jewel. The grenade always presents us with an open door to discover these aspects of our jewels. *This is the pathway to personal transformation: the journey from pebble to grenade to jewel.* We will not find it if we go from pebble to grenade and back to the world of pebbles (the external world). After we mine the jewels within our grenades, then we are ready to go back to the world of pebbles.

- One pathway to self-mastery is the belief that events manifest the hand of destiny. These events trigger the grenades, which become the footprints for reading the specific qualities of the jewel in us.

- I have detected two main errors in response to painful grenades: first, the attempt to find a quick fix, and second, getting mired in the intensity of the emotional weight. The quick fix is journey from pebble to grenade and back to pebble again in an attempt to change the outside world and finding salvation there. On the other hand, we could wallow in our emotional morass and get mired in it. Either case reflects a failure to stay in sufficient contact with our grenades to mine their jewels.

- The best way to understand a grenade is to see it as a response to a perceived violation or celebration of a facet of our jewel. The pebble is important. It triggers an opportunity for discovery and for learning. But it is not an adequate explanation of our response. For that, we need to understand our grenades and jewels.

- I define jewel as a precious stone within your soul. Jewels reflect pockets of soul sensitivity. Most religions portray a creation myth that depicts the soul as an emanation from the essence of God. Just as the soul is a facet of God, the Great Diamond, so a jewel is a facet of the soul.

- We are unique. Our soul carries a specific blueprint that is revealed by destiny, not created by the events and experiences of life. We are not simply the product of environmental forces. **Need.** Jewels reveal themselves first as needs. These are soul demands. Let us not confuse needs with being needy. A need is a yearning for a certain quality of the soul to be expressed in some way.

  Capacity. The core of the jewel is the capacity: that native talent or innate quality we possess. The need naturally points to a capacity. Desire cannot exist without the capacity for realizing it.

  Empathy. When we are in touch with our grenades and our jewels, we develop a profound sense of empathy for those with similar jewels. When these jewels are violated in others, we understand the nature of their pain. Conversely, if their jewels are affirmed, we are able to empathize with their joy and are able to join them in celebrating their gifts.

- The concept of grief as a natural emotion goes along with the idea that feelings come from the soul and from God. They may be painful, but they are not bad. This emotional faculty of the soul will bring about the healing we need from any loss, if we let it take its natural course. Loss triggers that ancient, core anxiety of being separated from God, our source of security and identity. Every loss, therefore, is a chance to get in touch with our primary mission in life: to find our true identity on the way back to God.

CONCLUDING NOTE

The Framework for Personal Transformation has emerged out of my daily work with individuals, couples, and families. I have also been able to teach it to the therapists I train. Since I watch these therapists from behind a one-way mirror while I am training them, I can influence the course of therapy while it is going on. I can test to see if the ideas are working or not.

I have also applied these ideas in the corporate setting, but with a different emphasis. In the work setting, the process of personal transformation is often best done quietly and privately. The payoff for this inner work will manifest in the quality of the communication and negotiation that follow.

This framework has been a significant boost in the lives of those I counsel, consult with, and train. My faith in the process of contacting the soul through grenades and jewels has been strengthened significantly. I invite you to test these ideas in your own life. At first, it seems like a lonely and burdensome journey because the framework always asks us to go within. The little child in us prefers a magical solution, where a prince/princess or a mom/pop figure takes care of us. Wilber has eloquently warned[4] us about falling into this romantic but regressive trap.

Hopefully, the rewards of self-transformation will keep us going inside oueselves to explore the riches of the soul. Our best contribution to the universe outside is to take care of our universe inside. In the long run, I believe we will all discover that inside and outside are intricately connected.

[1] Hillman, J. (1996). *The Soul's Code*. New York: Random House.

[2] Kubler-Ross, E. (1984). "Unfinished Business." In J. C. Hansen and, T. Frantz, Eds. *Death and Grief in the Family*. Rockville, MD: An Aspen Publication.

[3] Ibid. See Footnote 1.

[4] Wilber, K. (1995). *Sex, Ecology, Spirituality*. Boston: Shambhala Publications, Inc.

Chapter 6
COMMITMENT AND ACTION
Mastering the Will (1)

THE THREE PARTS OF THE MIND

THINKING, FEELING, AND WILLING

What are the connections involved in thinking, feeling, and decision making? Do we jump from thought to action? From feeling to action? From decision making to action? What about attitude? Is it just a thought or a feeling? What about the difference between a thought and a commitment? Is conviction more than a group of strongly held thoughts? When someone asks for our position on an issue or a plan, what, specifically, are they asking us to reveal? Is it a question of thinking, feeling, or willing?

In Western culture, it is difficult to express one's awareness other than as thoughts, feelings, or actions. Awareness about our cognitive or thinking life is well developed. Our affective or feeling life is also in the forefront of our awareness, even though its expression may be stifled by our cultural expectations.

The will is often taken for granted, however. It is viewed simply as a byproduct of our thinking and feeling process. In other words, our actions are seen primarily as the result of the mix of thoughts and feelings influencing us at a given moment. This assumption hides a significant part of our divine nature as human beings: our free will.

Philosophers, theologians, and mystics in past centuries gave much greater attention to the will than psychologists do today. This is unfortunate, as the will, after all, is the faculty through which we manifest our freedom to choose a course of action. *The self comes through in the act of will.*

Psychologists today give primacy to cognitive, emotive, or behavioral aspects of human experience. One often gets the impression that there is an automatic equation that looks like this: thoughts + feelings = action. According to this view, actions are best explained by studying the content of thoughts and feelings. Others, like sociologists, would add the impact of social and cultural forces to this equation. So now, we have social/cultural forces + thoughts + feelings = actions.

In any of the scenarios, decision making as a function of will is left nonexistent or, at best, viewed as a token blur on the psychological screen. This may be another consequence of the nature-nurture debate that has dominated the human sciences in this century. The person is left on the periphery of the human forest.

Among the pioneers in psychology, a notable exception is the work of Roberto Assagioli, whose psychosynthesis framework puts the will at the core of human existence and functioning. I have used some of Assagioli's ideas to highlight the concept of position, which I have developed and utilized in my counseling and consulting work with individuals, families, and organizations. This chapter will focus on the concept of position more than on any other aspect of the willing process.

THE NATURE OF POSITION

The person interested in mastering the self will do well to grasp the concept of position to the point of absorption and integration. Doing this will lead to greater clarity and flexibility in negotiating decisions and actions.

A VIGNETTE

Imagine, one evening, that I ask my wife if she wants to see a movie. As she is considering my request, I see her eyes roll up and then move from side to side. I interpret these cues to mean that she has mixed thoughts and feelings about going to the movie. I do not consider the possibility that she is in the process of decision making. She then says, "Yes, I want to go see this movie tonight." She took a position. Since I think that she has mixed thoughts and feelings about going, I say, "You don't really want to go, do you? It's, okay, you can tell me straight. I can take it."

That is an interesting response. Actually, this is a common response in interpersonal situations. In this vignette, I make at least two erroneous assumptions. One is that position is simply the result of a grouping of thoughts and feelings. This is a common error. This view assumes that my wife's decision is "simply" the addition or net effect of the thoughts and feelings she had at the moment. It is *she* who decides—not the group of thoughts and feelings influencing her.

The second error is that I assume my wife's motives must be pure in order for her to "really want" something. In other words, mixed thoughts and feelings would negate her ability to make a genuine choice. If my wife thought that there were other things she could do that night besides going to the movie, then her "yes" could not be spontaneous or genuine. Moreover, if she was slightly tired and felt like staying home in addition to feeling pulled to see a movie, then she could not "wholly" choose to go with me.

THE CONCEPT OF POSITION

The concept of position, if correctly understood, allows us to cut through this kind of fuzzy thinking. It frees us to accept the diversity of our thoughts and feelings and still make a genuine choice. A choice is an act of will. It is qualitatively different from thinking and feeling. It is natural for my wife to have a variety of thoughts and feelings about a request and still be able to say yea or nay. And since I made the request, it would be wise for me to accept my wife's act of will (her position) and respect her right to think and feel as she does.

This vignette reveals an aspect of position as commitment. Position, then, can be a commitment to an action. It can be as simple and straightforward as an agreement to go to a movie, either by myself or with someone.

If somebody asks what our thoughts are about an issue, we may offer our thoughts, pro and con. The person may then ask, "But where do you *stand* on this question? *Will* you support/promote this matter or not?" This is an altogether different question than what we think or feel about the matter. However, our language is not always clear.

I am not implying that understanding thoughts and feelings is unimportant. It is crucial in any relationship or task. Our paradigms have a great bearing on our behavior as we saw, for instance, in relation to causality and self-responsibility. I am saying, however, that there is a qualitative difference between thinking and feeling, on the one hand, and the *act of* willing, on the other.

When people ask where we are on issue, they are asking for our position. This is the concept of position as stance. It is an expression of a stand we take on a certain matter. A stance is more than a thought or feeling. It is even more than a conviction (a strong belief, usually backed by evidence). The word *attitude* probably conveys a position. The dictionary defines it as a posture or position. More graphically, attitude is "the tilt of a vehicle measured in relation to the surface of the earth as horizontal plane (space flight)."[1] The word *tilt* visually captures the concept of position because position is a relational idea. It depicts the position of a person in relation to another person or issue. A position always evokes a relationship that someone has toward someone or something, so that the self is defined in relation to something or someone else.

Position, as an act of will, occupies a different dimension than motive. Motive is essentially a push-pull experience triggered by the configuration of thoughts and feelings in relation to a certain issue or action. We experience motive as a directional tug towards a position or action. No one single image, sound, word, or feeling determines the position we take. *We* take a position through an act of will. We, you and I, are free beings. We have the capacity to choose. It is not our will that is free. It is *we* who are free. The will is the faculty through which we exercise that freedom.

HIGHLIGHTING THE SPECIAL CHARACTER OF THE WILL

Let us highlight the differences and the links between position and motive. Let us notice that motive is already a configuration of thoughts and feelings that provides a tug toward an action.

Position and Motive: Definition and Connection

A position is an act of will. It is a choice to take a stand on some issue or make a commitment to do something. Action is the child of a position. Position embodies motive, but it is independent of motive.

Motive provides the push-pull toward a certain issue or action. It is triggered by the configuration of thoughts and feelings (including images, sounds, words, and visceral feelings). Motive provides the heart and soul of what we commit to do. It offers the inspiration for our commitments. Still, the act of will, through which the self takes a position, transcends any aspect of our motives. We may even go against the strongest inclinations that our motives provide. The self remains free.

Through an act of will, a person takes a position that is not determined by any single thought or feeling. Our soul informs us through our thoughts and feelings, but our soul does not determine our positions. It is the self that takes a position. We are not determined by any one thing. We are free beings. It is not really our will that is free. *It is we who are free.* The will is the faculty through which we exercise that freedom.

The illustration to the right shows us a diagrammatic representation of the three faculties of the mind: thinking, feeling, and willing.

In the next chapter, we will expand this diagram, naming it The Communication Pyramid. For now, we will use it to highlight the qualitative difference between the will and thoughts and feelings. It is vital that we etch this special place of the will within the family of our inner faculties. The dotted line in the diagram depicts the difference between motivation (thinking/feeling process) and position (decision-making process). Let us periodically review the following highlighted portions:

The Three Parts of the Mind
Willing
(position)

Thinking ◄ *motivation* ► Feeling

The culmination of the willing process is a decision.
The decision defines the position of the self in relation to something or someone.

The will is the faculty through which the self governs the soul, which is the realm of the physical, the emotional, and the mental. The function of being the governing faculty of the self gives the will a special character in our interior life. That character is embodied in the act of taking a position through a process of decision making.

In the following illustration of how this concept can help guide us through some knotty territories, keep the diagram in view.

When couples come to see me for a marital issue, I try to sift out the position that each partner is taking vis-à-vis the relationship. "Are you in or out of the relationship?" This is not the same question as, "What does it feel like to be his wife?" or "What do you think about your marriage?" I usually ask the following question in the first session: "Where are you on a scale from 1 to 10, '10' meaning you are strongly committed to work on improving this relationship despite the pain, and '1' meaning that you have already made an irrevocable decision to divorce your spouse?" Any choice from 2 to 10 means that a person is still "in the marriage."

There is a qualitative difference between 1 and any number above it, including 2. That difference is a matter of position. A number "1" represents a commitment to divorce. *A position has been taken.* That person has already crossed the threshold of marriage and is now on course towards becoming single. The numbers "2" through "10" represent *one* position, but with varying degrees of motivational strength. That person is still "inside the marital arena" despite the pain and the difficulties experienced.

My *position* as a therapist will vary depending on the couple's relative positions on this commitment scale. If they are both within the 2 to 10 range, it is possible to have a marital therapy contract, granted that both persons make a commitment to work with me. If the person on the lower end of the scale is hesitant to commit to therapy, he or she may still be willing to explore the desirability of doing marital therapy. So, a few sessions of exploratory work may be agreed upon. If one partner has already decided on divorce, there are several possibilities: divorce therapy, no therapy for either, or individual therapy for coaching the committed one to seek "to win back his/her spouse".

These are all matters of taking a position, not just having mixed feelings or thoughts. It is even possible to take a position that counters a strong, opposing thought. A CEO could say to a vice president, "I don't think this approach will work, but I'm willing to try it. Whether or not this project succeeds, you have my full backing to test it." This illustrates how an act of will can transcend thoughts or feelings.

This idea is sometimes caught in the expression: "Despite my better judgment, I went along with the plan." In other words, despite a person's thoughts or feelings about a planned course of action, she decided to "go along with it." We may even go against our intuition in favor of some logical argument or in favor of a strong desire to do something. Or, we may follow an intuition that goes against our logical or emotional grain. It is a luxury when all parts of the mind are strongly aligned in one direction.

In any case, the self is alone at the very moment of that decision that leads to a position. But it is also during that moment of aloneness that we are most free, for it is precisely when the self, in the act of will, comes through. It is a moment when, as image and likeness of spirit, we manifest divinity in kosmos.

STAGES OF THE WILL

INTRODUCTION

Like Jung, Roberto Assagioli concludes that we human beings have a Higher Self. He says that the "I" or the conscious self is a projection of the Higher Self into the three-dimensional world. When we are asleep, the conscious self disappears and is assumed into the

Higher Self. This self is the permanent center, which is the source of the "I." The higher unconscious proceeds from this center and becomes the source of our higher aspirations and inspirations. It is indeed the manifestation of God-in-us. The self is the spark of individuality created in "image and likeness of God."

Assagioli spoke of an apparent dilemma that the experience of "two selves" brings for us humans. Existentially, we may experience a duality of these two selves, thinking that there are really two centers of being, which often contradict each other. It is true that the conscious self, in response to contradictory thoughts and feelings, sometimes takes positions that counter the inspirations (intuitions) of the Higher Self. Assagioli, in fact, raised this duality as the central problem in the human experience. He offered the following solutions to this dilemma:

- Knowledge of one's personality (through self-exploration or with a therapist)
- Management of one's thoughts, feelings, decisions, etc.
- Realization of one's true self
- Psychosynthesis—the reconstruction of the personality around its true center, the Higher Self.

As a core technique to understand the nature of the self, Assagioli uses a process called disidentification. The self is regarded as pure consciousness—the knower, not the known, the observer, not that which is observed, or the seer, not the seen. The self is essentially dissociated from any thought, feeling, decision, or action.

The exercise of disindentification involves saying things like: "I have thoughts, but I am not my thoughts. I have feelings, but I am not my feelings. I make decisions, but I am not my decisions. I perform actions, but I am not my actions. I am I, a being of pure awareness." Since the conscious self is regarded as a projection of the

Higher Self in the universe of matter, life, and mind, it is regarded as essentially unmodified by any specific characteristic. It would then be an oxymoron to associate the verb "to be" with any specific quality. Assagioli alerts us to the proper and improper use of the verb "to be." Instead of saying, "I am depressed," we are asked to say, "I feel depressed." The "I am" form is to be used only for our essential qualities, not changeable ones. Assagioli shares the following principle:

We are dominated by everything with which our self becomes identified.
We can dominate and control everything from which we disidentify ourselves.
–Roberto Assagioli, M.D.,
Psychosynthesis, 1971

I suggest revising Assagioli's language of "dominance and control" to the more "self-responsible" concept of managing only one's response. We cannot control another person's actions. Although we can have influence and impact on others, we cannot have unilateral control of their mind or their actions. In fairness to Assagioli, I must point out that he was speaking only of managing the self, not managing others.

With that revision in language, the principle of disidentification can be helpful in thinking clearly and in keeping the self free from being unduly controlled by thoughts, feelings, and intentions. The will becomes a clearer instrument of the self for taking positions independently of any specific thought or feeling. I have a will. I am not my will or any of its activities, just as I am not my feelings or thoughts.

Disidentification also helps to prepare the self to begin making the Higher Self the unifying center of all of our activities. This recentering of the personality around the Self, instead of the conscious self, is one of the goals of self-mastery.

THE SIX FUNCTIONAL STAGES OF THE WILL

Assagioli described six stages of the will. It is helpful to know these stages in order to have a clearer understanding of position. The following is my paraphrasing of his description of the sequential stages of the will in action. I have taken the liberty to integrate Assagioli's framework into my conceptual view of position.

ROBERTO ASSAGIOLI'S SIX STAGES OF THE WILL[2]

1. **Purpose, Aim, or Goal, Based on Evaluation, Motivation, and Intention.** A volitional act is characterized by the existence of a purpose to be achieved. In other words, there is an aim or goal to reach. Purpose is more than just floating images in our mind. A vision is not necessarily part of the will in action. An aim must be evaluated and assessed. If the aim is assessed as valuable, it will likely arouse motives, which trigger the intention to achieve it.

2. **Deliberation.** This is process of determining which of the possible goals is preferable. Goals are the specific aims that could fulfill a purpose. Deliberation is the foundation for choice.

3. **Choice and Decision.** A goal is chosen and a decision is made to pursue it. In essence, the self has commanded the will to strive towards a specific goal and to set aside other goals.

4. **Affirmation: The Command or "Fiat" of the Will.** The choice and decision must be confirmed by an affirmation. This affirmation is designed to activate the energies needed to reach the goal. It is as if the will is commanding the "opposing" thoughts and feelings to "get in line" and join the team.

5. **Planning and Working out a Program.** The plan and program are based on the means and phases of the execution of the plan through time and the existing conditions and circumstances.

6. Direction of the Execution. The will is director, not the actor, in the execution of the program. More correctly, the self, through the will, directs our thoughts, feelings, and body towards action. The will exercises constant supervision of the execution. At this point, all of our parts—thoughts, feelings (motives, urges, and impulses)—must be adapted and subordinated to the underlying purpose.

In my framework, Steps 1 and 2 belong to the realm of thinking and feeling. It involves the harnessing of motivation into an intention. It is in Step 3 that the self truly begins to take a position in the manner I am defining it. This position is reaffirmed in Step 4 before the actual striving[3] begins. In Step 6, the will continues its involvement as director of the execution. The other faculties, along with our physical body, are the actors in this drama.

Assagioli outlines these stages of the will as a "guide to complete and purposive action." It is not intended to be a description of every decision-to-action sequence. Many of our intentions are not carried out into willed acts in this clearly purposive manner. He offers us a valid description of what could be an ideal guide for bringing will into action. His description is also a good framework for developing the Congruent Mind—all parts of the self working together for a common purpose. It is clear that this framework is important on the path of self-mastery.

Here is a simple illustration of the stages in Assagioli's words. Talking about the head of a foundation who has just decided to fund an activity, he writes:

> At noon the same man may shift his *aim* to having lunch. He will quickly *deliberate* on the various possibilities, *choose* one among several nearby restaurants, and *decide* to go there. Perhaps he may

meet a friend on the way and chat with him. After a while, if the acquaintance leaves, he may remember that before getting side-tracked he had decided to go to the restaurant. So he *affirms* to himself that he will now proceed without allowing himself to be further interrupted. He rapidly *plans* the road to follow, and gets on his way.[4]

It is important not to have a strictly linear understanding of this sequence. If I deliberate about whether to lose ten pounds and keep that weight off for life, that goal requires much more than deciding on lunch today. It requires that my will be locked in to that goal through several weeks or perhaps a lifetime. It has to do with a much larger purpose—a purpose to which I will need to recommit periodically. If my vision of that purpose fades, I may not be able to direct the will towards actions that will continually manifest the goal.

Hence, the importance of purpose. If purpose is important in the matter of losing ten pounds and changing our lifestyle so that we continue to keep the weight off, what about keeping clear the vision of our life's purpose? The Jewish Scriptures say: "Without vision, the people perish." The will, as the servant of our vision, is destined to wander aimlessly without a clear vision of the purpose. Let us think of the consequences of a life without a clear sense of its overall purpose, without a clear grasp of its calling. No surprise about the effects on a people where the science and the culture are, in Wilber's words, "gutted of Spirit."[5] There will be a slowing down of the realization of our true purpose: union with our Higher Self. There will be no experience of Atman, just the prolonged suffering of the Atman project.

POSITION: THE SELF IN EXPRESSION

PURPOSE, VALUES, MOTIVES, AND INTENTIONS

Assagioli considers purpose, values, motives, and intentions as all part of the same stage of the will in action. He defines *purpose* as the will to reach a goal. To be a goal, something must be valuable. It must also be valued enough to trigger a movement or motive that impels us toward a goal. The direction of the motive is given by an intention of the self through the will.

In reality, these processes are not always in sequence or in logical order. We may be aware of some feeling that moves us to consider some values not yet clear in our mind. An event may trigger an emotional grenade that reveals a jewel in the form something we need or want. We may then intend to reach a goal that would fulfill that need or purpose.

Since thoughts and feelings are pieces of information from our soul, they reveal yearnings for experiences we need in order to fulfill our purpose. These yearnings may be steps needed to fulfill our mission. We must direct these thoughts and feelings in order for those values and motives to become intentions directed toward a goal. The will is our faculty for doing this. Through the will, we are the directors of this entire drama.

At this point, the crucial role that overall purpose plays in the direction of these intentions becomes obvious. That is why authors today make so much about the significance of creating a personal mission statement. Such a statement makes explicit our *meta*-purpose: the purpose of all the other purposes. Assagioli alludes to this when he says that motives and intentions are based on evaluations and that evaluations are based on the meaning attributed to life. He writes:

But this meaning, in its turn, is given by the aim or purpose of life itself, and by its achievement. Therefore it is very helpful for putting the will into operation to have a positive conception of the meaning and purpose of life; to admit, first of all, that life *has* a purpose which is meaningful; second, that this purpose is positive, constructive, valuable—in one word, that it is *good.*[6]

SELF AND POSITION IN RELATION TO THOUGHTS AND FEELINGS

It is important to redefine the concept of position now that we have described the stages of the will. Since I distinguish position as qualitatively different from thinking and feeling, it may be confusing to place the concept inside Assagioli's framework. He talks about purpose, meaning, and motive as elements of these stages of the will. I defined position earlier as an act of will: a choice to take a stand on some issue or to make a commitment to do something. It is in Step 3 (choice) that position emerges.

Through affirmation, that position is clarified and strengthened. Through planning and the execution of the plan, one's position becomes manifest in some form.

Position actually reveals the self in action. In taking a position, the self has, more or less, taken thinking and feeling into account. I say "more or less" because each person takes these messages from the soul in varying ways and degrees.

We do not always listen to the messages behind our spontaneous thoughts and feelings, which are indeed the mouthpieces of the soul. These thoughts and feelings do not determine our position. They influence and inform the self but they do not determine the choice that triggers the taking of a position. A few more definitions may help to clarify things further.

Under the term *thinking,* I include reasoning, beliefs, interpretations, meaning, and values. Reasoning refers to the process we use to analyze and evaluate things. Beliefs are our conclusions, while values reflect those aspects of life we consider worthwhile. Interpreting is the process we use to make meaning. Within the term *feeling*, I include our emotion. Motive, implying movement toward something, is best seen as a combination of thinking and feeling. It is interesting to play with the hyphenated word *e-motion*: a movement with energy or energy in motion.

MIXED MOTIVES AND CONTRADICTORY THOUGHTS

Our human experience daily reinforces the reality that we have a multiplicity of motives and a tremendous variety of thoughts, some of which contradict each other. I may go to lunch with my colleague because I feel hungry, want to discuss something with him, to fulfill an obligation, or because I enjoy his company. (Note that once we describe life in action, it is impossible to extricate thinking from feeling. All the motives mentioned above have a thinking and feeling component. The feeling component of motive provides the energy that "tugs" on the self, clamoring toward fulfillment of an intention. Since I am already describing an action, the description also includes elements of execution of the plan under the direction of the will.)

The motives described above are different but not necessarily contradictory. In the drive to be authentic, we might erroneously chastise ourselves for having mixed motives. You might hear a voice inside saying, "The only reason you went to lunch with him was *because* you were hungry. You really didn't want to be with him." This is like the scenario with my wife in which I might conclude that because she had thoughts other than just going to the movie with me, I assumed "she *really* did not want to go."

The point I wish to emphasize is that although position embodies motive, it is independent of motive. The *self makes the choice*. The self is not the puppet of the energy that may be pulling on it. We are truly free. The act of will is a sacred act through which the self is manifested. Our actions are not simply the product of our impulses, thoughts, and social pressures. It is true that people manifest different degrees of selfhood in actions. But it is still, finally, the self that comes through—more or less burdened by the onslaught of internal and external pressures.

Assagioli has some important reflections on authenticity that are relevant to our understanding of the relationship between position, on the one hand, and thoughts and feelings, on the other. He suggested a technique, which he dubbed "acting as if." He was criticized for suggesting such a technique because some thought it hypocritical to act kindly toward someone if you felt resentful toward that person, for example.

Assagioli did not think that hypocrisy was the real question involved. The more relevant question was the multiplicity that exists within us. It would be hypocritical to use the technique *if* we were attempting to deceive others for selfish ends or if we fooled ourselves by denying that we did not have any lower motives. He writes:

> But if, when an impulse or motive of hostility and resentment against someone arises in us, *we,* our true, our genuine self, do not approve of it and refuse to identify with it, then our *real will* is to choose the better motive and to act benevolently *in spite of* the impulse that urges us to treat the person badly. We can *choose* the motive to which we give free course.[7]

Assagioli is, by no means, advocating repression. He does not recommend denying that a person may have hostile feelings. The alternative, however, is not impulsive aggression. I think he would support the method for managing feelings that I am advocating in this book. He advocates transmutation and sublimation as ways of dealing with these feelings and motives. Turning a grenade into a jewel is a form of transmutation. Utilizing the capacities (jewels) for enlightened action is a way of sublimation. These processes give us more choices. That is the whole point of differentiating the function of the will from that of thinking and feeling. Assagioli says: "Authenticity does not consist in giving in to a bad motive simply because it exists."[8] We do have a choice about which motive to give expression and whether to give direct expression to a deeply felt anger or hurt.

He then adds a brilliant and profound statement: "Furthermore, in making this choice, this decision, we can make use of the resources of clear understanding as well as of the guidance of the Transpersonal Self."[9] The Transpersonal Self is another name for the Higher Self, the Higher Mind, or the spirit in us that is made in the image and likeness of God. Jung called it the superconscious mind.

As soon as we introduce the Higher Self into our understanding of the human being, we have introduced another layer of influence beyond just thinking, feeling, or social pressure. The Higher Self is the source of inspirations and lofty aspirations. If God is the Great Diamond, then we are a facet of that Diamond as the mind of God within us. This means that we have additional choices on the menu of possibilities.

This introduces a deeper understanding of choice and self-responsibility. The choice I make is an expression of me but it is not me. The self is pure consciousness. It has a capacity to choose but it is not determined or defined by its choice—although the self is responsible for its choices. If someone yells at me, I will probably feel grenades of hurt and anger. But I do not have to yell back. My Higher Self has repeatedly confirmed the wisdom of the injunction to "love our enemy." I also happened to learn that belief from my religion. But unless my Higher Self confirms it and inspires me to follow it, that belief may not hold much clout in my hierarchy of values.

IN A NUTSHELL

Thinking clearly about the will reinforces for me the principle of self-responsibility. I am responsible for my actions and reactions. This is not a burden but a celebration of true freedom. We really do have a choice. That freedom to choose does not mean cutting off from the impact that our thoughts and feelings have on us. And these can be very powerful. In life, there are many issues that are confusing and not easy to think through. Some of our feelings are like grenades that explode with the force of a nuclear weapon. They are nevertheless messages for us from our growing/groaning soul. It is best that we stay in touch with these inner meanings and feelings.

These meanings and motives inform us, but they do not determine us. We are free to determine ourselves. This is also true with regard to the social pressure we encounter in the world outside, our world of pebbles. We defined destiny as the facts and events that confront us daily. They are the pebbles thrown into our pond. Yes, we do ripple and sometimes feel grenades at the bottom of our pond. But those ripples and grenades reveal our nature: the nature of our sensitivities, which reflect our jewels. It is still *us* that is revealed by those pebbles of destiny.

We can remain intact through the conscious, responsible exercise of our will. Just as we have a Higher Self and a conscious self (lower-case "s"), so we have a Higher Will and a conscious will (lowercase "w"). Our spirituality and our religious traditions can remind us about this inner treasure. We can pray, meditate, and remain open to this great source of inspiration, intuition, and light. Deepak Chopra is correct in saying that a belief in a Higher Self is a necessary ingredient for effective living. He also says that we must each discover and fulfill our personal mission in life.[10]

The will is a glorious faculty, but only a faculty. It is obedient to the directives of the self—you and me. When the self is in touch with its purpose and becomes committed to that calling, true freedom is possible. Freedom is a capacity for self-directed action. But it becomes empty when there is no purpose for which it can mobilized towards the achievement of an overall purpose. Within the umbrella of this overall purpose, there are thousands of exciting smaller goals to achieve.

Congruence is the mobilization of all of our parts towards the fulfillment of our mission. Congruence in the service of our mission is the structure of self-mastery. It is the path of sainthood.

[1] *The Wordsworth Concise English Dictionary.* (1994 Edition). Hertfordshire: England.

[2] Assagioli, R. (1973). *The Act of Will.* New York: Penguin Books USA, Inc. This is a paraphrase of Assagioli's ideas, though stated mainly in his own terms.

[3] The striving part of the mind is called the *conative,* in contrast to the cognitive and affective faculties. Few people are aware of the word these days. The classic philosophers and theologians were much more aware of these parts of our human functioning: cognitive, affective, and conative. Conative is often used synonymously with action precisely because it is the striving part of the will that produces action. Conative, however, is best regarded as the process of striving—the how, rather than the end result of our actions. Ken Wilber uses the word conative extensively, particularly in describing the qualities of the stages of personal development. See Wilber's *The Atman Project.* (1980). Wheaton, IL: Quest Books. The theorist who has done the most to study the conative aspect of the mind is Kathy Kolbe. Kolbe sees the conative process of the mind as the *instinctive way we strive to create.* She has developed an instrument to measure instinctive action trademarked as the Kolbe Conative Index. See Kolbe, K. (1990). *The Conative Connection.* New York: Addison-Wesley Publishing. Also, Kolbe, K. (1993). *Pure Instinct.* New York: Random House, Inc.

[4] Assagioli, R. (1973). *The Act of Will.* New York: Penguin Books USA, Inc.

[5] See Wilber's discussion of the dignity and the disaster of modernity and post-modernity in Wilber, K. (1995), *Sex, Ecology, Spirituality.* Boston: Shambhala. See also Wilber, K. (1998). *The Marriage of Sense and Soul: Integrating Science and Religion.* New York: Random House.

[6] Assagioli, R. (1973). *The Act of Will.* New York: Penguin Books USA, Inc., p. 141.

[7] Ibid., p. 142.

[8] Ibid., p. 143.

[9] Ibid.

[10] Chopra, D. (1994). *The Seven Spiritual Laws of Success.* San Rafael, CA: Amber-Allen Publishing, pp. 95-103.

Chapter 7

THE ART OF NEGOTIATING CHANGE AND CONFLICT

Mastering the Will (2)

POSITIONING FOR GRACEFUL NEGOTIATION

In the last chapter, we saw how taking a position on a certain issue is qualitatively different from expressing our thoughts and feelings on the matter. Yet we kept in mind the importance of staying in touch with our thoughts and feelings. We will now apply our insights about the three parts of the mind to the area of communication. Special focus will be given to that important aspect of communication called *negotiation*—the gentle art of promoting change and resolving conflicts in relationships and groups.

NEGOTIATION AND THE CONCEPT OF POSITION

We will start with a number of concepts and principles that set the foundation for good negotiation. Using the three parts of the mind, we will build a framework called The Communication Pyramid (TCP). We will then learn to build mutual understanding through the use of the Deep Empathy Model (DEM). Finally, we will deal with the heart of negotiation itself: promoting change and resolving conflicts. For this, we turn to the Synergy Model for Change (SMC).

But first, a couple of stories to illustrate the use of position in negotiation. The first is a parenting example, and the other is about a couple defining their position in their marriage.

VIGNETTE: Coaching Parents

I have coached many parents to bypass intense power struggles with their children. The key was to distinguish *behavior management* and *mind control.* I told them never to negotiate their child's thoughts and feelings, only her actions. However, it was crucial to listen to their child's thoughts and feelings and, in fact, to "amplify" their child's need to say what was on her mind and heart. The parents learned to apply the process of achieving deep empathy by sincerely crawling inside their child's skin, seeing through her eyes, and hearing from within her ears, so they could get a feel for the world of their child.

The goal to this step was to generate understanding and, hopefully, a belief, on the part of the child, that the parents had some level of empathy. The main guideline was that there were to be no power struggles about thoughts and feelings. "What if they argue with us?" some parents asked. My response was that it takes at least two to continue a power struggle. Under no circumstances were they to reason with the child, nor persuade the child in any way, not even to instruct the child in any way.

After a reasonable, but limited, length of time of listening to the child and amplifying her thoughts and feelings, the parents paused to ask her a question: "Would you be willing to hear our thoughts and feelings about this?" If yes, the parents were to share their own thoughts and feelings, briefly. If the child interrupted the parents, they were to stop the discussion at that point with the words, "We will take your thoughts into consideration, and we will come back with a plan of action."

In presenting the plan some time later, the parents were to emphasize to the child that she did not have to like the plan. If the child was willing to negotiate the plan respectfully, she was invited to do so. With or without the child's ideas, the parents made the final decision, and the plan was to be put into effect. I would tell the parents to be calm but firm enforcers of the plan. It was better for them to expect that the child would not "like" the plan, yet they were to expect the child to follow it. Otherwise, there would be consequences.

I remember an interesting incident when our daughter Anna-Lisa was between four and five years of age. I told her to go take a bath. She responded by saying that she didn't feel like taking a bath. I then said to her: "I'm so sorry, Anna-Lisa. I didn't make myself clear. I didn't ask you *to feel* like taking a bath. I just want you to go get one. And while in you're in the bathtub, please feel free to cry and to hate it. That will be okay with me."

I don't think Anna-Lisa was very happy about it. But at least I tried to honor her right to feel what she felt, while exercising my parental leadership. I did this by managing her behavior, not her mind. This is a cardinal principle to live by in the area of parent-child negotiation.

VIGNETTE: A Marriage Example

Tom and Mary came to see me for marriage counseling. They were on the verge of breaking up their ten-year marriage. I asked Tom where he stood on a scale of 1 to 10, with 10 being highly committed to work on improving the marriage and 1 being at the point of divorce. He said he was at a 2. Mary was at a 10.

Tom showed no warmth toward Mary during the interview. He said he had recently changed his position with regard to the handling of his adult children (from a previous marriage). He used to "go along" with Mary's approach, which he found harsh. He blamed her for the distant relationship he now had with his own children. In the last three months, he had taken a completely independent stand and had made a number of unilateral decisions in relation the children.

At the end of the first session, I asked them if they would be willing to do two or three exploratory sessions to see if they were willing to give the marriage a real try. In essence, I asked them if they would agree to take an exploratory position with regard to doing marital therapy.

Marital therapy would require at least ten to twelve sessions over six months with a strong commitment to give their best effort to improve the marriage. Tom was clearly not ready for that. His reluctance to commit himself to therapy was not just a matter of having negative thoughts and feelings about the relationship. He had been experiencing those for several months by then. It was now a matter of his position in the marriage, as we shall see. But Tom agreed to a few exploratory sessions. And so did Mary, who was hoping desperately to save the marriage.

In the next session, Mary was especially sad and tearful. She said that the exploratory contract had not had any impact on Tom at all and that he was very cold and distant. Tom did not deny it. I had a hunch as to why, but I needed to prepare them for the question. I explained the three parts of the mind: thinking, feeling, and willing. I shared that it was in the willing dimension of the mind that we took positions and that it was from those positions that our actions emerged.

I then asked Tom, "If you showed warmth toward Mary, like giving her a hug or even sharing some lighter moments with her, would she interpret those actions to mean that you might be changing your position with regard to the marriage?" Tom said, "Yes. If I did those things, Mary would probably think things were better and that I would be committed to her again. She'd relax and go back to doing the same old things."

I suggested to Tom that he and Mary agree right here that acts of kindness and friendliness would not be interpreted to mean a change of position. Those acts would be encouraged simply because they were desirable in any relationship—exploratory, committed, or divorced.

They agreed that kindness would not mean a change in Tom's position of being on the verge of leaving Mary. Tom became visibly relaxed, including a softening of his facial muscles. I saw this as a sign of increased flexibility on his part.

Tom had worked hard to get to this position of clarity in relation to his children and in relation to Mary. It took a while to convince Mary that he was seriously questioning their relationship. He was not about to give it up, even if it meant going against some of his values about being kind and pleasant. Defining and affirming his position allowed him to increase his behavior repertoire while preserving the position that he valued highly.

DIFFERENTIATING POSITION AND ACTION

Differentiating position and action allows us to increase our behavioral flexibility. Specific actions do not have to be linked to a specific position. So, I can be kind to someone in the process of beginning a relationship or while ending it. Clarifying where I stand with someone prevents many misunderstandings. Our actions will be less subject to misinterpretations. This is a principle we need to keep in mind.

KINDS OF POSITION

The concept of position covers a wide scope of our reality. It can be as specific as saying yes or no to an invitation to do something, like going to lunch. It can be a position in relation to a thing: this is mine or this is yours. Position can also define your relationship to a person: "I am your friend, your competitor, your date, your father."

Position can be a *location* within an organization, such as president, sales director, or mother. In this case, it is good to remember that roles are attached to a position. There are specific sets of expectations that cultures or groups attach to a position that is part of an organization, like a corporation, or an institution, like the family. For example, parents are expected to be disciplinarians and children are expected to follow along.

Position can also be captured in our attitudes about certain issues. Our stance with regard to men, women, race, ethnicity, age, disability, and so on, reveals our position *in relation to* those matters. Since it is a position, an attitude is already a choice and, hence, an act of will. In time and in relevant circumstances, an attitude will take on a plan and will be executed under the direction of the will. The direction of the execution will be more or less conscious depending on the person's level of awareness.

To sum up, position can define:
- Our decision about an event
- Our relationship to something, such as ownership
- Our relationship to a person
- Our location within a social structure, such as mother or corporate president
- Our attitude or stand toward certain issues like race, gender, or taxes

In any case, position is a declaration of the self in some aspect of life.

THE COMMUNICATION PYRAMID (TCP)

A GUIDE FOR BUILDING UNDERSTANDING AND NEGOTIATING CHANGE

The figure on page 159 is a diagram of the framework I call The Communication Pyramid or TCP for short. It embodies the ideas around the three parts of the mind and the concept of position, along with its related principles and techniques. TCP, however, makes us aware of the communication and negotiation uses of these insights. So, we will use it as a negotiation model or guideline for living these ideas in our interaction with family members, friends, and associates in business and community settings.

HIGHLIGHTING PRINCIPLES EMBODIED IN TCP

Here are a few principles to guide us in navigating the waters of negotiation:

1. As human beings, we get stuck when we seek a cure for our grenades in the world of pebbles because these are two different levels of reality. The world of pebbles is the external world of the here and now, whereas the world of grenades and jewels is the internal world of our innate soul-level qualities. These qualities have been activated in our contact with past events (pebbles). Consequently, there are vital themes rooted in our past—themes that presently reside inside us as conscious and unconscious memories and tendencies. However, these themes now belong to the internal world of grenades and jewels.

2. We get into serious trouble when we confuse our personal, soul-level issues (grenades/jewels) with our jointly created interaction patterns (pebbles) in our present relationship systems. My grenades/jewels are "my" issues and your grenades/jewels are "your" issues. Our interaction patterns (world of pebbles) are "our" joint issues.

The Communication Pyramid

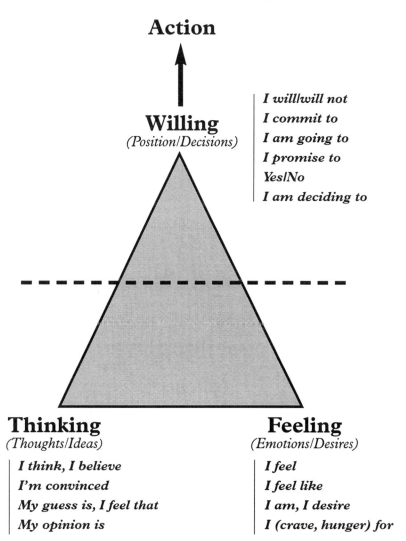

Action

Willing
(Position/Decisions)

I will/will not
I commit to
I am going to
I promise to
Yes/No
I am deciding to

Thinking
(Thoughts/Ideas)

I think, I believe
I'm convinced
My guess is, I feel that
My opinion is

Feeling
(Emotions/Desires)

I feel
I feel like
I am, I desire
I (crave, hunger) for

**TCP IS A MODEL FOR BUILDING UNDERSTANDING
AND NEGOTIATING CHANGE**

3. We can negotiate our relational pebbles—the realm of communication and interaction in the here and now—but not our jewels and grenades, which reside within us. This means that we negotiate only positions and actions, not thoughts and feelings. This distinction in captured by the dotted line dividing the pyramid in TCP. In this principle, the specific distinction is between external focus (world of pebbles) and internal focus (world of grenades). Although position, as an act of will, resides inside the person, it is already connected to the outside world as a commitment to action.

4. We cannot logically negotiate grenades and jewels as these are feelings and innate qualities that simply are. It would be like saying to someone, "I don't like the fact that you need oxygen. We need to talk about this."

5. We can talk about our grenades and jewels with each other. In fact, this is the arena of soul-level communication that generates deep levels of intimacy and empathy. This kind of in-depth contact is part of the repertoire of intimacy. Still, each of us must deal with those issues ourselves. If we do not do this soul work by attending to our grenades and mining their inner jewels, no amount of contact and togetherness will fill up the soul. We will become bottomless pits, endlessly draining our mates, children, and colleagues of their precious soul energy.

6. Relationships with our mates, families, and associates can be a cocoon for nurturing our jewels and supporting our personal mission. Our relationship to a mate is a primary arena for us to experience love and to express safely the fullness of who we are individually. Hopefully, we, too, are able to offer that kind of love. Issues in relationships, intimate or business, are negotiated more skillfully if we keep the boundaries of responsibility quite clear: we *personally* take care of our internal issues while we *jointly* negotiate the patterns of our interaction.

7. It is such a simple principle: *negotiate only positions and actions, not thoughts and feelings.* It is also one of the hardest principles to apply. We often live with the belief that if another person only agreed with our ideas, it would make us function better. This kind of belief leads to a fusion of selves, rather than a celebration of unique differences. Goodwill has not much to do with having the same ideas. It has much more to do with mutual respect of minds and with a willingness to negotiate actions for the greater good of all.

USING TCP TO BUILD UNDERSTANDING AND EMPATHY

Communication involves output and input of information. In engaging one another, we receive and give messages to each other. As we saw earlier, every time we communicate information about anything, we are also metacommunicating: we are giving messages about the nature of the relationship. This is inevitable. It is part of the human experience. All the more important then that we communicate accurately and effectively.

Developing accurate understanding is an essential foundation for wise negotiations because it gives people vital information about each other's experience. Three significant distinctions need to be made if communication is to be effective.

- Differentiating understanding from negotiating
- Distinguishing what is negotiable from what is non-negotiable
- Distinguishing between understanding and empathy

Understanding and negotiating. *Understanding* is the process of obtaining accurate and relevant information from others about their thoughts, feelings, and positions. These are the internal dimensions of their awareness about issues being discussed. *Empathy* is a common byproduct of understanding. Empathy requires a deeper level of caring and connecting with another person's internal world. Empathy includes the quality of compassion, in addition to accurate understanding.

It is crucial to note that understanding does not imply that we "agree" with the thoughts, feelings, and positions presented. *Seeking agreements* (in positions/actions) is part of the negotiation process, not part of building understanding. *Negotiating* involves the process of coming to terms with positions and actions about which the parties to a dialogue are willing or not willing to make commitments.

What is negotiable and what is non-negotiable. Again, we need to emphasize that thoughts and feelings are non-negotiable. Only positions and actions are negotiable. However, understanding people's thoughts and feelings as information from the depths of their being helps to build the empathy for successful negotiation of positions and actions. Negotiation built on the foundation of empathy has a much better chance of being mutually beneficial and synergistic.

Understanding and empathy. *Understanding* involves accuracy of perception—that we know what other people think, feel, and want. We can develop understanding without caring about those with whom we are communicating and negotiating. Furthermore, the others may not even be aware that we understand them. *Empathy* includes two additional ingredients beyond accuracy of perception.

First, is an attitude of caring about the dignity and the welfare of those with whom we are interacting. Let us remember that attitude is a position, a stand or tilt, in relation to something or something. This is an act of will. Second, empathy includes the successful communication to the other parties that we understand and that we care. In other words, they need to know that we know and that we care.

HERE'S THE POINT

Relieved of the burden of agreeing or committing to anything in the beginning, we are freer to focus on the task of building empathy as a foundation for negotiation.

REMINDER

Thoughts and feelings are informative, not directive, or negotiable.

Only after mutual understanding has been achieved should negotiation of positions start. It is tempting to influence the other person's position at the start of the communication. If the issue being discussed generates emotional intensity, our ability to develop empathy and to negotiate effectively will be jeopardized severely.

It is important for us, as practitioners of self-mastery, to commit to the effort of building empathy, even if the other parties to a negotiation do not show the caring and understanding we would like. This is out of our control. But we are in charge of our positions and actions. One of those positions will, hopefully, be an empathic attitude. Whether or not others take our attempts graciously is beyond our control as well.

TCP AND THE DEEP EMPATHY MODEL

When people are relaxed and respectful of each other, the dance of understanding and negotiating takes place easily and naturally. The flow from generating understanding to negotiating positions can proceed quite effortlessly. Let us take a simple example to illustrate this easy transition from understanding to negotiating, following the communication between Derek and Allison:

Derek:	"I'd like to eat out tonight. Want to join me?"
Allison:	"Oh, I thought you had too much to do for tomorrow's meeting. Did I misunderstand you?"
Derek:	"No, you didn't misunderstand me. I appreciate your concern. The truth is I'm just tired of preparing for that meeting. I don't think I can look at another spreadsheet. How about you, are you up for it?"
Allison:	"You bet I am."
Derek:	"Great. I sure need a break."

Notice the ease with which Derek and Allison achieved understanding about their thoughts and feelings. This accuracy helped them to negotiate a change in their positions about the way they were to spend the evening. It happened quite effectively.

However, when we are dealing with issues that trigger intense emotions, we need to slow down the communication by setting the groundwork for negotiating. When grenades are involved in an interaction, it is difficult to build empathy. The flow from understanding to negotiating takes much more effort, caring, and skill. In these situations, it is helpful, along the path of self-mastery, to have some specific guidelines to build empathy. Here's a quick refresher on The Communication Pyramid.

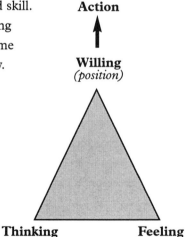

TCP

Action

↑

Willing
(position)

Thinking   **Feeling**

Highlighting Aspects of The Communication Pyramid (TCP)

- To begin with, TCP reminds us of the three parts of the mind: thinking, feeling, and willing. These are the three faculties we use to navigate the waters of life, including the world of relationships.

- This diagram also gives us some of the phrases used to communicate the awareness that comes from each of those faculties.

- The will is placed at the top of the triangle to remind us that we manifest the self by taking a position.

- Position is the point through which the self emerges into action. Position is an act of will. The will directs the actions that proceed from a given position.

THE LINK BETWEEN EMPATHY AND OUR GRENADES AND JEWELS

In a previous chapter, we saw that empathy is one of the fruits of staying in touch with our grenades and jewels. Here's a recap of two relevant points for our discussion:

1. **Empathy for Another's Pain:** If we stay in touch with your own grenades, we will develop natural empathy for those who experience similar grenades.
   - Staying in touch with our grenades means that we welcome our feelings without denying those feelings or getting buried by them.
   - Denying feelings means we have cut the soul's communication system with us.

2. **Empathy for Another's Joy:** If we mine the jewels within our grenades, affirm them, and nurture them with care, we will develop natural empathy for the good qualities of those who experience joy and success. How is this relevant?

- Without this kind of empathy, we are vulnerable to feelings of envy and jealousy. If we do not mine the jewels within these feelings, we may end up acting on them by putting others down.

- It is important to have the ability to support others, to praise their positive qualities, and to join them in the happiness of their accomplishments. That is part of connecting with people in significant ways. That is part of a relationship.

- When we affirm our own soul qualities, we naturally develop the ability to see those gifts in others and appreciate them with a natural sense of understanding. We know those capacities by experience, not just in theory.

These principles are foundational because they are prerequisites for living the concept of empathy. Empathy gives us the ability to connect with another human being while maintaining a clear sense of our individuality. It supports the two primary forces in life: our need to belong and our need for individuality.

DEFINING EMPATHY

The word *empathy* comes from the Greek: *en,* which means *in* and *pathos,* which means *feeling.* So the root meaning of empathy brings up the image of being *inside the feeling.* That is an accurate and helpful definition of the word. The dictionary definition is also helpful. The *Wordsworth Concise English Dictionary* defines empathy as follows:

Empathy: *n.* the power of entering into another's personality and imaginatively experiencing his experiences: the power of entering into the feeling or spirit of something and so appreciating it fully.

Both the root words and the dictionary meaning of empathy are accurate in describing what happens when we enter the empathic state. Here is the way I would describe the process of empathizing:

Empathizing means that we are, figuratively speaking, seeing, hearing, and feeling the world of events from within the other person's eyes, ears, and skin. We make a bold attempt to experience the world "as if" we were the other person, much like a good actor does in a movie or play. To do this in true life requires love and respect.

THE ROLE OF PERSONAL TRANSFORMATION IN BUILDING EMPATHY

A BRIEF STORY

I remember a friend of mine talking about how painful it was for him to be shut off by his wife when he was trying to tell her something important. Even in the retelling, he would shed tears of deep anguish. The pebble thrown in his pond was his wife's action to cut him off from the dialogue. The grenade had to do with his feelings of rejection and pain that came from being shut off and misunderstood.

In addition, he felt trapped, believing that if he were honest about his thoughts and feelings, she would get upset and cut him off again. He did not like being cut off, nor did he like the idea of keeping his thoughts from her.

I invited my friend to journey into his emotional grenades (misunderstanding, feeling trapped) to find out what those feelings said that he needed. I asked him to imagine also that his feelings could talk. What would these feelings say he needed? He answered, "I need to be heard, to be understood, and to be accepted as I am." These are the jewels manifesting as needs.

"What would happen if you got this from your wife—if she understood and accepted you for who you are?" He paused for a moment and said, "I would feel *at peace, confident,* and *free* to be me." These are the jewels manifesting as capacities although they were phrased as desires that my friend had.

THE TASK OF PERSONAL TRANSFORMATION

My friend needed empathy from his wife. What he failed to understand was that he needed to have empathy for himself as well. This is one byproduct of personal transformation—by mining the jewels within his grenades and nurturing those jewels, my friend would experience natural empathy for his wife's grenades and good qualities.

A NATURAL BYPRODUCT OF PERSONAL TRANSFORMATION

Staying in touch with our grenades opens the door to our jewels. By mining the jewels within our grenades and nurturing those soul sensitivities, we experience natural empathy for those who suffer or triumph in similar ways. This is a common byproduct of our personal transformation work.

Empathy, as we saw earlier, is the state of mind that allows us to feel, hear, and see the world from within another person's eyes, ears, and skin. It is much easier to define empathy than to apply it. The difficulty rapidly increases when we are emotionally involved in the matter that is concerning the other person. The reason for this difficulty is that the process of empathy requires that we put total focus on examining the world "as if" we were the other one.

It was not too difficult for me to empathize with my friend because I was not involved in triggering his pain. I could devote my energies to his situation. My emotional flexibility was at its maximum. It would be a different matter if my wife were telling me about how my actions triggered her pain. The difficulty increases if her actions triggered my own grenades. To develop empathy, I would have to set my feelings aside for the moment so that I could devote my entire energy towards "walking in her shoes."

I have often used the words of Jesus to help me be empathic in difficult moments: "Greater love than this no one has, that one give up life itself for a friend." The way I apply these words is to think of my life as my agenda. So I die to my agenda first, set it aside, so that I can more fully see, feel, and hear my wife's world through her eyes, ears, and skin. This is love in its highest expression. In other words, I momentarily "die to my agenda" for the sake of my friend. This is not easy to do.

When we are still "grenading," so to speak, it is not the best time to engage our spouse, friend, or colleague in developing empathy. We first do our personal transformation work by "polishing" the jewels that those grenades are revealing. So, we begin by mining the jewels within our grenades. After meeting our needs and affirming our jewels, then it is time to attempt the process of deep empathy.

St. Francis prayed in this manner. His prayer is captured in one of Stephen Covey's *7 Habits of Highly Effective People.*[1] Habit Number Five reads: "Seek first to understand, then to be understood." It is worth reading this chapter in order to deepen your appreciation for the benefits of empathy.

INGREDIENTS NECESSARY TO DEVELOP EMPATHY

How does one develop empathy? The technique itself can be taught and practiced, as we shall see shortly, but the living of it requires other ingredients.

The emotional and spiritual strength needed to live empathically requires a different kind of preparation.

1. It demands the will to be real and the will to honor others for who they are.
2. In close relationships, it requires *the commitment of will to give the relationship our best,* including the *honesty and integrity to live our mission and to support our loved one's mission.*
3. It requires practicing the process of personal transformation in order to develop the natural empathy needed to apply it in relationships.
4. Finally, it is helpful to learn a technique and to practice it.

THE DEEP EMPATHY MODEL

Empathy, then, requires a deep level of self-acceptance. This is the best grounding for putting the process of deep empathy to work. However, it is helpful to have a specific guideline for applying this quality in our negotiations. For this, we offer The Deep Empathy Model.

This method carries the adjective *deep* in order to emphasize that its purpose goes beyond simply the accuracy of perception needed to navigate the everyday world of conventional tasks.

Deep empathy is most useful when we want to:
1. Develop true intimacy
2. Give or receive significant support from others
3. Prepare for effective conflict resolution
4. Develop new patterns in relationships or organizations

PUTTING THE DEEP EMPATHY MODEL IN CONTEXT

We will talk about two roles in describing this technique:
- **The Role of Empathizer:** This is the person who is doing the empathizing—the one who is attempting to "crawl into the other person's skin."
- **The Role of Subject:** This is the person who is describing his thoughts, feelings, and positions.

AGREEING TO PARTICIPATE

Ideally both parties agree to develop mutual empathy and follow a process designed to accomplish this. This needs to include agreement about time, topic, and method—when, what, and how to go about it. The parties need to be clear on the goal of the initial conversation: to build mutual empathy.

If only one party is committed to do it, it is still possible to generate a good deal of understanding. However, that person needs to realize that it will probably be a one-way flow for a time. If one is able to empathize without demanding that the other also take on the role of empathizer, some useful work could be done. It will probably not be as productive as it could be if all parties were willing to participate in both roles.

The technique described here will assume that all parties have made a commitment to participate willingly.

THE DEEP EMPATHY MODEL

THE ROLE OF EMPATHIZER

1. Focus on the other person as the subject of empathy.
2. Understand the subject's thoughts, feelings, and positions regarding the issues being discussed.
3. Trust the subject to lead you to areas that are important to her. Your *main intent* is to follow the subject's lead. However, give yourself the freedom to probe into areas of the subject's thoughts, feelings, and positions that you think are important to grasp.
4. Actively participate in the flow of interaction through questions. Use open-ended questions followed by specific probes.
5. Use the diagram of TCP to guide your questions and probes.
6. Check out your understanding by periodically paraphrasing what you hear.

THE ROLE OF SUBJECT

1. Accept your role as the focus of the conversation—the attempt to develop deep empathy. Remind yourself that the other person has agreed to "walk in your shoes."
2. Remember that you agreed to discuss the issue at hand. This includes *your* decision to discuss a matter that the other person may want to know about.
3. Be helpful to the empathizer by providing as much information as he/she needs to understand your *thoughts, feelings,* and *positions* on the issue.
4. Encourage the empathizer to probe into areas he/she wants to understand. This probing may be helpful to your own understanding of the issue. Be ready, though, to guide the empathizer to the most relevant thoughts, feelings, and positions you hold.

5. Remind your partner not to share his/her own thoughts, feelings, and positions about the issue until this process is completed.

The end of this process is determined by the subject when he/she is understood, or when a certain agreed-upon time limit has been reached.

HOW TO USE THE DEEP EMPATHY MODEL

The roles outlined in the model will be our primary guidelines. There are three main steps to follow as we take the roles of subject and empathizer. After that, a few guidelines may be helpful in going through these steps.

STEPS IN THE DEEP EMPATHY MODEL

STEP ONE: Subject shares information from the three parts of the mind. The empathizer listens and participates actively by asking questions.

STEP TWO: Empathizer paraphrases the sender's essential message. The subject offers feedback to guide the empathizer.

STEP THREE: Confirmation of the empathic connection: the empathizer describes the "gist of the subject's experience" about the issue. The subject gives feedback about the accuracy and depth of the partner's understanding.

These three steps summarize the core of the process involved in the Deep Empathy Model. This process may look innocently easy, or perhaps even naïve and unnecessary. However, my experience tells me that family members, spouses, business partners and associates often take this empathic stage of negotiation too much for granted. *If we take care of the relationship, the task will get done more efficiently and with greater care.*

Task and relationship are manifestations of the two primary forces in human life: belonging and individuality. Both dimensions need our attention. If we do not build the relationship through the bond of empathy, the task at hand will suffer. Our specific spot in a relationship or organization may be challenged, and our freedom of expression and action may be thwarted or unsupported.

Here are a few guidelines to keep in mind when using the Deep Empathy Model:

- **Identify your desire to get into the roles of empathizer and subject.** Whoever thinks that there is good reason to use this technique can identify the need. That person then tells the other person what the nature of the issue is.

- **Agree to use the technique.** Ask the other one if he is willing to talk about it. It is important that there be a willingness on both sides to engage in the process. It works best when there is an explicit agreement, so no one is feeling dragged into it.

- **Agree on time, place, and process.** *When, where,* and *how* are not necessarily clear just because the question of *whether* to talk about it has been settled. Have some idea about how much time is available for the conversation—to make sure you do not "overstay" in each other's emotional space.

- **Alternating roles.** Stay in the role until the subject indicates that he is understood or until there is agreement between the parties that a role switch may be useful. It is sometimes desirable to attempt a series of switches in order to achieve partial "chunks" of understanding. The empathizer needs to check this out along the way. However, the empathizer can inform the subject if he needs help in making the process of deep empathy more productive. Either party is free to call a "time out" to discuss how the process is going and if any adjustments need to be made.

- **Feedback checks.** Giving and asking for feedback is useful. The subject can ask, "Tell me what you hear." Or the empathizer can paraphrase the message received and then ask the subject to confirm or modify the interpretations.

- **Clear role boundaries.** The empathizer focuses only on expressing thoughts about the subject's thoughts, feelings, and positions, not her own. The focus is always on the subject's awareness of the issue at hand. In the role of empathizer, we "die to our own agenda" for the sake of our friend. We do not share our own thoughts, feelings, or positions. In other words, we use only the thinking part of our mind to paraphrase our grasp of the subject's experience of the issue.

- **Personal transformation.** We each discern whether we need to do some personal transformation work before, in between, or after these deep empathy sessions. Our guide for this determination is the depth and persistence of the grenades that the issue triggers in us. Even if we were able to participate effectively in the process, the impact of the conversation may still require us to mine the jewels within the grenades we felt. This is part of the deal.

- **Ending.** The ideal ending to this process occurs when the subject is convinced that he is profoundly understood. This is the goal of the empathy model, even if it is not always possible. In the process, it helps to aim for the "gist of the subject's experience" of the issue. We may not always hit the nail on the head. So, sometimes we may table the process with a sense that there is only a partial grasp of each one's understanding. Some issues are too large to settle in one sitting and may call for an ongoing dialogue that can be marked by a series of deep empathy sessions.

WHEN TO USE IT

Like any good technique, this one can be put to good use or it can be misused. There is no substitute for a good heart that is driven by love. That is always a given. On that soil we build the foundation of clear thinking and effective skills. We can use this model:

When we are making an important decision: Let us be watchful for what we could call structural issues: issues that involve the patterns in our life. For example, job issues or changes that affect relationships, schedules, money, mission, colleagues, and perhaps even geographical changes.

When we want to change a relationship or organizational pattern. The DEM could be useful if we find ourselves in a rut, repeating interaction sequences we do not find useful. For example, I make suggestions and my friend typically comes up with more alternatives. I feel irritated and find myself questioning his motives, which leads me to abandon further planning, aborting the activity altogether. I may wish to find a better pattern.

When we have to manage crises or transitions. A crisis usually brings change in meaning and in behavior patterns. If a parent is ill or dies, there will be emotional implications. Job crises bring shock waves to the job holder in addition to issues of money, lifestyle, geography, and self-esteem.

When we are working on a personal issue. We may ask a friend or spouse to help us by taking the role of empathizer as we sound out our thoughts, feelings, and intentions. We reverse roles so we can hear our friend's thoughts and feelings about what we're going through. No formal process is required here. After a while, the conversation will likely just become a free-flowing dialogue.

THE SYNERGY MODEL FOR NEGOTIATING CHANGE OR CONFLICT

A MODEL FOR CONFLICT RESOLUTION

How do we incorporate these insights into a workable method for conflict resolution? Just as grenades challenge us to dig deep into our souls, so conflicts in our relationship challenge us to grow in both intimacy and self-definition. Mates choose one another in powerfully mysterious ways. Work associates also find themselves with people who have a knack for triggering some of their most sensitive grenades. Destiny has manifested and is embedded in a relationship and an organization.

The relationship or group carries its own wisdom and its own life cycle. I respect it in all of its aspects, including the conflicts that arise. Conflict is universal and it emerges at a moment when we are invited to "love more" and "be more."

It is important to have effective ways of utilizing and resolving conflicts. Therefore, the model I offer has two primary goals: utilization and resolution. David Mace, mentor to the whole field of marriage enrichment, used to say, with a twinkle in his eye: "Never waste a conflict."[2] These words capture the spirit of utilization.

TWO IMPORTANT FUNCTIONS OF CONFLICT

1. Conflicts trigger grenades, which provide opportunities for personal growth by pointing to our jewels.
2. Conflicts also point to areas in the relationship or organization that need to change. They are like windows into potential solutions.

CONFLICT UTILIZATION FOR PERSONAL GROWTH:
The Pebble-Grenade-Jewel Connection

The following is a model for utilizing interpersonal conflicts for personal growth. It incorporates the model for managing feelings (Chapters 4 and 5) involving a relational situation at home or at work. It is designed for conflicts that trigger grenades. Not all conflicts trigger grenades. There are a good number of conflicts that we can handle without much emotional intensity. In those situations, we remain present-centered and are able to negotiate our positions and actions quite reasonably. This pattern of conflict utilization offers us questions and suggestions for tracking the pebble-grenade-jewel connection. By now, we will find the first part of this model quite familiar.

QUESTIONS TO TRACK THE
PEBBLE-GRENADE-JEWEL CONNECTION

1. What does the other party do that gets to me? This question detects the pebbles that tend to trigger our grenades. Although pebbles do not create our grenades, it is important to track the hand of destiny in our relationship environment. That way, we become astute about the kinds of triggers that reveal our areas of oversensitivity.

2. What meanings and feelings do I experience? This question elicits the nature of our experience at the level of thinking and feeling. Although the grenades emerge more intensely at the feeling level, there are important thoughts connected to them. So it is important to examine the pattern of thoughts and feelings involved. We recognize this as the FEEL IT step in the model for managing feelings.

3. What do the grenades say that I need? This question is quite effective as a way of mining the jewel within the feeling. We can imagine talking to the feeling as the "mouthpiece of the soul." After asking the question, we remain quiet for a moment listening carefully to the message our soul may offer. We recognize this as listening to our feelings and as a way of mining our soul jewels.

4. What can I do to meet that need? This question gets to the heart of soul healing. If the soul tells us that she needs to be heard, then we need to listen to her thoughts and feelings without judging them as good or bad. We provide what she needs by listening to her. As we learned earlier, this is the most crucial part of inner healing. As a representative of the Higher Mind, we are helping to connect the soul to God, the source. We remember this as the first part of Step III in the model for managing feelings.

5. Is there something my partner can do to help me nurture this need? This question takes us back to examining the world of pebbles to find resources and solutions. It is important for us to be an effective "representative of the soul." It our responsibility to act on the message we received from our soul. We could, for instance, inform the other party about our experience and ask to dialogue. The crucial factor in this step is acting on the message (not on the feeling). In this case, we asked for dialogue. Our healing does not depend on the other person's response. We've already done our healing. If the response we get is also nurturing, we can consider this a blessing for our soul. It is not the crucial factor. But it is good for us to remember how helpful a loving response can be, because it can heighten our own sensitivity to providing this blessing to others.

This conflict-utilization process embodies a high level of self-responsibility. Taking care of ourselves is a mark of self-responsibility. When we do so, our colleagues and loved ones do not have to over-function and rescue us. Overfunctioning in order to prop us up for a time would tax their own resources. Although overfunctioning is present in all relationships, it is good to take steps to minimize it. Otherwise, all parties suffer.

Utilizing a conflict for personal growth is also the best preparation for the conflict resolution phase.

CONFLICT RESOLUTION FOR INTERPERSONAL GROWTH:
A SYNERGY-ORIENTED PROCESS

Here is an outline of the phases and steps involved in negotiating conflicts using model based upon a synergy-oriented framework. The framework is explained below.

PHASES OF CONFLICT RESOLUTION

A. Preresolution Phase: Contracting and personal preparation.

B. Resolution Phase: Understanding, setting criteria, and negotiating.

    1. Develop understanding and deep empathy.

    2. Dialogue to discover each person's vision of the desired outcome and to explore mutual advantages and disadvantages for self and the relationship.

    3. Negotiate positions and actions best able to meet those needs.

C. Evaluation Phase: Testing the fruits of the tree.

Let us keep this outline of the phases of conflict resolution in mind as we go through the following ideas. We will return to these steps after a brief discussion of the paradigm shift involved in going from a consensus-to a synergy-driven model of negotiation.

FROM CONSENSUS TO SYNERGY: An Important Paradigm Shift

Some communication models emphasize consensus as the desirable outcome of conflict resolution. Consensus-oriented negotiation emphasizes agreements instead of understanding. It often presupposes that the beginning positions of the parties are set. In the consensus model, the main task is to find common ground (among initial positions). Then, through a process of "mutually giving in" (compromise), parties work to remove the differences in those positions until the first common denominator is reached.

The consensus model subtly makes a god out of agreement and, at best, temporarily tolerates the existence of differences. The process has a built-in bias to remove differences instead of utilizing those differences.

The synergy-oriented model, on the other hand, involves some significantly different assumptions and processes. Synergy incorporates the notion that the whole is qualitatively different than the sum of the individual parts. The starting positions of the negotiating parties are seen as parts involved in the evolution of the whole. The differences in the thoughts, feelings, and positions of the negotiating parties are considered the necessary ingredients in cooking the whole meal.

Differences are viewed as desirable starting points—but only as starting points. The pain experienced in response to these differences may not be seen as desirable. But it triggers the search for jewels and provides the impetus for seeking a "more effective interaction pattern" within the relationship or organization.

The goal of the synergy model is to discover a new choreography in the relationship that leads to a more aesthetic and effective dance. Through a dialogue that utilizes these multiple views of an issue, people can arrive at a new set of positions that might meet their needs in a better way. Gregory Bateson uses the fact that we have two eyes as a metaphor for achieving "depth perception" in a relationship. It is difficult to gauge the distance of an object with just one eye. Each party to a negotiation carries one eye. Together, in dialogue, the parties have greater depth perception. Bateson calls this idea "double description," drawing from the metaphor of binocular vision. He writes:

> Let us consider another simple and familiar case of double description. What is gained by comparing the data collected by one eye with the data collected by the other? Typically, both eyes are aimed at the same region of the surrounding universe, and this might seem to be a wasteful use of the sense organs. But the anatomy indicates that very considerable advantage must accrue from this usage ...

> From this elaborate arrangement [of the optical processes involved], two sorts of advantage accrue. The seer is able to improve resolution at edges and contrasts; and better able to read when the print is small or the illumination poor. More important, information about depth is created. In more formal language, the *difference* between the information provided by the one retina and that provided by the other is itself information of a *different logical type*. From this new sort of information, the seer adds an extra *dimension* to seeing.

> ... In principle, extra "depth" in some metaphoric sense is to be expected whenever the information for the two descriptions in differently collected or differently coded.[3]

It is vital to keep this metaphor in mind. Each person brings a different code or description into a situation, a relationship or an organization. The synthesis of the different views brings a new level of information—a new point of view. We need to get beyond our own point of view, allowing the other person's perspective to influence, not dominate, us. It is the synthesis that provides depth of vision to the parties.

The synergy model may be difficult for couples, executives, or team members to learn, but it is potentially more rewarding than the consensus model. Like any interpersonal strategy, the synergy approach requires that there be a common vision that includes all parties in the dialogue. It is also important to have a set of measurable criteria for knowing whether or not people are progressing toward their common vision.

Once we enter the synergy framework, we realize that greater emphasis is placed on the common vision than on common ground. *Ground* refers more to the starting point, vision points more to the goal or the outcome. In the synergy framework, differences are utilized, not removed or avoided.

A. PRERESOLUTION PHASE

Contracting. Before starting the conflict resolution process, it is crucial for the parties to have a "contract"—a willing commitment to resolve a specific conflict. We can describe this as "an agreement to discuss a disagreement." The question is, "Are you willing to discuss this matter?" Through a "yes" or a "no," we elicit the person's position. If yes, we determine when and where to discuss the issue. For the vast majority of issues, the contracting phase is implicit. When dealing with grenade-level issues, however, I recommend that this phase be made explicit. We do not need to dramatize or belabor it. We just need to be clear.

Personal preparation. One of the best ways to prepare for the conflict resolution phase is to make sure we go through the first four steps of the Conflict Utilization Model. If we do this, we will have quieted our emotional system and, having mined the jewels within our grenades, we will be ready to represent our soul more clearly and effectively. We will have gone to the "closet to pray." By doing our personal transformation work, we will be ready for empathy and for self-definition.

This kind of commitment to excellence in our personal and professional lives is the staple along the path of self-mastery. The false ego within us will question why we have to do such personal preparation work when "those people obviously don't deserve any hearing whatsoever." The false self lives in the shadow of a power-based world and is unable to see the whole in the part or the part in the whole.

We need to be alert to these power-driven voices: they may come from the persona or shadow aspects of our being. We need to own them, listen to them, and accept them as parts of us. This we do by going through the Personal Transformation Model. By mining the jewels in our grenades, we will be transmuting and sublimating the soul energy behind these voices.

B. RESOLUTION PHASE

1. Develop understanding and deep empathy. Now we enter the conflict resolution phase. We recognize this first step as the process of building understanding and deep empathy. So only a brief description is given here. This is the time to use the Deep Empathy Model.

While one person shares his thoughts, feelings, and positions, the other listens and participates in the experience of deep empathy. The listener gets into the shoes and the skin of the other person and begins to look and listen from within the other's eyes and ears. There is no evaluation of the merits or demerits of the other's experience. The effort is to understand, not to agree or disagree. An attitude of caring is a requisite for developing empathy.

2. Dialogue (a) to discover each person's vision of the desired outcome and (b) to explore mutual advantages and disadvantages for self and the relationship.

(a) At this point, the conversation becomes more exploratory and more possibility-oriented. The parties share their hopes for what they want personally and relationally. This step is still focused on developing understanding, not on negotiating. But the focus now switches to possible commitments and actions. Yet dialogue toward mutual understanding is still the key element here. When this dialogue occurs openly, without maneuvering or persuading, the synergistic process takes a significant step forward. The partners are already mutually enriching each other in the process of sharing their vision.

(b) The dialogue also explores how a person's vision affects the other. Each person asks the question, "If my vision were realized, what impact could it have on you? Please spell out the positive and negative aspects of your view." The listener goes through the deep empathy process again. The listener (empathizer role) is the one who asks the question. Going through the empathy procedure will inform the listener in a significant way. This is another big step along the upward synergy spiral.

It is important for each person to verbalize clearly the perceived negative impacts as much as the perceived positive impacts. Each soul has protective tendencies that will be registered as concerns or even grenades. Furthermore, the listener may not be aware that her position could include some of those negative impacts. This awareness may or may not shift that person's position. But it could lead to new information.

3. Negotiate the positions and actions that are best able to meet those needs. If the partners have done the first two steps well, the actual negotiation could be the most logical, straightforward step in resolving the conflict. Ideally, this step takes on a solution-focused, problem-solving approach. The partners discuss actions and interactions that could improve their personal and relational lives. As they explore various options, they declare their positions: commitments to do or not to do something. The faculty of the will is quite manifest in this step.

A commitment reveals an inner position: a stance supported by an act of will. The action is the external manifestation of a position. Positions and actions are the proper subject of the negotiation step in conflict resolution. Each of these positions needs to be evaluated in light of the goals set by the partners earlier.

These commitments are the only truly negotiable items in this entire process. The core of negotiation itself is captured in the question: "Are you willing to do this or not?"

EVALUATION PHASE

What follows is a discussion about how the parties will know whether they are making progress toward their individual and organizational/relational goals. This is where they can reexamine the criteria or indicators of progress. In the strategic approach to family therapy, for instance, great importance is given to these signs of change. Signs of progress need to be specific, observable, and minimal. Minimal indicators are those early manifestations of change that can easily go unnoticed or can readily be discounted by the parties to a negotiation.

Minimal indicators of change open up the possibility of encouraging gradual or incremental steps toward the goal. It is a great antidote to perfectionism—an attitude or position that accepts only unflawed or unadulterated performance. Life is developmental and gradual.

Like love, life is a many-splendored thing—rarely pure and homogeneous. People and relationships are unfinished products in the process of seeking the true, the good, and the beautiful.

[1] Covey, S. (1989). *The 7 Habits of Highly Effective People.* New York: Simon and Schuster.

[2] David Mace was a pioneer in the marriage counseling field in England and in the United States. David and his wife Vera Mace were the original founders of the Association of Couples for Marriage Enrichment (ACME). The major part of their professional work focused on marriage enrichment. The words I quote were spoken in a marriage enrichment conference in Kansas City in the early 1980s.

[3] Bateson, G. (1979). *Mind and Nature: A Necessary Unity.* New York: E. P. Dutton, pp. 69-70.

Chapter 8

OF ATOMS AND MOLECULES

On Seeing the Relationship Dance

THE ILLUSION OF SEPARATENESS

The path of self-mastery naturally orients us toward focusing on the individual self. This is especially true when we begin to emphasize the fulfillment of our mission. The journey requires knowing our purpose for being and the ability to master thinking, feeling, and willing toward the realization of that major purpose. But a life of mastery brings many challenges and puzzles in the form of pebbles in our world of destiny that trigger emotional grenades. It is a bumpy journey. That is why we need the support of viable relationships, especially of the close kind.

As students of self-mastery, we need clear lenses to understand the terrain of relationships and organizations where we team up with other, either one-on-one or in groups. This chapter will equip us with those lenses in broad strokes. In the subsequent two chapters, we will find guidelines for mastering the self as mate, friend, and child. These are tremendously important ideas and skills to have along the spiritual path.

Relationships have a major impact on our lives. Our bodies bear the evidence of their importance. Dean Ornish has gathered scientific data to show that relationship is the strongest single factor affecting the "quality of life, incidence of illness, and premature death from all causes."[1] We need to be able to understand our individual nature, as well as our social nature. This chapter will lay the foundation for being able to see the dance *and* the dancer. It will help us to see the atom as a part of the molecular dance.

Besides, a mission-based life always involves service to others. Service takes us beyond ourselves and brings us into contact with others. As we grow in self-mastery, we also grow in our capacity to transcend the ego. Ken Wilber noted that the movement from the lower to the higher stages of self-development is marked by a correlated movement from egocentric to ethnocentric to worldcentric.[2] He is convinced that a prerequisite for entrance into the transpersonal levels of development is the identification of the self with at least a world-centric view of life. It is the ground floor of mysticism.

The great mystics of East and West tell us that the essence of mysticism is the experience of interconnectedness—that everything in the universe has one source. Bruno Borchert, in his book *Mysticism*, writes: "Thus a mystical experience is *all-embracing* ... It is a realiza-tion—with one's whole being—that all things are one, a universe, an organic whole into which the self fits."[3]

This way of thinking challenges us to "see" structure in the flow of seemingly disconnected events in our lives. It prods the artist or mystic in us to detect "patterns" in apparently random events. When we see people interacting in groups (whether in family or business organizations), our eyes deceive us into seeing these individuals as separate entities, acting independently and randomly. This is the illusion of separateness. The human eye can detect only differences in the visual field, such as shape, color, size, location, and motion. We are lulled into believing that those differences are boundaries that separate things from each other.

Our human sensory experience continually reinforces the idea that things and events are separate realities. We see only atomically, unable to see the molecule as an *organization* of interconnected atoms. We have to see with our inner eye in order to grasp the "pattern which connects," to borrow a phrase from the great anthropologist Gregory

Bateson.[4] It takes a paradigm shift to think like Bateson and to be able to observe patterns among random events. What, for instance, are the patterns that connect the world of living things? What connects the great blue heron to the lobster and to the rose or to you and me?

Once while teaching a group of students at the California School of Fine Arts, Gregory Bateson showed them a freshly cooked crab. He challenged the students "to produce arguments which will convince me that this object is the remains of a living thing ... How would you arrive at that conclusion?" He told them to imagine they were Martians who had never seen crabs or lobsters. The students first came up with the observation that it is symmetrical—the right side resembles the left. Then they observed that one claw was bigger than the other, and therefore, revised the view that it was symmetrical.

In response to differences in size, one student said that "yes, one claw is bigger than the other, but both claws are made of the same parts." Bateson exclaimed:

> Ah! What a beautiful and noble statement that is, how the speaker politely flung into the trash can the idea that *size* could be of primary or profound importance and went after the *pattern which connects*. He discarded an asymmetry in size in favor of a deeper symmetry in formal relations.
>
> Yes, indeed, the two claws are characterized (ugly word) by embodying *similar relations between parts*. Never quantities, always shapes, forms, and relations. This was, indeed, something that characterized the crab as a member of *creatura*, a living thing.[5]

The key to seeing structure or organization among seemingly disjointed events is pattern. Organization may be described as the "pattern which connects." The functioning of an organization is the invisible dimension of a system. An organizational chart of a corporation is only a pale map of the reality that it attempts to describe. Seeing it requires a vision that goes beyond space and captures "patterns of behavioral sequences through time." We, the observers of those sequences, are ones who mentally organize the seemingly random behaviors into a pattern that connects. We will learn to see with that inner eye.

PATTERN: The Key to Seeing Structure

Why do we continually buy books? They all contain the same twenty-six letters of the English alphabet. If you have seen one book, you have seen them all. So why the ongoing fascination with books? If twenty-six individual, isolated letters is all we see in this book, then we might as well put it down. We've already seen it all. But we continue reading because we see the pattern in the sequence of letters. We see the organization. Put the letters together in a certain sequence and words emerge. Put those words in a certain order and sentences appear conveying new ideas. Gather those sentences in certain ways and they create paragraphs, pages, sections, chapters, and volumes. But switch two letters in a word and we get nonsense or a new word.

If we put a hand under an electron microscope, we soon realize that the skin is not as solid as our senses show us. In fact, if we had a microscope powerful enough to see the atoms in our skin, we would observe that the body is mostly space.

Deepak Chopra points to an amazing fact: "the void between two electrons is proportionately as empty as the space between two galaxies."[6] And this is at subatomic levels—the space within an atom. So what makes a hydrogen atom different from an oxygen atom? The organization of the subatomic particles. What makes the skin different from the wood on the floor? The organization of atoms and molecules.

Note that hydrogen and oxygen are gases in their separate atomic states. Yet, when combined as H_2O, they produce a liquid called water. As a molecule, water has different properties than either of its component atoms. But hydrogen and oxygen are still present in water. It is from the organization of the component parts that a new entity emerges.

THE UNIT OF ANALYSIS: The Atom and the Molecule

We will use the analogy of atom and molecule in discussing person and relationship: *atom* will be to person as *molecule* will be to relationship. In order to see the dance between two or more people, we must be able to see the connection between the dancers. Focusing only on one dancer will cloud our ability to see the dance patterns. This would be like studying the properties of water through an atomic analysis of oxygen in its gaseous state. The whole is different from the sum of its individual parts. We keep one eye on the part and the other on the whole.

For instance, the husband who feels rejected may start pursuing his wife with such intensity that it triggers some reactive distancing on her part. Her distancing may, in turn, trigger an even more intense pursuit on his part. And the dance continues. At the level of self (the atom), the husband may feel hurt and unloved. He may be convinced that his wife no longer cares for him. The wife, on the other hand, may feel suffocated and controlled. She may see the husband as possessive and controlling. This is "atomic" analysis. The focus is on individual behavior.

At the relational (molecular) level, we see a curious mutual triggering of dance steps that neither person enjoys experiencing. The pursuit/distancing dance is a relational phenomenon. In order to see that the husband's pursuit is connected to the wife's distancing, we need to observe the dance at the molecular level. We note that distancing, in turn, invites more pursuit. The ability to see the circular link requires systemic thinking: seeing the molecule or the dance at a higher level of abstraction. We don't lose sight of the individuals as we notice the sequence of behaviors that lead to relationship structure. The husband's motive ("to have more intimacy") is best understood as an internal individual reality (atomic level). And so is the wife's motive "to seek independence." These are important to understand. But individual motives will not give us the full picture at the relationship level (molecule). The pursuit-distancing cycle is best viewed as a systemic pattern—a relational reality that transcends individual motives and behavior. This kind of analysis is designed to detect structure—recurring patterns of behavior sequences. Structure in an organization acts much like an infrastructure of highways in a city.

We cannot explain a relational quality by examining a personal trait. That would be like explaining the qualities of a molecule by looking at the qualities of an atom.

Gregory Bateson had a curious definition of "lack of wisdom." He defined it as "a partial arc": a frame of mind that sees only a one-way connection between two events.[7] This is what we called, in Chapter 2, the linear causal view. When I was a young boy, I liked my father more than my mother. I saw him as benevolent, happy, and fun to be with. My mother appeared strict, unpredictable, and sometimes harsh. When my mother and father had problems in their relationship, I usually saw the difficulty as being caused by mother. My father was the victim of her anger. This is "partial arc" thinking. I couldn't "see" my father's part in the relationship.

By contrast, wisdom consists of seeing the whole circuitry (circularity) of a relational transaction. The capacity to view pursuing as a trigger for distancing, and vice versa, leads to wisdom because it encourages perceiving the interconnection of the dance steps. If we blame the wife's distancing as the sole cause of the sad state of the marriage, then we are looking at a partial arc (i.e., a sector of the whole). This, to Bateson, is erroneous thinking and will lead to lack of wisdom. A partial arc view is akin to nonmystical thinking. This would be like someone looking at the pieces of a mobile without noticing the strings connecting all the pieces, and thinking that the movements are totally independent.

In the case of my parents, I did not realize that my father's lack of leadership "danced with" my mother's sense of desperateness. His unwillingness to take charge at certain times "triggered" my mother's overfunctioning. My immaturity and my limited view (atomic only) narrowed my repertoire of responses. At times of stress, I tended to ally with my dad against my mom. Since I could not appreciate her position, I was unable to empathize with her. Instead, I sympathized with my father and distanced from my mother.

I was looking only at the atoms and did not see the molecule. If I had taken a molecular view, I could have related to them in a number of other ways. As it was, I recoiled in fear of my mother's wrath and would distance from her at the first sign of impatience. At the same time, I idealized my father and became blind to his shortcomings. It impoverished my understanding of him as a real person. I underrated my mother and failed to appreciate some of her contributions to the family. Furthermore, I did not include myself in the analysis of the situation. I was, in fact, part of the interaction "molecule." I had no idea that my views, as observer, influenced my actions, which became part of the interactions.

This view also constrained my early responses as a husband, occasionally defining my wife's legitimate complaints as insensitive. At those times, I did not perceive the marriage molecule in its wholeness. I, therefore, could not see my part in the marital dance. Once again, if I could have included myself as *part of* the marriage molecule, instead of a seeing each person as a separate atom, I could have understood the person-relationship dynamics better. With that part-whole view, I would have had more effective handles and options for change. A few vignettes will illustrate the different levels of analysis.

MEDICATION, THE INDIVIDUAL, AND THE SYSTEM

In one of my seminars, I remember a school counselor telling me about a six-year-old girl in her school who was diagnosed with Attention Deficit Disorder (ADD). The girl's mother, who was suffering from depression, was at her wit's end about how to handle her daughter Annette. There were also an older boy and a younger girl in the family. The father was distant from the emotional center of this turmoil, refusing to accompany his wife and Annette when they went for a visit to the psychiatrist who put the little girl on Prozac.

Prior to taking the medication, Annette had intense power struggles with her mother, including tantrums, screaming matches, and defiant standoffs. If a parent or teacher praised someone else for anything, Annette would insist, in a whiny voice, that she too was good, capable, or pretty, depending on what the compliment was.

A few days after the medication was started, the mother recounted the following incident. She had just given each of the three children a treat when Annette asked her mother's permission to give her portion to her younger sister. This was an eyebrow-raising act, since Annette would previously have yelled out a complaint like, "You never get me what I want!"

At this point, the older brother, usually more stable, whined that he should have two treats as well. Annette then asked her sister if she could have her treat back and, after receiving it, asked her mother if she could give it to her brother. Peace was restored and more eyebrows were raised. The mother was ecstatic about the miracle that Prozac brought to her daughter.

This is a most interesting scenario because, if we view the problem simply in terms of the individual child, we could conclude that a giant step had been taken toward resolving the matter. From a systemic perspective (molecular), however, success at the individual level can sometimes cloud effective resolution at the organizational level. Since the mother viewed Prozac as the solution, she concluded that the problem was "obviously" some kind of chemical imbalance in her daughter. Case closed. In this type of scenario, general psychiatric approaches would confirm the mother's conclusion.

Neglected in all this would be the structure of the situation. For example: How was the girl's behavior maintained and reinforced by the family system regardless of what triggered it? Annette's behavior—whether triggered by what she ate, by a biochemical imbalance, by an attention-getting motive, or by an unconscious attempt to distract parents at war—impacts the family system and needs to be handled in some way. If the mother is anxious and overreacts, her anxiety will spread among all the family members, whether or not Annette suffers from ADD.

If there is no adult in the family who will handle matters effectively so that "the emotional buck stops here," even normal children will not feel safe. If there is no effective leadership when children misbehave, anxiety spreads even more and someone will react, perhaps with a symptom. We do not have to assume that someone is neurologically sick for this to happen. The neurology is simply a part of the equation. If we put all the blame on that single part for the entire sequence of interaction, we have empowered one element in the system (molecule) and dis-empowered every other part.

When Prozac entered the family system, it became another factor to be accounted for in the family dance, not the only causal factor. The cold war between the parents, the father's lack of involvement in the children's issues, the mother's depression and lack of leadership skill are additional factors to be accounted for if we are to understand and gain mastery in this matter.

The wisdom to perceive the whole circuitry of a transaction is an important component of self-mastery.

Even if we assume that Prozac helped Annette to calm down and to focus better, we must still be alert to the effects of the divided and ineffective leadership within the family. If, for instance, Annette's misbehavior had become a distraction away from the marital tension, her good behavior could leave a problem vacuum into which another child could step and become the "identified patient." Or, the marital relationship could become the issue, assuming Annette is no longer the focus of the family worry.

If the marriage became the focal problem, things could get better or worse depending on how the parents handle it. The marital war could escalate and lead to greater family tension, more divisive coalitions, or even divorce. On the other hand, the couple could find effective solutions to resolve their pain, get closer, and even find a way to unite as a supportive parental team. Systemic thinking encourages us to look for the relevant factors all throughout the sequence of interaction. Here's how Bateson puts it: "What is the case is that when causal systems become circular …, a change in any part of the circle can be regarded as *cause* for change at a later time in any variable anywhere in the circle."[8]

Note that, when we look at the dynamics of the family as an organization, Prozac becomes only *one* of the factors in the larger puzzle. The implication here is that if Prozac has a beneficial effect on Annette's behavior while the organizational structure remains the same, a symptom could still emerge somewhere else in the system. It could emerge either in another individual, in a relationship, or back with Annette. In other words, the system could nullify the effects of the medication. It is as if the system has the capacity to transfer symptoms from one part of the system to another. This can be quite confusing to members of the system, as well to helpers of the family members.

When medication "works," it is tempting to conclude that (1) the individual was sick and (2) the rest of the system had nothing to do with it. In a word, one person takes all the blame for the problem and the rest are excused or totally absolved as having anything to do with it. This lack of wisdom (partial arc) can lead to negative effects. If we saw Annette's behavior as simply the result of ADD, we would interpret her actions as sick or neurologically impaired. We would reduce her struggles to a diagnostic category and render her actions meaningless and totally out of context. Within the linear causal view, we would scapegoat one element in the system as the sole cause of the problem.

In James Hillman's terms,[9] we would not see the acorn (the unique self) striving to resist or fulfill her mission. We could not appreciate the pursuit by Annette's Higher Self, relentlessly reminding her about her commitment to pursue her calling. We would not perceive the jewels sparkling within those grenades. We would see only pathology.

Similarly, if we viewed only one factor as the cause for the entire pattern in a system, we could not perceive the environment as part of destiny's hand—pebbles provoking the acorn to manifest its uniqueness. Without perceiving the molecular dance, we could not notice nor appreciate the organizational patterns of interaction of which Annette was a part. We would not see the trunk that connects the leaves and the branches to the roots embedded in the life-giving earth.

*The inability to see the whole ecology of person and
system (atom and molecule) limits our vision.
It could lead to disease and disaster.*

UNBINDING A MARITAL PARADOX

THE STORY OF A COUPLE AS ATOMS AND AS A MOLECULE

The marriage of Louise and Eric is an interesting story that beautifully illustrates the framework of atoms and molecules. The gist of this story lies in understanding their relationship paradox: Eric could not see himself as a happy husband (part of the marriage molecule) and simultaneously believe that he was an autonomous individual (atomic view). His solution was to deny passionately that he was in love with Louise, even while declaring that he would never leave her. Louise could not put the two positions together. When she pointed to actions that she defined as "happy" or "loving," Eric would immediately deny her interpretation.

Using the metaphor of hydrogen and oxygen atoms in the water molecule, we could state the paradox as follows: Eric accepted his identity as hydrogen atom but simultaneously denied being part of the water. The more Louise insisted that Eric was part of the water, the stronger his denials became. But if Louise accepted Eric's definition of his atomic individuality, she would have to accept his not being part of the water (marriage). On the other hand, if Eric accepted Louise's view that he was part of the marital water, he would have to deny his atomic independence (his individuality).

Here we see the classic "war" between the primary forces in life: the need to belong and the need to be an individual. Louise picked up the banner of belonging and Eric held the banner of individuality. Not realizing that this was a false dichotomy, they could not see the

199

circularity of these two complementary needs. As always, the story will give us a more compassionate view of this rather cold summary.

DEFINITION AND HISTORY OF THE PROBLEM

Louise and Eric are in their late twenties. They have been married for five and a half years and have a son who is almost two years old. Eric's family of origin sees him as the successful one in the family. He is a young lawyer in a reputable firm who is eager to make a reputation for himself. His siblings are viewed by the family as either mediocre or simply losers. Louise comes from a supportive, close-knit family who sees her as a good wife and mother. They are happy with the match, viewing Eric as a good companion to Louise.

Louise and Eric's problem is a rather puzzling one. For the first three years of their marriage, Louise thought they had a good, happy relationship. Eric did not show any signs of unhappiness. One month before she gave birth to their son, Eric announced that he was actually never in love with her and that he had never been happy. Louise was shocked.

ERIC'S VIEWS AND POSITION

Eric wanted Louise to understand that he was *not* in love with her. He recited a list of qualities he wanted in a wife. Louise had only a few of those qualities. This unhappiness, he said, started in the courtship years. This was news to Louise. He said the marriage was a mistake from the start. He felt forced to marry her because they had sexualized their relationship and because both families of origin expected them to marry. The pregnancy had further sealed his fate. He concluded that he should leave her but that this would be more costly than the price of staying married to her forever. The price he was talking about included the emotional, social, and economic aspects of their lives.

LOUISE'S VIEWS AND POSITION

Louise was devastated. She could not make any sense of his position. Her observations and experiences in the past simply did not add up. She was convinced that Eric loved her and that he was really not that unhappy in the marriage. In fact, she thought that he was more unhappy as a person than as a husband. She noted that he was not sociable. He never contacted his own family, not even to say hello. She was the one who made contact. Eric did not care to invite friends over to their place, or to go out with other couples. Louise tried to convince him that their marriage was good and that it had even greater potential. Eric shot down every effort she made to defend the marriage. He would say, "You just don't get, do you? I don't love you and I am not happy with you."

Louise had come in alone for the first session. In the second session, Eric came with her. I found out then that his parents had an extremely unhappy marriage, yet they stuck it out. Eric was the star of the family. He acted out the part of the good, successful boy who became the standard-bearer in the family. However, in his gut, he was always unhappy and often seething with resentment. I concluded that Eric's way of preserving his sense of independence and individuality was to be unhappy as a member of the family. In his family of origin, these feelings were rarely expressed. In his marriage, however, he was now expressing this pessimism openly.

Eric took pride in making it known to me that he understood the situation perfectly. He said he understood himself and Louise well. But there was nothing that could be done about it. He did not think any therapist could help. I praised him for coming to the session to share his insights. I told him that his unhappiness in the marriage was probably his most potent way of asserting his individuality inside this relationship. I also mentioned that, given his position, he probably would not be interested in pursuing therapy. He agreed. I accepted his decision. He was always welcome, of course, I told him.

I told him that I would work with Louise to help her deal with her unhappiness in the relationship. I said, however, that I might call on him in the future to get his insights about what was going on with Louise and with their marriage. Eric readily agreed. In the third session, Louise told me that Eric felt I was the first person that truly understood him and his ideas. The reason for Eric's positive response may not seem apparent on the surface. Louise was, likewise, responding positively to my approach. This may also be puzzling, since I made no effort to convince Eric to change his stand on the marriage or the therapy.

The framework of atoms and molecules can help us to understand the couple's responses. In fact, it provides an intriguing view of the marital terrain. As we saw, there is a seeming contradiction in their relationship that can be understood if we look at two levels of the couple: the individual or atomic level and the relational or molecular level. Each level can be understood in its own terms; it can be seen as logical. Yet when we put the two levels together, there is a contradiction that is not logical. Let's go further in our analysis.

Every time Louise praises Eric as a husband, Eric criticizes the idea and criticizes her for not understanding him or the true nature of the relationship. When Eric criticizes the marriage, Louise defends it. Her defense of the relationship elicits another criticism from Eric. When Louise expresses happiness as a wife, Eric expresses unhappiness as a husband. This is their molecular dance.

At the atomic level, each is surprisingly content to be who they are. Louise is puzzled about Eric's unhappiness with her. She perceives herself as a good person, an attractive woman, and a loving mother. Eric sees himself as a competent person with many positive qualities. He even sees Louise as a good and attractive person. He can praise her as *an individual*, but never *as his wife*. Therein lies the difference. He can acknowledge the atom but not the molecule. If we grasp this principle, we begin to understand why Eric and Louise accepted my initial approach. I accepted each person's view and positioned myself in a way that did not violate either one's view.

I even told Eric that marriage therapy might be "disadvantageous" for him because, if successful, he believed it could take away his primary way of experiencing his individuality. He would gain at the relationship level (molecular) but fear losing something precious at the individual level (atomic).

With this distinction in mind, I was able to make precise recommendations to Louise in the third session. She came by herself. She told me that she loved Eric and that she would prefer to stay in the marriage if she could take it. There was a great deal of ambivalence on her part, at least in her thinking and feeling. However, her choice (will) was to stay in the relationship. She was asking for help to understand the puzzle in her marriage and to deal with the pain of rejection more effectively. Mindful of her goal and her decision to stay in the marriage, I gave her the following recommendations:

Ramon: Louise, you need to understand the dance in your relationship. Any time you praise Eric *as a husband* or defend your marriage, you will get shot down. Eric will tell you he is unhappy and that you do not understand him at all—proving his point that you are not the right spouse *for him*. If you wish to be more comfortable, you will have to give up two precious hopes you have. [Louise looked puzzled.]

Louise: What do I need to give up?

Ramon: Give up hoping that he would ever say "I love you" or that he would declare his happiness with you as his wife.

[Tears started to roll down her cheeks.] You will need to look at his actions and, secretly, find loving gestures there. These gestures are there. That is why you are puzzled by his words. Never expect him to admit that he has moments of happiness with you. You can praise him *as a person*. If he does something nice for you, you can thank him for his kindness, even if you realize that he is unhappy in the marriage. [There was a little laughter mixed in with her tears. She saw the absurdity of the mix between the atomic and the molecular.]

Louise: This is so strange [smile] ... But I know that he loves me. We've had good times [pained look].

Ramon: I know you've had many good times. That is not the problem. You need to realize that if you talk about it, he will contradict you and you will feel rejected. The more you defend the marriage, the more he will feel compelled to convince you that the relationship stinks and that you simply do not understand. I want you to recognize the dance. When you are optimistic about your marriage, he will be pessimistic about the relationship.

Louise: Will it always be like this?

Ramon: For the moment, yes. I do not know if it will always be that way. My guess is that, if you do as I recommend and keep your composure for a long time, he may become uncomfortable. This would be particularly true if you become accepting and calm about his not declaring his love and happiness. I'm really asking you to stop trying to change his views. You will, however, need to be patient with yourself because this will not be easy for you to carry out. When things are going well between you, you will be tempted to try your old dance and see if he might declare some level of happiness with you. At that point, I predict he will perform his usual dance and you will feel shot down again. He will, strangely, feel somewhat strengthened after declaring his unhappiness. Remember, this is his way of experiencing his independence.

The next session brought some confirmations about my analysis. Louise and Eric spent the weekend together in a resort area. She said that things were going well between them. In fact, she thought that Eric was comfortable, relaxed, and in an upbeat mood. At one point, she said something like this, "See, Eric, it's not so bad between the two us, is it?" Eric said, "You still don't get it, do you? I am here with you only because it's my duty, not because I'm happy." The rest of the weekend was a downer for Louise.

Every time I share this story with therapists in training, I get raised eyebrows from some people who say, "Why does she not leave this guy?" I translate that comment as coming from someone who does not perceive the dance and who is looking only at the individuals. The logical conclusion from the atomic view alone is to blame one person and to absolve the other as a victim. This is the partial arc Bateson spoke of. But when we put the molecular perspective beside the atomic view, we are able to give each level its unique place. We can still see the absurdity of the mix. But it is easier to navigate the territory if we know where we are treading. Here is what I told Louise when she relayed the incident.

Ramon: How did you feel when Eric told you that you guessed wrong about his feeling happy?

Louise: Awful. I just don't understand it. He looked relaxed and happy [tears].

Ramon: Louise, in a way, I'm glad this happened. Besides showing quite clearly that, as a person, Eric can actually be content with you now and then, the incident is also a reminder to you that he will not admit that he can be *happy as a husband*. It would be nice if he could accept being happy both as a person and as a husband. At the moment, he will not do that. He has too much of his individuality invested in being unhappy in the relationship.

Louise: But will I never be able to hold him accountable for what he does?

Ramon: You certainly can and you should. Give me an example of an area for which you want him to be accountable.

Louise: He never wants to have friends over to the house. It's always just the two of us and our son.

Ramon: What would you like instead?

Louise: I want to invite some friends over, but he says he won't enjoy having them over. I feel stuck.

Ramon: Here's what I recommend. Tell him you have decided that you want to invite friends over, even if he will not enjoy the occasion. However, you want him to help you get ready for the event and you expect him to act as a decent host. Tell him, though, that you will not expect him to *enjoy himself*. Accept his willingness to do *his duty* as a husband. He will do it for duty's sake, not for love's sake.

There was a smile again in Louise's face. The smile did not show total contentment with her situation, but enough recognition of the pattern to find her way through it. I gave her precise instructions about how to say things that would honor their individual experience without praising or defending the relationship. I told her that if he looked happy, she could say, "I know you're unhappy with our marriage, but it's nice to see you smile." I would expect him to accept that kind of compliment without triggering the dance of pessimism. You might ask: What are her options? It seems somewhat limiting for her to live under such narrow limits. Actually, if Louise is truly willing to give up verbal confirmation of Eric's love for her, she can exercise quite a lot of freedom. She can extend the approach used in inviting friends to many areas in their lives. This is not to deny that Eric's position imposes a drastic limitation on their relationship repertoire.

Recently, when Louise was expressing ambivalence about staying in the marriage, I gave her three options to think about: (1) to keep the old dance going (the relationship as it existed prior to therapy); (2) to stay in the marriage with the approach I recommended and assess it in six months; or (3) to separate immediately, but propose to Eric that they work together in therapy to change the dance altogether. The third option could put their relationship in jeopardy, depending on Eric's response.

Louise chose option two. She applied my recommendations for about six or seven months, at the end of which she decided on option three. She left Eric for a month, taking refuge with her family of origin. Interestingly enough, Eric had a "change of heart and mind." He admitted that he was wrong about his assessment of the marriage. He wanted her back and agreed to do individual and marriage therapy. They started their sessions with me as soon as Louise came back to town. It's been a two years since their last session. They seem to be doing well. Like every other couple, they have certain issues. But these issues are no longer as mysterious as the previous ones.

HIGHLIGHTING

It is helpful to recognize the difference between personal and relational levels of reality. Although these realities are linked and affect one another, they need to be viewed as operating at different levels. The metaphor of atoms and molecules helps to understand the difference in a graphic way. The metaphor is much like the difference between the dancers and the dance.

The story of Eric and Louise is a dramatic illustration of this idea. It would be difficult to understand their relationship patterns if we looked only at the personal or atomic level of analysis. When, for instance, we realize that Eric's way of experiencing his individuality was tied to being unhappy in the relationship, we can feel compassion for his apparent arrogance in the way he talked about Louise as a wife. Yet, he could praise her as an individual, but not as his wife. This opened the door for Louise to see that, through his actions, Eric was saying "I love you." Flexibility was the fruit of this framework. Any movement in that direction is a good sign.

TECHNIQUE AND STRUCTURE

APPLYING THE FRAMEWORK IN THE FAMILY SYSTEM

The framework of atoms and molecules takes on additional significance when applied to parents and children in a family setting. Again, let us view the individuals as atoms and the family system as the molecule. I will use the term *technique* to refer to the behavior of parents in response to their children, the term *structure* to refer to the patterns of interaction in the family system. To extend the metaphor, *technique,* therefore, is at the atomic level and *structure* is at the molecular level of analysis.

When talking to parents about managing children, I routinely make the distinction between technique and structure. Examples of technique would include imposing logical consequences for children's behavior or using a system of rewards and punishments for given behaviors. Many parents become confused about the nature and impact of these techniques because sometimes they work and sometimes they backfire. One reason for backfiring has to do with what I call structure. *If the structure is not right, the technique will often not work.* In fact, things could get worse.

If the structure is not right, the technique will often not work.

If there is a rift in the marital relationship so that husband and wife do not experience an adequate level of closeness and support, they will not likely be cooperative as executives of the family. So, if mother and daughter have a conflict over a certain issue, the father might lend his support to the daughter and form an emotional alliance with her against the mother. In systems theory, this particular dance is called a *triangle*. A triangle is essentially a coalition of two against one. It is especially devastating if the allies come from two different generations, as in the parent-child coalition. (The details of this concept will be covered in the next chapter.)

If the daughter feels her father's support, she will be empowered by this alliance and get enough strength to "attack" mother. She may even have a fantasy of "getting" mom for dad's sake and expect to be rewarded by her father in subtle ways. Father may give her many privileges, become overly permissive, and even criticize mother for being unduly harsh toward their daughter. This would be akin the alliance between a vice president and a manager against another vice president of a company.

Within a dysfunctional structure, even the best techniques for childrearing will most likely fail. The structure will nullify the technique. Since the structure forms the context of the technique, it will influence the meaning of the technique. Since technique is carried out through individual behavior, it is at the level of self (the atom). And since structure refers to an organizational pattern, we view it at the level of system (the molecule).

The same technique will, therefore, take on different meanings in different structures. Logical consequences used by parents who are united and who support one another will mean something different from consequences imposed by parents who are divided in a triangle with a child.

TECHNIQUE AND STRUCTURE

Within a dysfunctional structure, even the best management techniques will likely fail. The structure will nullify the technique. Since the structure forms the context of the technique, it will influence the meaning of the technique. Technique is at the level of self (the atom) and structure is at the level of system (the molecule). This is true in family or business systems.

Those who develop the capacity to see things at the level of self and at the level of system will have many more options from which to choose. If you are the father in the above example and you are convinced that your daughter, at age sixteen, needs a little more freedom, you may be in favor of extending her curfew from 11 p.m. to midnight. These are your personal thoughts.

Your wife disagrees, however. You also realize that the more you push your point of view, the more your wife digs in. You notice her getting harsher toward your daughter and more distant from you. Your daughter, in turn, becomes more belligerent. You are aware that you are part of a dance pattern (the molecule). The pattern becomes clearer if you momentarily become an observer and watch the dance like a movie, seeing yourself as one of the dancers. This will help you see the whole circuitry of the interaction, not just a partial arc. As a dancer, you are part of the choreography—an atom *within* a molecule.

The dancers, if examined carefully as individual atoms, will give the observer clues about what each needs. Mother may need father's support as strongly as father needs her to listen to his ideas about managing their daughter. The daughter may need for the parents to be clearer in their leadership, along with her need for some trust from her parents. Close examination may even reveal that the chink in the parental armor means that the marriage needs more attention than the couple has given it in weeks.

The systemic (molecular) view reveals aspects of the structure that may need change. These changes in structure will trigger shifts in the interaction patterns of the members and will, in turn, impact the personal experiences of each one involved. If we do not develop a systemic eye, we will miss seeing the dance and, with it, the capacity to choose options that could prove helpful.

Consider another scenario.

Mother and ten-year-old son have developed a close relationship. Father, a busy businessman, has grown distant from his son and his wife. His discomfort in the role of father shows up in his impatience toward his son. Mother's emotional life is more entwined with her role as mother than as wife. Her joys and sorrows are more calibrated to the ups and downs in her son's life. A triangle is born, which may be diagrammed as follows:

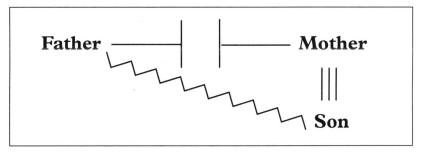

This triangular pattern may not be obvious when things are relaxed in the family. It becomes more apparent when tension is running through the system. It is important to realize that everyone "cooperates" to maintain a given pattern, even the outsider in a triangle. Assume that one Saturday morning a minor miracle takes place: father and son go fishing together and happen to enjoy each other's company. They arrive home in a jovial mood.

They bring their catch of the day through the kitchen entrance and in the process of filleting the fish, father and son notice that mother is in a somber mood. Note the shift in alliance: mother is the emotional outsider for the moment. Suddenly, mother gets upset with her son for his inept handling of the fish. The son yells at his mother. Father enters the fray by yelling at his son for talking to his mother disrespectfully. Then mother scolds father for being too harsh with their son. Father leaves the scene while mother consoles her son. The usual triangle becomes reestablished.

The members are so caught up in the content of the drama that no one realizes how each contributed to the process of moving back to the dominant pattern of the family. The structure in a system contains "train tracks" through which dozens of issues run in the course of time. The train cars and their cargo may differ from day to day, but they go through the same old tracks. Let us keep an eye on both the cars and the tracks.

STRUCTURE AND ISSUES
The structure in a system contains "train tracks" through which dozens of issues are run in the course of time. The train cars and their cargo may differ from day to day, but they go through the same old tracks. Let us keep an eye on both the cars and the tracks.

SELF, SYSTEM, AND SYNERGY

AWARENESS AND SOCIAL CONDITIONING
Awareness has the power to change aging, but awareness is a two-edged sword—it can both heal and destroy. What makes the difference is how your awareness becomes conditioned, or trained, into various attitudes, assumptions, beliefs, and reactions.

–Deepak Chopra[10]

In this quote, Chopra is putting forth, in different words, the same ideas about the relationship between our psychology and sociology. The conditioning through the social system in which we are embedded breeds an intricately woven net that is invisibly nested into the fabric of our awareness. This is reality. This is not wrong. It would be an error to define social conditioning per se as the culprit. It would be like blaming the right foot for a swelling on the big toe or blaming air for the existence of pollution.

The social fabric is a given. The nature or quality of this fabric may vary in desirability. We get support and criticism through the same medium. If a toe is infected, we should try to heal the infection rather than amputating the foot, if it can be saved. If our parents were the source of some ineffective conditioning, let us try to heal the conditioning and redefine those relationships, rather than cutting them off from our social sphere.

THE SOCIAL FABRIC OF AWARENESS
The conditioning we receive through the social system in which we are embedded breeds an intricately woven net that is invisibly nested into the fabric of our awareness. This is reality. This is not wrong.

Awareness is the substance of our maps that form the landscape of our thinking, feeling, intending, and doing. If mind and body interact in a mutual causal dance, and if social system and mind are similarly interconnected, then social system and body are likewise causally linked. We can visualize the link as an infinity sign or as concentric circles. See diagram on the following page.

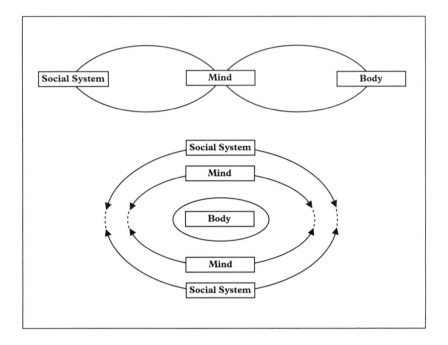

It is important to understand how the interactive dance between self and system breeds symptoms or synergy. Synergy is a group effect where 1+1=3. Symptom, also a group effect, leads to something less than the sum of the individual parts (1+1= -3). When two or more people come together for some purpose, the system will produce noise or music or a combination. When "two heads are better than one," you have synergy. When "two heads are worse than one," then symptoms appear in a person, relationship, or both.

Symptom and synergy are qualities of the system, the molecule.

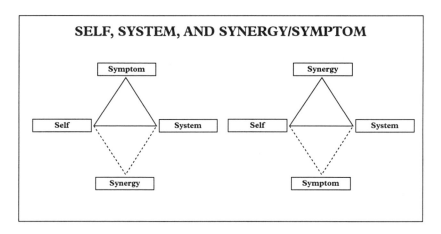

SELF, SYSTEM, AND SYNERGY/SYMPTOM

This diagram depicts the connectedness of self, system, and synergy/symptom. When the dance leads to synergy, symptom is in potential. That is why the dotted lines are there to form the lower triangle. If the dance leads to symptoms, let us remember also that synergy is a potential. One can be converted to the other. This capacity of transformation resides is each person as well as in the system.

Symptoms are signals of the need for synergy.
Symptoms are potential pathways to synergy.

ANOTHER STORY ABOUT ATOMS AND MOLECULES: A Girl with Sleeping Difficulties

A few years ago, I invited Harry Aponte, a family therapist, to conduct a workshop for mental health professionals. As part of that workshop, Harry worked with a family who had an eight-year-old girl named Melanie. The family described Melanie's symptoms as follows: crying sporadically without any apparent reason, difficulty sleeping, sleepwalking, and difficulty getting up in the morning. The girl was being seen by a social worker at a mental health center. She was given a diagnosis of childhood depression. No one else in the family had been involved in the previous therapy.

Lori, the mother, was on her third marriage. She was twenty-five years old. Her second marriage brought Contessa, age four. David, Lori's husband, was twenty years old and an immigrant from Mexico. They had been married for about a year and had been living together for two and half years. David, Lori, Melanie, and Contessa were living in an apartment with Lori's mother and grandmother. In other words, there were four generations represented in this apartment: from Melanie to her great-grandmother, Margarita.

Melanie had lived with Margarita and Nita, the grandmother, since the day she was born and Lori had been coming in and out of this household during the eight years of Melanie's life. At the time of the interview, Lori and David had been back in the household about a month. Melanie (the self) lived in a structure (the system) in which the great-grandmother and grandmother had been the constant caregivers, not the mother or the fathers. Melanie has regular visits with her father.

During the interview, Mr. Aponte asked a revealing question: "How are decisions made about Melanie in this family?" The picture that emerged was one of a confused hierarchy. Grandmother recounted a time when Margarita, the great-grandmother, was assisting Melanie with her spelling lesson. Meanwhile, a friend came asking to play with Melanie. Lori insisted that Melanie go out and play—against great-grandmother's wish. Caught between the two, Melanie went out to play.

The instructional videotape that I edited based on this session is called "Tres Madres," meaning "Three Mothers." That title captures the essence of Melanie's system. If one connects the self (atom) and system (molecule) in Melanie's world, it is not difficult to understand how she might feel like suddenly crying or unable to relax enough to sleep. The sleepwalking is an especially telling symptom. It "speaks" of a self in which one part is actively seeking to do something while the other refuses to cooperate consciously.

Mr. Aponte's primary recommendation hits the crux of the "molecular system." He tells Lori that she must be a different kind of mother. She needs to be the "Chairman of the Board" in a "corporation of parents" who need to work together as a team in charge of raising Melanie. The "atoms" in this family "molecule" are good people with good intentions. However, the structure of the system is flawed. It is the symptom in Melanie that raises the flag, signaling the kind of change needed. Every atom in this molecule is suffering even if only one is currently showing obvious signs (symptoms) of distress.

It is at this point that the role of expert diagnostician (therapist, priest, shaman, minister, medicine man, or witch doctor) becomes crucial in the evolution of the system. At one point, Aponte looks at Melanie and says, "You cry and your mother cries. You are not sick." This was a modern "exorcism" of sorts. This is the fruit of seeing at least two levels of reality—the individual atoms and the systemic molecule. It is a step along the mystical path of seeing the full arc— the whole, not the illusion of separateness.

IN A NUTSHELL

Through a number of true-to-life stories, we saw the real dilemmas that some human beings face when confronted with the paradoxes of life. We saw how Louise was puzzled by her husband saying he didn't love her and that she was wrong for him. Yet, he not only stayed in the marriage, but also did things that portrayed love and commitment. Eric himself suffered unhappiness in the relationship, but felt he was stuck. Louise found relief and saw some behavioral options by distinguishing between the atomic and molecular levels of analysis. This helped her to grasp the difference and the interconnectedness between personal and relational functioning. Eric finally found ways not to use his unhappiness in the relationship as a way to solve an individual issue—the need to experience an adequate level of individuality. It took a lot of dedication, loyalty, and courage on Louise's part to finally take a stand in relation to the marriage. Fortunately, Eric chose to work on his individual issue within the marriage molecule.

In the life of Annette, who was diagnosed with ADD, we saw the dangers of labeling one person with some disease or character disorder and then seeing that person's condition as totally disconnected from the larger system of relationships in the family (the molecule). Using the same framework, we were able to distinguish between technique and structure in parenting. This distinction helped to integrate technique and structure in a way that gave us more options to deal with parenting issues. There are many applications of the concept for organizational development as well.

It is useful to link person and system (atom and molecule)—this is a holy act: wholeness in action. There is no implication that the structure (molecule) causes individual health or disease. The molecule is the context or environment in which the atom is revealed in its unique nature. In the same way, the relationship system is the environment in which the nature of the self is revealed.

It is true that the molecule/relationship affects the functioning of the atom/person. However, one can also say that the behavior of the atom/person affects the nature of the molecule/relationship. The interconnectedness is circular. To put all the "blame/credit" only on one level is to cut up the pie—an unholy act: the illusion of separateness in action.

Both levels of reality are important in their own right. Holiness is the act of perceiving and dancing with the wholeness of life.

This is the dance of the mystic—the goal of self-mastery.

[1] Ornish, D. (1998). *Love and Survival: The Scientific Basis for the Healing Power of Intimacy.* New York: HarperCollins Publishers.

[2] Wilber, K. (1995). *Sex, Ecology, Spirituality.* Boston: Shambhala Publications, Inc.

[3] Borchert, B. (1994). *Mysticism.* York Beach, ME: Samuel Weiser, Inc.

[4] Bateson, G. (1979). *Mind and Nature: A Necessary Unity.* New York: E. P. Dutton, p. 11.

[5] Ibid., p. 9.

[6] Chopra, D. (1993). *Ageless Body, Timeless Mind.* New York: Harmony Books.

[7] Bateson, G. (1979). *Mind and Nature: A Necessary Unity.* New York: E. P. Dutton, Chapter Four.

[8] Ibid., p. 60.

[9] Hillman, J. (1996). *The Soul's Code.* New York: Random House.

[10] Chopra, D. (1993) *Ageless Body, Timeless Mind.* New York: Harmony Books, p. 51.

Chapter 9

RELATIONSHIP KNOTS AND THEIR SOLUTIONS

Mastering Relationships (1)

SELF-MASTERY AND INTIMACY

We identified the ability to develop viable relationships as one of the requirements of self-mastery. This and the next chapter focus on the nature of intimate relationships. In this one, we examine relationship knots and how to unbind them. Much attention will be given to the concept of triangle: the coalition of two against one. The triangle is the mortal enemy of the two-person relationship, which is the basic unit of intimacy. In the next chapter, we will give attention to the self as mate and as child in the family of origin.

For true intimacy to develop, we need the skills to sustain a person-to-person relationship in which self encounters self. If our relationship is united by a common focus outside of our twosome, then our closeness is suspect. Is our alliance simply externally fashioned because of a common enemy or worry? Or is it glued by a love that is based on true knowledge about each other? It is important to detect the patterns that foster the experience of true closeness.

Spirit is manifested everywhere, including our relationships. The mystical view alerted us to the presence of God everywhere: in matter, in life, in mind, in relationships, in communities, in cultures, and in nations. In detecting the patterns that breed love and intimacy, we will be seeing the fingerprints of Spirit. The language of science and logic need not blind us to the spiritual action of God in everything, including relationships.

The mystics often remark that marriage is an outer symbol of the "alchemical" wedding of the soul to God. Ultimately, we seek union with God. Along the way we need to learn to love Spirit as manifested in everything and everyone. The injunction to love our neighbor is universal. Loving a mate demands that we transcend the ego so that the two find a larger whole (molecule) without losing the uniqueness of self (atom).

CLOSENESS AND INDEPENDENCE IN BALANCE

To understand functional balance in a relationship, we need to keep in mind the interplay of the primary life forces: belonging and individuality. These forces are universal: we find them in all human beings across cultures. In the words of Carl Jung, we would say that they are archetypal: part of the warp and woof of our psyche. These two complementary needs manifest themselves in the relationship as closeness and independence. These two patterns, like the needs they reflect, are also universal. We find them etched in all relationships.

It is important to remind ourselves that belonging and individuality are mutually enhancing forces. The stronger the one, the stronger the other. If one is diminished, the other will be undermined as well. This is true within the person (the experience of belonging and individuality) and in the relationship patterns they manifest (the qualities of closeness and independence).

CLOSENESS AND INDEPENDENCE IN THE EFFECTIVE RELATIONSHIP

In the effective relationship, there is a flexible balance in the patterns of togetherness and independence. The two people in the relationship have a comfortable and satisfying level of contact, communication, fun, and conflict resolution. They are also comfortable with the level of space and tolerance provided for independent action. If one feels too controlled or crowded by the other, she can send signals that are received effectively. If she feels that the other is not invested enough in the relationship, she can send signals that effectively restore the desired balance.

This balance in the relationship patterns may be diagrammed as follows:

	Husband	Wife
Togetherness	→	←
Apartness	←	→
Restoring closeness	←	←
or independence	→	→

The first set of arrows depict moments when two people are together willingly and are able to be real with each other in their verbal and nonverbal contact. The communication may be playful, casual, or serious. The serious conversations may involve exploring issues or negotiating changes in certain areas. Some of these exchanges may even be uncomfortable, but they are open and honest. The second set of arrows portray moments when two people are engaged in independent action, whether or not they are in the same space. In other words, there is a willing tolerance and support to let each other engage in independent activity.

The last two sets of arrows show moments when one is "inviting more closeness" or "generating more independence," depending on which one is feeling uncomfortable with the temporary imbalance. The one who first feels a need for more closeness or more independence usually initiates action designed to correct the imbalance.

These restorative moves are important. In well-functioning relationships, these balancing acts are done with tolerable levels of stress, accomplishing the adjustment without overly depleting the couple's fund of goodwill. This is the ideal picture, the mental template that guides us.

CLOSENESS AND INDEPENDENCE OUT OF BALANCE

I do not believe it is possible for any relationship to sustain this kind of balance at all times. The goal is to aim for it and to make periodic corrections along the way. When we perceive a threat to our belonging or individuality, we experience a level of anxiety. As a result, we will begin to make moves to protect what is valuable to us. This is true of all relationships, especially those with a great deal of emotional significance for us.

Our attempts to restore balance may lead to undesirable outcomes, despite our best motives. Let's remember again that personal realities (atomic) operate at a different level than relationship dynamics (molecular).

At the relationship level, these negative outcomes may be diagrammed as follows:

	Husband	Wife
Ongoing pursuit/distance	→	→
Mutual distance	←	→
Ongoing conflict	〰→	←〰
Over-/underfunctioning	↑	↓

In the course of our lives, we have probably seen many examples of these patterns. A brief description will suffice for our purposes here. In the ongoing pattern of pursuing and distancing, one person feels either left out or crowded by the other. The attempt to pursue triggers more distancing and the attempt to distance triggers more pursuing. Although each person is motivated to restore the balance, his or her mutual attempts trigger a dance that leaves them with less of what each wants.

This is where it helps to distinguish the atomic from the molecular level of analysis. If we focus on the motives of the persons involved in the dance, instead of observing the interaction patterns, we miss the dance. If we pay attention only to what is going on individually (atomic), we will miss the interplay (molecular).

The same is true for the mutual distancing, conflict, and over-/underfunctioning patterns. Let us take the ongoing conflict pattern as a focus. When two people engage in ongoing power struggles, they are often unaware that they are simultaneously attempting to experience closeness and independence. The battle between them provides the contact that they need. But the battle also amplifies the differences in their positions. These differences serve to give some sense of independence. Even if this couple's experiences are unsatisfactory, the benefits of the conflicts may be better for them than the net result of avoidance or distancing.

For some couples, fight is better than flight. For others, however, mutual distancing is the preferred coping pattern. Distancing temporarily cools off the anxiety. The distance often gives people breathing room and the illusion of independence. We see this illusion of independence most graphically in the dance between a young adult and his parents. When a young man is away from home, for instance, he may have comfortable conversations with his parents over the phone. Yet, when he visits, the sparks start flying within a few hours of his arrival.

The over-/underfunctioning dance is an especially interesting relationship knot. In this coping pattern, one member gives up too much individuality within the relationship, in the hope of finding more peace and a greater share of belonging. The one who capitulates and placates is seen as the loser. The overfunctioner is first perceived as the winner and the recipient of the relationship helm. This turns out to be a double-edged sword because along with the helm comes the responsibility of being in charge of the other person's life.

One classic example of this pattern is the alcoholic and the codependent spouse. The alcoholic is the underfunctioner who depends on the spouse to nurture, scold, protect, or clean up after him. One becomes the doctor and the other becomes the patient. After a while, the caretaker feels constrained by the burden of the responsibility, even if she has a great deal of decision-making freedom. The "patient" gets less and less positive nurturing and more negative attention. The sense of belonging becomes corrupted and unrewarding.

The attempts, by either side, to correct the imbalance are usually met with resistance and resentment from both. For the underfunctioner, the idea of being responsible for one's own life and the conflict that independence may trigger cast darker shadows than the codependent pattern. For the overfunctioner, the loss of control may be feared more than the burden of caretaking. True partnership has its own challenges, not just its own rewards.

All of these patterns are examples of people's attempts to preserve the need to belong and the need to be an individual. It is truly astonishing to perceive these two life forces in everything we do, especially in our encounters with the people we love or with whom we work.

Murray Bowen, a psychiatrist and family therapist, has been one of the great contributors to our understanding of these primary life forces. He believed that the forces of individuality and togetherness are biologically rooted—that they are more than just a brain function.

In other words, these forces are instinctive and, therefore, written in every cell of our beings. I would translate the "biologically rooted" idea into the concept that these forces are "soul-rooted." They are etched in the glow of our inner jewels.

Bowen's description of the way these forces work in a relationship is a good slice of systems theory:

> The relationship balance is not static, but is in a state of *dynamic equilibrium* ... Each person carefully monitors the other for signs of change, signs of "too little" or "too much" involvement ... Signals interpreted as signs of "too little" involvement automatically trigger actions designed to restore a "sense" of adequate attachment and signals interpreted as signs of "too much" involvement automatically trigger actions designed to restore a "sense" of adequate separation. Each person's signals and actions are in response to the other's signals and actions and so neither person's functioning can be adequately understood out of the context of the relationship.[1]

Bowen's comment about not being able to understand a person's functioning outside a relational view is especially important. This is the molecular or systemic view we have been discussing. The dancer and the dance need to be brought together in our analysis. If we assign blame to one and absolve the other, we will see only atoms. The molecule will become invisible.

CLOSENESS AND INDEPENDENCE: A More Precise Understanding

In talking about intimacy, we often hear people pitting closeness against independence. The impression is that the more closeness we experience, the less independence we have in the relationship. This is the kind of thinking that leads to those tongue-in-cheek metaphors about marriage like "tying the knot" or "taking the plunge."

We hear people using expressions like, "I'm afraid of getting too close because I might suffocate or lose my independence." Another might say, "I feel lonely in this relationship because my wife is too independent." A false dichotomy is subtly hidden in this kind of thinking. The dichotomy can be expressed as closeness versus independence. It may be diagrammed as follows:

Closeness ———————————————————— **Independence**

If we view closeness and independence at opposite ends of a pole, we tend to view high levels of either in a suspicious way. The more of one, the less of the other. Within this paradigm, "effective" relationships will manifest moderate levels of these two qualities of the human experience. Intense levels of intimacy and amazing manifestations of independence will be considered enemies of the relationship. "Too much" closeness would be defined as dependency and "too much" independence could be labeled as selfishness, lack of love, or fear of intimacy.

This viewpoint is deeply embedded in the culture and even in the thinking of psychologists and sociologists. It is important to clarify our thinking in this area in order to understand the true nature of intimacy. The best way to clear the confusion is to think in terms of two continuums:[2]

Closeness ———————————————— **Coldness/Distance**
Independence ——————— **Enmeshment/Intrusiveness**

In other words, the polar opposite of closeness is not independence. It is coldness or emotional distance. Enmeshment, not closeness, is the opposite of independence. *Enmeshment* is an apt word because it carries a flavor of melting boundaries: a fusion of personal boundaries leading to a confusion about where one person begins and the other ends. The active side of enmeshment may be described as "intrusiveness." The passive side shows up as "dependency."

Closeness and independence go together; they are on the same side. If you diminish one, you diminish the other. The more secure couples are about their commitment to each other, the greater their experience of belonging and connectedness. This strength of commitment usually allows them to have more courage to be themselves in the relationship. They can take more heat and more joy from the fire and excitement of differences in their relationship.

Coldness and enmeshment are two sides of the same coin. Relationship distance, as a manifestation of emotional coldness, is one way of coping with the pain of rejection or the fear of intimacy. Distancing or emotional cutoff is a way to avoid enmeshment. It is truly a coping response to a lack of independence. The person who cuts off is so insecure about being able to be himself in a close relationship that he distances in order to avoid feeling controlled. In this way, he gets the illusion of being independent and of not needing other people at all.

Enmeshment of the intrusive kind hides the fear of being independent. To be independent, we must face our mission in life, which can be scary and lonely at times. We are responsible for our level of success or failure in this endeavor. By intruding into somebody else's life, we can momentarily forget our mission and try to be responsible for another person's mission. This is the anatomy of codependency. Dependency is the other side of this: we allow another person to run our lives. We seek salvation outside ourselves, believing that our mate can relieve the anxiety we feel.

True intimacy is built on a strong foundation of closeness and independence. This is such a beautiful and rich paradox. The greater courage I have to be myself, to share myself, to risk my thoughts, feelings, and positions, the greater my capacity to experience closeness. On these twin pillars hangs the mystery of intimacy—the Spirit between us.

And now, let us take a closer look at how these forces are regulated in a relationship with ongoing conflict.

HOW CONFLICT REGULATES CLOSENESS
AND INDEPENDENCE: A Story

Peter and Sherry stand out in my mind as an example of a couple that used ongoing conflict to maintain a dynamic balance of closeness and independence. Their relationship was stable but miserable. They had three children in their teens. Sherry was the main complainant. She complained that Peter did not involve her in his decisions about money and about a number of other things that affected her, including the children. These were the kinds of pebbles that triggered emotional grenades.

She felt that he was generous to others but stingy with her. She managed the household and the children. The allowance she received for running the house had been adjusted for "cost of living" only once in the last fourteen years. Yet, she would find out, usually after the fact, that Peter gave generously to members of his extended family and to his church. She felt hurt and angry about being excluded from the decision making and about being relegated to the bottom of the totem pole. At this point, we can already sense the nature of her jewel, just by listening to the description of the grenade. The sparks of her jewel glow with a need to belong, shining through the pain of exclusion.

When I asked her what she needed, she said she needed communication and understanding. "If Peter talked to you and understood you, what would that do for you?" I asked. "It would make me feel complete and that I'm part of a team." I then asked her how she would know if she were an important part of the team. "Peter," she said, "would involve me in his decision making and he would be as generous to me as he is to his family." Another clear sign of a belonging jewel.

Let us recall that although both life forces sparkle in each of us, each person tends to reflect one quality a little more brightly than the other. Sherry shined brightly with the capacity to become connected as an important member of a partnership.

Peter's emotional grenades were triggered by two kinds of pebbles that Sherry threw into his pond. One was her criticism of his decisions about giving money to his family and to charity. The other was that she would override a number of the positions he would take. In other words, in areas outside finance, Peter felt that Sherry would simply negate his positions and proceed on the basis of her own views. He felt that she cared about him only in his role as provider and father to their children, not as a unique person. He felt rejected and dejected.

What did his grenades say he needed? "I need for Sherry to be aware of what's going on within me, to understand me, and to trust and love me as I am." His fantasy was to have a wife who implicitly trusted his motives and who would support him in his decisions. Instead, he believed that Sherry had no confidence in him at all. His jewel of individuality was constantly violated in their ongoing arguments.

Peter and Sherry, though married for nineteen years, no longer had moments of positive closeness. They did not express affection toward each other. Sexual contact was rare. Yet, there was no divorce talk. Their relationship was characterized by almost constant conflict. They argued about everything. Peter's power was lodged in the financial area. Sherry took the reins in the running of the house, the managing of the children, and in the level of affection and sexual contact.

As Peter and Sherry fought, they were aware mostly of the "rightness" of their positions or the "unfairness" of the other person's actions. Neither one was aware of the circular function of their dance: that in the midst of fighting, they were making contact and defending their individual positions. We could say that the relationship carried the symptom, as they each unloaded their anxiety on the other. Neither one was aware of how they simultaneously maintained the ongoing war.

Peter and Sherry were a classic case of people who tried to find the solutions to their grenades in the world of pebbles. Sherry would accuse Peter of caring more about others than he cared for her. She would argue her case passionately and plead for more generosity on his part. She believed that if only he would include her in his decisions or even give her more money, she would be happy and would be able to shower him with a lot of affection.

The more she argued her point, the less accepted and understood Peter felt. In fact, Peter felt that he would be more controlled by her if he gave in to her demands, including giving her more money. Besides, he felt he was already generous.

Peter, for his part, believed that if Sherry would just trust him and his decisions regarding money, he would be quite content and cooperative. The "reason" he was combative and unfriendly (effect) had to do with Sherry's blaming and controlling behavior (cause). If Sherry would be warmer, friendlier, and more sexually giving, then the relationship would take a jump on the marital satisfaction scale.

Note the equation in their thinking: "I'm unhappy because of you and I fight because of you." This is the mindset of a victim. This mindset is partially maintained and fueled by the equally false premise: "You can make me happy, if only you would change." These personal beliefs (atomic) blind them to their role in co-creating the dysfunctional patterns (molecular) in the relationship.

231

BALANCING CLOSENESS AND INDEPENDENCE
IN THE RELATIONSHIP

The dysfunctional patterns discussed above make a relationship vulnerable. The lack of success in creating a workable balance between closeness and independence puts the relationship at risk of either breaking or "overflowing" into a triangle. The concept of triangle means that the unresolved anxiety in the relationship gets tangled up with a third person who gets roped in to form a coalition with one side against the other. What does it take to keep the balance? How do triangles develop and get resolved?

Self-mastery is precisely what is needed to develop and maintain a healthy balance of closeness and independence in a relationship. This state of being assumes that a person practices the principle of self-responsibility: *I am responsible for my thoughts, feelings, positions, and actions, but not for another person's actions.* There is also an acceptance of the principle of co-responsibility: I and my partner are *jointly* responsible for the patterns of our interaction. In other words, I participate in the processes involved in "our dance of interaction."

To do our part in balancing the forces of closeness and independence requires great self-honesty, courage, and the ability to be aware of our own thinking, feeling, willing, and acting. We must be in touch with the deepest levels of soul functioning, without denial, blame, or avoidance of the issues within us and with others.

Self-mastery also requires great awareness in detecting the ripples that our actions trigger in our sphere of influence. Saying that we are not responsible for another person's response does not remove us from the dance. We are part of the interaction even if we do not control the other person's response.

Self-mastery also implies a healthy dose of self-directed behavior. Self-direction presupposes that we have a goal—a purpose or mission in life that is meaningful. It is this spiritual commitment to our soul blueprint that drives our independence. This belief in a transcendent view of our life's purpose feeds our individuality. It gives us the courage to take independent action even when our need to belong is threatened. Without this clear purpose, we may make too many compromises for the sake of our need to belong.

THE BIRTH OF A TRIANGLE

WHEN TWO PEOPLE CAN'T HOLD THE BALANCE OF CLOSENESS AND INDEPENDENCE

When two people are experiencing too much anxiety about the lack of belonging or individuality, it means that they are not effectively managing the balance of closeness and independence in their relationship. They may be making costly compromises. One could be "giving in" too much just to keep the peace while the other gets a false sense of individuality. Or the conflict they are experiencing may have gotten so intense that the stability of the relationship is in doubt. It could also be a case of too much distance, a situation where they are both avoiding their issue by not engaging one another in any significant way. That too could threaten the balance.

One "solution" people use to correct imbalance in a relationship is to involve a third person in the process. We did this even as little children. I remember when my "best friend" and I had a common enemy. The two of us may even have had a good number of laughs about how silly and dumb this other person was. I instinctively knew not to be caught befriending this enemy, otherwise my friend would get upset with me.

That was the essence of a triangle: two against one. In a triangle, there are two "insiders" and one "outsider." The two insiders are close to each other. Typically, one insider has a conflict with the outsider. The other insider is distant from the outsider by virtue of his alliance with the insider who has a conflict the "odd man out."

Triangle as Gossip System. A triangle involves a gossip system: two people talk to each other about a third person and feel an artificial bond in their common dislike. They may not be sure that a person-to-person relationship can work for them. It is easier to talk about somebody else than it is to talk to each other about each other. A person-to-person relationship is more risky business.

PRESERVING WITHOUT RESOLVING

A triangle emerges as a way to manage the unresolved anxiety in a relationship. Between two people, there is only one relationship. Bring in a third person and we have three relationships. There is then "more room" for the anxiety to float around. A triangle can maintain a two-person relationship without resolving the real issues between the two.

CLASSIC PATTERNS IN TRIANGLES: The Affair and the Troubled Child

Certain patterns govern the functioning of a triangle. Let us take a look at how triangles emerge around an ineffective marriage. There are two classic situations I would identify as attempted solutions to a difficult marriage: the affair and the troubled child.

The Affair. The affair is a good way to begin understanding how triangles work. Let us take the case of Peter and Sherry and create a hypothetical situation. Although I am not aware of any affairs in his relationship, Peter is in a system that would be vulnerable to having an affair. He does not feel much warmth coming from Sherry and, in addition, he is feeling powerless inside the relationship.

His power currently resides in his control of the money. If Sherry succeeds in sharing more power in that arena, Peter's last bastion of individuality could be invaded. Lack of power diminishes the independence of a person and, therefore, his experience of individuality.

Let us say that Peter falls for his assistant at work. Laura is an attractive, warm young lady whom Peter sees as competent, self-assured, and understanding. She is able to be quite objective with Peter and is able to provide closeness without blaming or clutching. Peter thinks he has found the ideal match. They are comfortable with each other and, above all, they "open up" and are able to "talk about anything." Meanwhile, at home, things have gotten worse. Sherry does not know why she is feeling much more powerless these days. Her tirades and her moves to take charge do not seem to have any effect on Peter. He seems much calmer and quite emotionally removed. The structure of this triangle may be diagrammed as follows:

Laura is satisfying Peter's need for closeness. The contact between

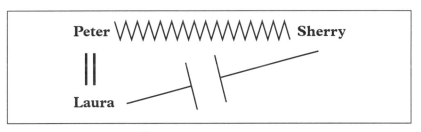

the two of them seems comfortable to him, particularly when he notices that his independence is totally respected. Since he has less investment in his closeness to Sherry, Peter has no fear about throwing pebbles into Sherry's pond and triggering grenades. It does not matter much anymore whether or not he gets her affection. He feels ecstatic about his newfound freedom, thinking himself invulnerable. He will now think that he has outgrown his wife who appears to be a pathetic figure. He also thinks that Laura provides the perfect balance between closeness and independence.

If we look at all the parts of the relationship system, we see some enlightening patterns. The two insiders, Peter and Laura, have little awareness that many of their conclusions about the situation are distorted. Peter thinks that he is no longer emotionally dependent on Sherry. He "does not really care." His need to belong is adequately met by Laura. Since he is not married to her, Peter does not feel much, if any, of the obligations about meeting her needs for security, for support, or any of the chores of daily life.

While he lives with Sherry, Peter's emotional space is "structured": he still goes home at night and the weekends. His meetings with Laura have to be in secret. Peter is shielded from easy intrusions by his paramour and comes to believe that this is the way she really is. He believes he has become the paragon of the self-actualized human being.

When Peter and Laura talk about Sherry and her "obvious" short-comings, they feel a bond that is almost free of any dyadic tensions: no sense of unresolved issues between the two of them. Most of their problems have to do either with Sherry or the difficulties encountered "because of the situation." In other words, the difficulties they perceive are mostly outside their relationship, not anything inherent to their two-some. This is the "illusion of a solution" people get from a triangle. It is not a true resolution of the issues involving any of the players.

Another dimension of this illusion is captured in the conversations Peter and Laura have about each other. They are able to see each other in positive terms. Their conversations are pure delight. Any seemingly negative response that either of them gets from the other is quickly excused and viewed as caused by the difficult circumstances surrounding their secret affair. They believe that "if only they were living together and free to be a couple openly," such difficulties would not exist. In other words, other than the social limitations, "there really are no difficulties."

It is useful to view a triangle, at least for a moment, as if it were a closed system with no outside interference. This is, of course, not true because other people around the triangle (children, for example) are making their own moves to accommodate. But in this pretend closed system, one can see that the Peter-Sherry side of the triangle is expressing most of the negative tension, the Peter-Laura side is experiencing most of the closeness, and the Sherry-Laura side is the most distant, naturally.

Even if Sherry is not aware of Laura's role in the triangle, she is still "relating" to Laura as part of the group. All Sherry may be aware of is that the "equation" between her and Peter has changed. She has noticed that things are quite different between them.

We find some important observations as we look inside each "point" or person in the triangle:

- Sherry is feeling threatened by the lack of closeness in her marriage. Prior to the affair, the conflict between Sherry and Peter affected him in significant ways. She believed that he cared about their issues and her responses to those events. Although there was not much warmth between them, there was heat and emotional contact. Now, it is different.

- Peter, as we stated, is feeling independent and emotionally unhooked from Sherry. This is especially true in the early phase of the affair when the excluded spouse often makes moves to generate more closeness. Peter would show disinterest. He would probably view his lack of interest as further proof of his growing independence.

- Laura's independence is intact at this point. Her sense of belonging is not as strong as she would like it to be, assuming she intends to marry Peter in the future. Although Laura feels emotionally loved by Peter, the structure of the triangle allows only limited access to Peter. Certainly, she cannot yet take "her place" socially, legally, and economically. As time goes by, she may begin to put pressure on Peter to take more definitive steps to leave the marriage.

It is at this point that things could start activating another phase of the triangle. As Laura puts pressure on Peter, she will become more or less happy depending on Peter's response. If Peter starts to talk about divorce, Sherry's sense of belonging will be further threatened. Her anxiety will rise and she will begin to take more drastic steps. She may, at first, throw caution to the wind and pursue Peter with an intensity he had not seen before. In response, Peter may slow down his moves to end the marriage.

Laura, in turn, will likely feel angry, become unhappy, and could threaten to end the relationship. This is the time when some dyadic tension could show up in the Peter-Laura side of the triangle. In the middle phase of the affair, Peter may still experience Laura's demands as passionately romantic and exciting. This phase can last a long time depending on the Peter-Sherry side of the triangle. If Sherry continues to tolerate Peter's distance and still pursues him with positive energy, he may be able to withstand Laura's demands with grace and benign patience. Otherwise, this phase may be short-lived.

The Troubled Child. All kinds of scenarios could emerge from the drama unfolding in the triangle. Sherry could start involving the children in a series of interlocking triangles. She may, for instance, invite one of her daughters to become her confidante as she worries about what to do with her marriage. That child will be "invited" to side with Sherry against Peter, her father. Now we have Sherry and daughter as the insiders, with Peter as the outsider.

The father-daughter side could remain distant for a time. However, conflicts between father and daughter could gradually emerge and detour the conflict away from the marriage. Peter may experience pain in the parent-child relationship that even the relationship with Laura cannot alleviate. The conflicted side may eventually shift more permanently from Peter-Sherry to the Peter-daughter side.

If the daughter dysfunctions socially or academically, her problems may lead Peter to reconsider the whole affair. His guilt may be more intense in the parental role than in the marital area. He could even end the relationship with Laura and focus his energies on helping his daughter. This shift could, in turn, lessen the tension between Peter and Sherry. They could then unite in their efforts to help their daughter cope with the challenges of growing up into a happy and productive young woman.

The original triangle will probably subside and remain inactive for a while. This inactive phase does not mean the triangle has been resolved. The marital issues may, in fact, remain submerged during the childrearing years. More commonly, the stress in the marriage periodically breaks out when the child in the middle does better. When the marriage gets heated, the child usually gets worse until the balance is restored.

SEEING THE TRIANGULAR DANCE

THE TRIANGLE IS THE MOLECULE OF RELATIONSHIP DECAY.

The triangle is the enemy of the two-person relationship—the structure of intimacy. Intimacy is based upon a person-to-person encounter in which one talks to the other about each other. The triangle is a corruption of intimacy. It is the impostor of intimacy. And yet it is present in all relationships and in all organizations.

One can, therefore, also say that the triangle is the molecule of organizational decay. If the president of a company is allied with a manager against one of the vice presidents, this triangle will wreak havoc on the organization. It would be like a family in which the grandfather is in a coalition with his grandson against his own son, who happens to be the grandson's father. There will be confusion.

The triangle is the molecule of relationship decay.
The triangle is the impostor of intimacy.

In order to see the triangular dance, it is important to make a distinction between being *moral* and being *moralistic*. Being *moral* implies that you live according to your moral principles. Being *moralistic* denotes a judgmental attitude toward a person, stating that a person "should" not have done something. The moralistic attitude implies personal involvement in the situation, with elements of side taking.

A moralistic view prevents the observer from seeing the dance patterns because, in taking one person's side, the observer has blamed one and absolved the other. The minute we assign cause to one person in a relationship, we do not see the circularity of the interaction. We will conclude that one is the victimizer and the other is the victim. In order to see the molecular dance, we need to look at the interaction, the circular process involving a series of actions and reactions. To do that, it is helpful to leave the atomic level of analysis for the moment. Then we will see patterns that can help us grasp the reality of a relationship in much broader terms. The triangle will emerge more clearly.

PATTERNS IN THE DANCE OF TRIANGLES

There are certain rules that govern the dance of triangles. They are only rules of thumb and, as such, they are maps for observing aspects of the relationship territory. Useful as these maps are, they can never fully describe the richness of the relationship world. However, they are great starting points and reference points along this journey.

It is important to give tribute to Murray Bowen at this point as the primary originator of the triangle concept. Seeing people as "threes" rather than as "ones" or "twos" was considered a tremendous break-through in our understanding of human functioning. Bowen did the pioneering work on this whole concept and tested it through many years of observation and therapy.[3]

The primary patterns of the triangle are as follows:

- When the triangle is active, one side is close (involving the insiders). This side expresses much of the closeness in that group or system. However, the closeness of the relationship is part of a coalition: the two are together primarily in relation to their common enemy.

- Another side is calm but distant. Although relatively free of any obvious conflict, this relationship is characterized more by distance than by calmness. The early phase of the triangle involving Peter, Sherry, and their daughter is an example of this. Father and daughter were not in conflict initially, but this did not signal true peace. Neither did it signal closeness.

- The third side is conflicted or tense. This is the most obvious activity of the triangle. Conflict alone does not necessarily spell the existence of a triangle. However, if the conflict is ongoing and unresolved, it is a good guess that a triangle is lurking in the background.

- The coalition of two against one is the essential configuration of the triangle when it is in the active phase. Triangles are not always active.

- Unless the triangle is resolved, you can think of the "area of the triangle" as staying rather constant. If two points get closer, the third point will move in such a way as to maintain the same total area of the triangle. It is interesting to observe these patterns in your own immediate family or in your family of origin.

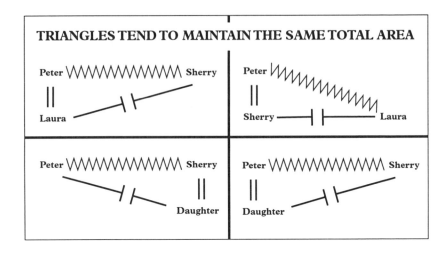

RESOLVING TRIANGLES: From Triangles to Triads

It is helpful to have a few maps about how triangles operate at the level of molecule. Although good motives are essential in relationship development, they are not enough to ensure skillful conflict resolution. People generally have good motives, especially when dealing with family members. We still need to be astute about how relationship patterns impact people despite their good intentions.

WHEN TRIANGLES BECOME PROBLEMS

Everyone faces difficulties in life, including differences of opinion in relationships at home, at work, and with friends. The potential for conflict is perennial. Since our need to belong and to be unique is universal, our relationship patterns are always shifting in order to accommodate the desire for closeness and independence. All of us, therefore, experience the anxiety of loneliness or suffocation now and then. It is during our attempts to alleviate this anxiety that triangles emerge.

All families and organizations experience at least mild to moderate degrees of triangulation. Only when triangles become rigid and persistent should we refer to them as dysfunctional. Here are some the ways that triangles can be destructive:

- When the intensity of a triangle begins to constrain our individuality and our behavioral options, difficulties start. For instance, if Peter wants to give money to charity and he gets into trouble with Sherry who questions his love for her, Peter feels restricted in doing something that he considers important. In the future, he may give to charity behind Sherry's back. If he does this, he may feel guilt for sneaking the act or resentment for feeling constrained by her position on the matter.

- Sherry, for her part, may hesitate to voice her concerns about the way money is being spent or distributed for fear of being accused of trying to control Peter's decisions. A triangle exists between two people and an issue: Sherry, Peter, and a charitable organization. Peter and the organization are characterized as the emotional "insiders" with Sherry as the "outsider."

- In the Peter, Sherry, and daughter triangle, the constraints of the triangle are more obvious and more destructive. Once the daughter becomes Sherry's ally against Peter, this coalition restricts the independent actions of father and child in their relationship. The child is in mother's "camp" as a support to Sherry who feels rejected by her husband. The daughter's loyalty is to the mother. She would naturally feel guilty if she went to the other "camp." That is the nature of a two-against-one coalition.

- If conflicts between Peter and Sherry are always resolved, then, by definition, there is no triangle. Since these conflicts have not been resolved satisfactorily, however, one of them reached out to a third person. First, Peter developed an affair with

Laura, his office associate. Later, Sherry recruited their daughter to be her ally against Peter. Once a third party enters the picture, the conflicted side can last longer precisely because the anxiety is diffused without any real change in the structure.

- Even the outsider in the triangle feels some relief. Peter, for instance, feels relief that he does not have to be the only one to provide emotional support to Sherry. Now the daughter often serves as Sherry's primary companion and confidante.

SIGNS INDICATING THE PRESENCE OF TRIANGLES

- **Gossip**: talking to someone about an absent member. Not every conversation about an absent member means that a triangle exists. The acid test is whether the two people conversing are willing to include the absent member.
- **Side taking**: taking sides on an issue that involves two others. Side taking means that we are in a coalition with someone against another. It means that we have lost neutrality on the matter. Neutrality is a position that allows us to "be for everyone, but against no one." It does not mean that we do not have any thoughts or feelings about an issue that is concerning two other people. Neutrality allows us to respect the right of two people in a relationship to negotiate their own positions.
- **Deceit**: hiding something from someone. Deceit is a power-based move. It is either an attempt to gain control over something by moving stealthily, or fear that an open approach may trigger opposition from a person in a relationship with us. In either case, this move signals a discomfort with a direct, person-to-person relationship.
- **Unresolved conflict**: ongoing conflict between two people that remains unresolved through time. This usually leads one

member to invite a third person into some kind of coalition.

- **Overfunctioning**: getting embroiled in the "third side" of a threesome. The overfunctioning stand means that we have crossed the boundaries of responsibility. If my spouse has an issue with her coworker, that matter is between the two of them. She may want to share the issue with me as a friend and as a sounding board. But if I impose my solution on her, I have diffused the boundaries. This would be more obvious if I took it upon myself to deal with her coworker myself.

HOW TO DETRIANGLE

The overriding guideline in detriangling is to have the courage and skill to communicate directly with the person with whom you have an issue. Developing a "person-to-person relationship" is the guiding framework in keeping triangles out of your relationship dance.

- Being direct takes more courage than talking to a third party about your difficulties with that person. Gossip is a fear-based approach to a relationship. When we enter the gossip road to relationship resolution, it is a clear sign that we have not done our personal transformation work. A coalition is an emotion-based move to gain support and emotional wellbeing. Rather than coming up with clear thinking and honest decisions about the issue, we go for emotionally safe and feel-good alliances. The false ego runs rampant in our dealings with others. The real self is submerged.
- The direct approach also takes more caring, since it means giving the person concerned a chance to explain the matter and to negotiate changes, if necessary.
- A person-to-person relationship requires a solid respect of people's boundaries. The two people with an issue to work out need to own that issue and deal with it inside that relationship.

If I am the third member of a threesome, I need to recognize and respect that an issue may belong to the "third side" of our triad. In that case, I leave it up to them to resolve. If I am invited to participate as a resource to their process, then I act as a friendly consultant, not as a player or full participant.

When We Are Invited into a Triangle

If a loved one talks to us about a third person, how might we handle it? This can be a delicate matter. Let us say that Peter talks to Sherry about his father and he unburdens himself of a great deal of negative emotion. How might Sherry handle this situation without getting caught in a triangle with Peter's father as the outsider? Here are some guidelines that may be helpful in handling this situation:

- Sherry will need to listen carefully and with a great deal of caring. She can develop deep empathy for Peter and still keep an open mind about his father. Her emotionally neutral stand will allow her to listen to Peter without distancing herself from his father.

- In other words, Sherry's relationship with Peter's father should develop on her own terms, not on the basis of Peter's view. That is the operational definition of neutrality. She can listen to Peter views but still keep in mind that she has her own relationship with his father—her own position based on her own observations and reflections.

- Sherry could ask Peter what *he* intends to do about these matters. It will be useful for her to focus on *his* thoughts, feelings, and especially his intentions. This path will keep the dialogue away from Sherry's own views about Peter's father. She can then encourage him to deal directly with his father. She could even offer to be there with him when he decides to talk to him.

- Sherry can also reassure Peter that she will work to keep a good relationship with his father and will try not to let his feelings get in her way of doing that. This position will free Peter to become more honest with her as his sounding board, knowing that he cannot unduly influence her position. This principle will stand even if Peter is initially disappointed that Sherry is not joining the "bandwagon of criticism."

What to Do When Our Neutrality Is Challenged

Sometimes, when we take a neutral stand, the person who wants support from us takes offense and accuses us of being unfeeling and unsupportive. Our neutrality will be severely challenged. When this happens, we need to keep the following ideas in mind:

- Remember that *taking a caring stand* is different from *taking responsibility*. Taking responsibility for an issue puts us in the middle of the action as a participant, not simply as a caring bystander. An issue can involve two or more people at the same time. If we are truly involved, then that is another matter.

- Among the most loving things we can do is to let people carry their own burden. And if we can do this with clarity, love, and caring, we will have done those people a tremendous favor. This is one of the clearest signs of self-mastery, especially when we have to endure criticism and questioning of our love. It takes humility.

- It is important to show caring and sensitivity without taking a position against the third party, in this case, Peter's father.

- It is tempting to ride the "bandwagon of negativity" just to appease a friend, spouse, or child. But if we do it against our own best judgment, then we are bending our truth and casting mud in our eyes. We would not be doing our friend a favor. For Peter to benefit from Sherry's role as friend and sounding board, he needs her to have her own set of eyes, ears, and brains.

- To be simply a "yes person" is not an enhancing role to offer a child, spouse, or friend.
- Sacrificing our own integrity does not build a strong foundation for a relationship. Spouses who are honest sounding boards for their mates do them a great service. When the going gets rough, their mates know that they can count on them to be real. This is the value of neutrality that is founded on both caring and integrity.
- It is this integrity that is sacrificed in the triangle involving an affair. When the going got rough between Peter and Sherry, the real live Peter actually stayed honest with Sherry and brought his issues to therapy. In the hypothetical example involving his affair with Laura, he would have sacrificed his integrity by avoiding his marital issues and getting emotional support from a coalition that was hostile to his wife.

KEEPING OUR SOLUTIONS DYADIC, NOT TRIANGULAR

Let us build another hypothetical scenario between Peter and Sherry. This time there is no infidelity involved. Sherry, however, feels lonely in the marriage and believes that Peter is more interested in his golfing buddies than in his marriage. Let us also say that her early pursuits of closeness in the marriage were met with coldness.

Sherry now moves to attack Peter's enthusiasm for spending time with his golfing friends. On a Friday night when Sherry becomes aware that Peter is going golfing the next morning, she gets upset with him and accuses him of caring more about golf than about his marriage. This is what we can call a *triangular solution:* the attempt to solve a conflict between two people by attacking the "third side" of a triangle.

Triangular Approach to Negotiation. Keep in mind that one of Sherry's motives is to get more loving closeness in her marriage.

She criticizes Peter's love of golf and his relationship with his golfing friends. She hopes that by her doing so he will distance himself from golf and move closer to her. Instead, Peter defends the sport and his right to be with his friends. He distances himself even more from Sherry. At this point, we can diagram the shape of the triangle as follows:

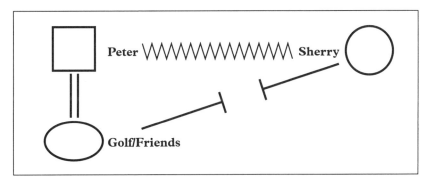

Notice that the dynamics of the triangle offer the same classic patterns:

- One side is conflicted: the relationship between Peter and Sherry.
- One side is close: the relationship between Peter and his golfing friends.
- One side is distant: the relationship between Sherry and the golfing friends of Peter.

In the triangular approach, the outsider attacks the "third side" and the insider defends it with vigor and passion. This approach is usually quite unproductive.

The Dyadic Approach to Negotiation. In this approach, the one who wants the change addresses the issue directly between the two people involved. Sherry, for instance, could say to Peter, "I am feeling lonely these days. I am hurt when I see you distancing yourself from me. I need some special time with you in order to reconnect with you and to talk about my feelings. When can we have some time together?"

Here are some characteristics of this approach:

- Sherry does not criticize golf or Peter's golfing friends. She is addressing the relationship between her and Peter in an honest way.

- She is also suggesting a solution that is positive and one that addresses the issue.

- She could even add something like this: "I like to see you excited about playing golf. I would like some of that excitement in our relationship. Can we do something together tomorrow night?"

Peter may or may not agree to accept Sherry's definition of the issue or even agree with her suggestion. According to this framework, that is not the crucial factor.

- His response may reveal that the erosion of their connection may be even more extensive than Sherry thought. This could be important information for both of them to realize. Perhaps, more drastic steps may need to be taken.

- The point is to keep the focus of the negotiation on the right place: the dyad in which the issue belongs.

- Attacking the "third side" rarely brings good results. Sherry needs to leave Peter's relationship to golf between him and the game. Tampering with that relationship puts her in the role of supervisor or parent.

We can put anything or anyone on that third point of the triangle and follow the principles above. It will be a helpful guide. But since we live in an interconnected system of relationships, none of the guidelines can be followed with the precision of a machine. They are to be used as maps guiding us through a complex and rich territory called life.

IN A NUTSHELL

We start life in a triad—our primary triad consisting of self, mother, and father. The threesome is, in fact, the basic unit of society. There is no "I" without a "You." And there is no "We" without a "Them." There is always a third point in our relationship life. We are indeed individuals with an essentially social nature.

The triad can be defined as the healthy threesome: three interrelated individuals who can work together as a group and as separate dyads. Each of the three dyads is viable. Each dyadic relationship, therefore, can achieve adequate levels of closeness, independence, and conflict resolution. When a dyad goes out of balance in any of these areas, that dyad will either break up or develop emotional triangles around it.

Strangely enough, a triangle can stabilize a shaky dyad. But it can also prevent true resolution of the issues between two people. Often, children become the balancing "third points" in a shaky marriage. The third person carries a lot of the stress that remains unresolved between the two adult players.

This chapter has given us a molecular view of the way triangles work, along with some suggestions for how to detriangle ourselves from unwholesome coalitions. Many well-meaning people, including those on a spiritual path, have fallen prey to triangles, simply for lack of awareness of how these patterns can limit relationships.

When relationships are dysfunctional, the individuals in those relationships lose behavioral flexibility. They become puzzled by the responses they get from people, despite their desire for peaceful and productive outcomes.

Self-mastery requires a binocular vision: one eye on the atomic level and the other on the molecular level. We need to watch the dance and the dancers. Only then will good intentions flower into truly successful and fruitful outcomes.

[1] Kerr, M. and Bowen, M. (1988). *Family Evaluation*. New York: W. W. Norton and Company.

[2] My own thinking has been clarified and enriched by the work of Green, R.-J. and Werner, P. D. (June, 1966). "Intrusiveness and Closeness-Caregiving: Rethinking the Concept of Family 'Enmeshment'." *Family Process*. pp. 115-136.

[3] Kerr, M. and Bowen, M. (1988). *Family Evaluation*. New York: W. W. Norton and Company.

Chapter 10
THE SELF AS MATE AND CHILD
Mastering Relationships (2)

This is another chapter on *viable relationships* as a requirement of self-mastery. After looking at some ways to unbind relationship knots, we now turn to ideas for deepening the two-person relationship. These concepts and techniques are especially important for developing a strong and lasting relationship with a mate. This is the first area we will look at. We will use the framework of pebbles, grenades, and jewels to dig into the guts of intimacy itself. We can use these ideas for developing lasting friendships, as well. True friendships have been described as treasures from heaven.

Then, we will examine the early environment of the self: the family of origin. If we can be genuine with the members of our original family, we can define ourselves more effectively with our mate, friends, and colleagues. We will explain a number of principles for defining the self in our family of origin. Not all of us become spouses, parents, or grandparents. But all of us are children, from start to finish.

We will, in essence, look at the self as mate and child. Developing viable relationships in these aspects of life strengthens our identity— the experience of self as manifested in the world of time and space. Success in our experience as mate and child will add confidence and substance to both our sense of belonging and individuality.

THE SELF AS MATE
Intimacy is a right-brain experience that can never be fully stated

in logical terms, thank God. However, it is useful to describe some of its dimensions and processes. The metaphor of pebbles, grenades, and jewels is useful in this attempt. Like mysticism, intimacy cannot be reduced to a set of techniques. However, following a framework and having a repertoire of useful techniques can prepare couples to discover the intimacy that is uniquely theirs. Let us follow the story of Drew and Kim.

INDEPENDENCE AND INTIMACY

Drew and Kim love each other. They are committed to each other for life. He is in his late forties and she is eight years younger. They have been married ten years: this is her first marriage but Drew's second. Drew has two grown children with whom he keeps contact. They are both highly educated, each making a good living in executive-level jobs that keep them busy. Their marriage is generally calm and is characterized by a mixture of independence and distance, but lacking in closeness and passion, by their own admission. However, periodically they get into arguments that leave them disturbed and dissatisfied, followed by more distance between them.

The independence they experience in their relationship is not satisfying to either of them because the closeness level falls far short of what they want. There is an imbalance between these two forces. Since closeness and independence go well together (as we just learned), when one of these is understated, the other cannot achieve its purpose. Independence without connectedness becomes hollow. It soon degenerates into some form of alienation, emotional cutoff, distancing, rebellion, or stubborn individualism. But togetherness without independence soon gets corrupted into suffocation, dependence, intrusion, control, bossiness, or submissiveness.

REMINDER

Identity is that mysterious reality that emerges out of the dance of intimacy and self-definition. Yet, identity is not explainable on the basis of either intimacy or self-definition. Identity is expressed in the interaction between intimacy and self-definition, but it is not explained by simply "adding up" the elements of these primary forces in life. Identity is at a higher level of reality than either of its components—in the same way that water (H_2O) cannot be explained by the characteristics of the individual atoms that compose it. H_2O transcends hydrogen and oxygen.

The student of self-mastery will notice that independence and closeness are the *interactional manifestations* of the need to belong and the need to be an individual. The need to belong drives us to seek closeness and to achieve a level of intimacy that affirms our connectedness with significant others. It is our way, as human beings, to experience being lovable. The need to be an individual, with a unique personal mission, moves us to maintain enough independence so that we may discover and actualize our talents in the service of our personal destiny.

CLOSENESS AND INDEPENDENCE

Closeness and independence go well together. If one aspect is understated, then the other cannot achieve its purpose. Independence without intimacy degenerates into loneliness, alienation, rebellion, and evasiveness. However, intimacy without independence soon gets corrupted into suffocation, dependence, intrusiveness, bossiness, or submissiveness.

255

FROM PEBBLES TO GRENADES: The Puzzling Connection

The framework of pebbles and grenades will help us to understand how two people create the imbalance between intimacy and independence. This map will also show us how to move toward a more dynamic balance. It will allow us to appreciate the way the soul works through the patterns of our relationships and the elements of destiny. We will again see the interconnectedness of the inner and outer dimensions of our lives.

REVIEW
DEFINING PEBBLES AND GRENADES

Let's keep in mind that pebbles are the events in the current world occurring outside a person. Destiny makes itself known through pebbles or the events that "come at us." Grenades are the emotional reactions experienced by someone at a level of intensity that cannot usually be explained on the basis of the pebbles alone. Grenades are soul-level responses and are manifested in important themes from our past.

Grenades, properly mined, will yield significant jewels that support and light up our journey back to God. These jewels reveal aspects of our soul blueprint that are salient at a given stage of our personal mission. Since grenades reveal jewels, they, too, are important mirrors of the soul.

Let us now trace the pebble-grenade connection between Drew and Kim.

I asked Drew what Kim did that really got to him. He said that he usually had negative reactions when Kim:

- was *absent* from,
- or *late* for, an event,
- or if she thoughtlessly focused on *things that did not take Drew's wishes into account.*

Kim, he said, had her own agenda, and unless he prodded and clamored to be included in that agenda, he would likely get left out in the cold. This was the world of pebbles as far as Drew was concerned. Although pebbles refer to events outside the person, the key to their impact on someone resides in that person's way of responding to those events. The thought that Kim did not take his wishes into account was Drew's interpretation. It may not match Kim's conscious motives. But that interpretation became an element that influenced Drew's response.

Drew's thoughts and feelings in response to this kind of pebble were powerful enough for us to classify them as grenades. He saw Kim's behavior as attempts to exclude him. To him, her actions meant that she didn't care about him, that she did not like him, and that she probably saw him as irrelevant in her life. He felt angry that she did not take him into account when making choices about her time and activities. He felt deeply unloved and lonely at these times. This is a brief sketch of Drew's world of grenades—the intense emotional reactions triggered by pebbles that Kim threw.

Drew's Pebble-Grenade Connection

Pebble		*Grenade*
Kim was absent, late, or focused on things other than Drew.	**T**	He believes he is excluded by Kim. She does not care about him and that she does not like him.
	F	He feels lonely and angry.

T = thought   **F** = feeling

What Drew did was to act immediately on his feelings, based on his first thoughts, and get locked into the world of pebbles. Drew got focused on the outside world of events instead of looking at the inner world of responses. By focusing on the event, a person can defocus from the world of feelings (grenade-level reality). The loneliness that came from feeling unloved was painful for Drew. It was difficult to pay attention to it and to listen to his soul. His way of coping was to rationalize the matter and to focus on Kim by questioning, blaming, and accusing her with a tone of controlled anger.

Let us note that Drew's words/actions now become the pebbles thrown into Kim's pond (self). Kim may or may not transform these pebbles into grenades, depending on her inner response. In this situation, she does transform them into grenades. We may diagram it this way:

Pebbles Thrown by Drew into Kim's Pond

Drew's Actions ➜	*Kim*
Questions Kim, then blames and accuses her of not caring about him.	

Let us see how Drew's actions become the pebbles that trigger Kim's grenades in a pattern so complementary that it boggles the mind of the observer. It is difficult for Drew and Kim to see this complementary dance, partly because they are viewing these actions only from their own vantage point. They are unaware of how their actions become the pebbles that trigger the other person's grenades. Another reason for this lack of awareness is that neither one is listening to their soul's groaning—the responses that contain the messages about what they need in order to grow from these experiences.

When I asked Kim what Drew did that truly upset her, she said that when he complained, he would use rational arguments that led to blaming and accusing her of not caring about him. Behind those arguments, she heard him saying that she was cold, uncaring, and downright selfish. He came across as righteous and condescending, giving her the impression that she was beneath him. This interpretation hurt her deeply and led to feelings of unworthiness (grenade). The little girl in her could not fathom how anyone, particularly her husband, could even think about questioning her motives. And yet she felt ashamed and unworthy of being his wife. These were responses she would mostly keep to herself.

Kim would then start excusing and defending herself. This usually led to an unpleasant argument during which Kim bolstered her position of innocence. Kim then distanced and withdrew—responses that would amplify her already strong tendency to act independently. The alert observer will note that Kim's distancing actions now become the pebbles that trigger Drew's grenades. Observe the complementary dance.

Kim's Pebble-Grenade Connection

Pebble		Grenade
Questioning, blaming, and accusing Kim of not caring.	**T**	Accused of having bad motives. Seen as uncaring and selfish
	F	Feeling hurt and unworthy. Low self-worth

T = thought   **F** = feeling

Kim's actions were often based on these grenade-level thoughts and feelings. She would explain, excuse, and defend her behavior as evidence for her good motives. The more she did so, the less in touch she was with her own pain and the needs that her feelings were trying to reveal to her. Distancing herself into a world of independent activities followed this denial. However, as we saw earlier, this kind of independence was not satisfying to her because it negated instead of complemented her need to belong.

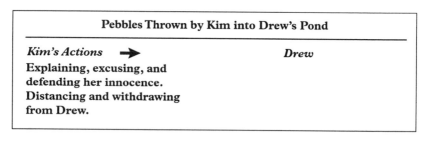

Pebbles Thrown by Kim into Drew's Pond

Kim's Actions ➔	*Drew*
Explaining, excusing, and defending her innocence. Distancing and withdrawing from Drew.	

GETTING STUCK IN THE PEBBLE-GRENADE CYCLE

Kim and Drew have fashioned a level of intimacy that has been adequate to keep their marriage stable throughout the years. However, they have both been dissatisfied with the quality of joy and support they have experienced together. There is enough kindness and courtesy to enjoy the companionship between them. Yet, they are often lonely. Both feel unfulfilled in their search for a satisfying relationship. They feel stuck. This is a danger signal for a couple: stagnating means depleting the reserves they have for giving support when the going gets rough. There are many ways to map out the pattern of stagnation. The pebble-grenade connection provides a helpful way of mapping the pattern and the solution. We saw how *couples get stuck when they seek a cure for their grenades in the world of pebbles.* If Drew believes that his need to be affirmed and to be loved should be filled mainly by Kim, then he will periodically be disappointed. He will not realize that the essential task in life is to seek self-love through our relationship with our Higher Self, the spark of God that is our true being. It is this inner relatedness that enables us to love others in return.

Our family of origin was the place in which we were to learn these lessons of healthy love of self and others. It was the setting for the formation of the basic sense of self at the psychological level. Our past is recorded as stories written in our minds. These stories contain themes that color our experiences. These themes are like filters that color our interpretation of the pebbles thrown our way. We need to recognize these filters and own them as part of the way we interpret outside events. This is one way we can reclaim our personal power, and not give pebbles undue clout over us. In essence, our soul is the proper area for the inner healing of our grenades—not the outside world.

We can state this thesis as follows: *Couples get into serious trouble if they confuse their individual, soul-level issues (grenades) with their jointly created interaction patterns (pebbles) in the present relationship system.* We need to take personal responsibility for our grenades while negotiating closeness and independence in our relationships. We can negotiate the way we deal with pebbles—relating and communicating with each other in the present. Grenades and jewels are non-negotiable.

Confusing one level of responsibility with another (personal versus joint) is a key to understanding the patterns of stuckness. Drew, for instance, may believe that he would be totally fulfilled and happy if Kim were simply to love him and show how much she likes being with him. That would be an error in thinking. The relationship can indeed be a supportive and, often, necessary ingredient in the healing of the soul. But it is never sufficient for the attainment of that inner peace we desire. Drew must find his own inner healing and connect with his soul in order to find inner peace. And so must Kim. If they each did that, then their relationship, if handled effectively, can become a great source of additional strength and will certainly contribute to their personal healing and happiness.

CONFUSING PEBBLES WITH GRENADES

We get into serious trouble if we confuse our individual, soul-level (grenades) with our jointly created interaction patterns (pebbles) in our present relationships. We need to take personal responsibility for our grenades and jewels while negotiating closeness and independence. Grenades and jewels are non-negotiable.

What most couples do is to loop endlessly between pebble and grenade, as Drew and Kim did. When he felt hurt by her seemingly uncaring behavior, he would blame her for it and accuse her of being cold and selfish. His anger eventually covered up the hurt by focusing on the outside world. Also, by putting responsibility on her shoulders for the hurt he felt, Drew disempowered himself by making himself a victim of Kim's actions.

Kim, for her part, did the same thing by defending herself. She believed that if Drew would only trust her and respect her as a person with good motives, she would feel loved by him and experience a sense of wholeness within herself. And this, she believed, would be her salvation from the loneliness she felt. She, too, would be disappointed, victimized, and end up in the idolatrous position of seeking God outside herself.

Kim's actions of explaining, excusing, and defending took her away from listening to her soul-pain by keeping her focused on Drew and his behavior. She kept focusing on the outside world of events, trying to change the environment without connecting with her soul. What is the way through this maze?

FROM GRENADES TO JEWELS—AND BACK TO PEBBLES

JEWELS

REVIEW

Behind every grenade is a jewel: a precious capacity that can propel us to heights of joy and accomplishment. Jewels are like pockets of energy deep within our souls. They reveal what is profoundly important to us. Like pure crystals, they radiate our unique qualities. Jewels are innate characteristics of our soul. Our early environment does not determine (cause or create) these jewels. Our early experiences reveal these properties of the soul. These experiences do not shape these qualities "into" us. We dance with our environment. Our environment is important because it reveals the hand of destiny. But we respond to destiny: it does not predestine us.

When we pay attention to our jewels, our self-esteem and natural creativity blossom incredibly. Our being demands that we honor these jewels. Our mate or friend cannot be held primarily responsible for nurturing these soul needs.

This idea is a key to understanding the method of managing feelings, as we discovered in Chapter 4. Paying attention to the feeling is a way of getting in touch with the grenade. And so is paying attention to our thoughts. Listening to the message within the feeling will lead us to the jewel (the need behind the feeling).

Let us examine Kim's grenade-to-jewel connection:

Kim's Grenade-to-Jewel Connection	
Grenade	*Jewel*
T Seen as having bad motives, being defective, and selfish.	Needs to be trustworthy, good and competent, a person with talent and with noble motives.
F Feeling hurt and unworthy. Shame and low self-worth.	
T = thought **F** = feeling	

At this point, we might wonder why this grenade is so profoundly powerful to Kim. Let us look at some patterns in her childhood that significantly reveal aspects of her soul blueprint. Kim grew up as "parentified" middle child. She acted more like a parent than a sibling. He older brother, Clay, was the black sheep of the family whereas her younger sister, Nancy, was the emotional baby of the family who clutched on to her mother's apron strings. Mother and father exhibited a tug of war.

Mother attempted to instill personal and social graces in the children, in contrast to father's immature rebellion against the standards of his social class. Kim was caught in the middle of this power struggle. Mother showed behavior that was civil, respectable, and proper. Father started to show signs of "blue-collar" behavior: greasy fingers from working on junk cars and "cruising" in and out of prisons.

By the time she entered early adolescence, Kim was, in effect, acting as the "father" of the family. She was allied with mother against father. In fact, she was ashamed to be identified as her father's daughter. Her parents eventually divorced. Father continued his slide down the social ladder while mother managed to maintain her sense of social dignity. Mother never remarried. Kim was eventually estranged from her father. He cut himself off from them as much as they cut themselves off from him.

The young adolescent girl felt a deep shame about the "defectiveness" or "lack of acceptability" of her background. Her response to these events reveals a deep sensitivity to the value of self-acceptance (jewel). It also reveals an oversensitivity to the feeling of being "defective" or "unworthy" (grenade). Both the grenade and the jewel are important to our discussion. The grenade (oversensitivity) gives her the capacity (potential) to empathize deeply with those who hurt in the same way. But this capacity will be actualized only if she maintains soul contact with her inner responses. These beautiful qualities can become hidden from her awareness if she doesn't feel these feelings and if she fails to mine the jewels within them. The jewels will also be hidden.

A BRIEF INTERLUDE ABOUT GRIEF

I wrote the first draft of this chapter soon after the death of Princess Diana and Mother Teresa. Commentators noted the tremendous grief felt around the world about the death of these two women. They noted that grief over Diana was triggered partly by the realization that she faced life-threatening emotional struggles, including depression and eating disorders. The public perceived Diana's strength in her revelation of these vulnerabilities, as well as in the way she applied the "lessons of her symptoms" to help the needy, the sick, and the oppressed. However Diana's personal history may be written, one thing is already clear: the people's response revealed more about themselves than about Princess Diana. They responded to *their image* of her sensitivity and heartfelt service to the less fortunate among us.

The facts and circumstances of Mother Teresa's life are vastly different. Yet, the people's response to Mother Teresa's death had enough similarities to that of Diana's. Mother Teresa's caring, empathy, and strength of personal mission touched them in a way that reveals much about the people's grenades and jewels. Those who deeply mourned her passing showed *their need* to be loved and to be noticed. We could assume that these were the jewels within the grenades they felt. We could also assume that those mourners who mined the jewels within their feelings probably transformed those sorrows into a greater depth of love and sensitivity for those in pain.

It is, likewise, interesting to note that Mother Teresa's ability to care for the poor of Calcutta showed that she, like Diana, was in contact with her soul sensitivities and her grenades. This is a person who must have suffered deeply. This is an inference—an educated guess, if you will. But I cannot imagine how a person can touch so deeply without having gone to the depths of her own soul.

Drew's childhood also reveals the dance between destiny and his soul blueprint. His family of origin reveals his need to be liked, accepted, and included. Drew grew up on a farm that was several miles away from the nearest town. After school, he either worked on the farm or played by himself. His siblings were older and did not see him as a buddy. His school friends either lived in town or lived on farms as well. So, Drew was essentially cut off from his significant social circle. He was also excluded from the emotional center of the family. When there were significant issues in the family, he was told to go outside while the rest discussed important family matters.

Young Drew felt the pain of exclusion. A number of years ago, I would have interpreted these events in his young life as the "cause" of his sensitivity—that these events "shaped" his sensitivity to being excluded. I now see his sensitivity as a quality of his soul that was revealed by his response to these "promptings of destiny." This view, incidentally, does not diminish the importance of context or environment in the drama of our lives. The circumstances and events in our lives are part of the interplay between soul and destiny. Destiny plays a necessary and crucial role in "triggering forth" aspects of who we are and what we are about.

I asked Drew to recall a moment or incident in his early years that reminded him of his need to be included. He prefaced his tale by telling me that he was emotionally distant from his father. He remembered many occasions when his father would tell him to go outside because the rest of the family needed to discuss something. He was about nine years old. He recalls sitting on the edge of their pond and dipping his feet into the water, whiling away the time by himself. He spent many hours there deep in thought.

I am not sure if Drew, even now, realizes how instrumental those hours may have been in drawing out of him the highly intellectual nature of his soul pattern. This country farm boy went on to become a highly educated and successful CEO of a large corporation. Drew's intellectual bent is his strength. And I utilized it in guiding him toward making contact with his feeling side.

I gave him a theoretical map of how he can deal with his grenades and then negotiate some changes with Kim. Every time he felt excluded, rejected, neglected, or unloved in the relationship, he was to "visit" the nine-year-old boy sitting on the edge of the pond. He was to "sit beside him, put an arm around him and begin a conversation."

INSTRUCTIONS FOR SOUL HEALING: What Drew Can Say to His Soul.

Say something like this to the little boy inside you: "Hey, Drew, *I am here* with you. I know you are thinking about many things. I would like you to know that it is okay to *feel whatever you feel.*" Be quiet for a while and give him time to think and feel whatever comes to his mind and heart. Then tell him: *"I am here* to listen to whatever you wish to share with me. Or if you wish simply to be quiet for a while, that's okay too."

Give him some time to speak or to be quiet. Whether he speaks or not, go ahead and ask him the following question, "What do you need right now?" Pause. Whatever he tells you, listen carefully, accept it as important and provide for that need in the best way you can. I do not know what he will reveal to you. But listen carefully. If, for instance, he tells you that he needs to be close to someone who will listen to him, tell him you would like to be that someone.

Make a commitment to him that you will listen to his inner promptings from now on. Tell him that you will especially listen to the grenades that may come in the next few months and that you will visit him here by the pond each time these grenades come. You would like his help to mine the jewels within these grenades. (It would have been nice, had it occurred to me then, to have young Drew throw a pebble into the pond and watch the ripples expand throughout the surface. It would have summarized for the right brain the meaning of the entire process I was teaching the adult Drew.)

Reassure young Drew that you will represent his needs well in the relationship with Kim, telling her what you need from her and then discovering (not controlling) the ripples of interaction she will offer you. You will then be in a much better place to negotiate things with her.

When Drew and Kim came back a month later, Drew mentioned that he followed this process about three times. After that, he said he didn't need to go through the entire sequence anymore. When he felt those grenades, he would simply think of the little boy. He would then begin to feel better and was able to negotiate calmly and without blaming. In fact, the night before the session, Drew came home and found that Kim was not there. Kim, thinking that Drew was going out of town, decided to run some errands.

By the time Kim got home, Drew was peacefully asleep. This would never have happened in the past. It would normally have triggered a grenade in him, and he would not be able to sleep until she arrived. In the morning, on the way to the therapy session, Drew mentioned in passing that it was hard for him to conceive that she forgot that he was not going out of town. Though said without any sense of blame, this remark triggered a grenade in Kim. It was that incident that led me to discover Kim's own grenade-jewel connection.

Let us learn from Drew and Kim to search for resources (jewels) within our joys and pains, not for what is wrong with us. Asking for "what's wrong" is like asking someone "how can I *not* get somewhere." There are an infinite number of ways to *not get somewhere,* but only a few good ways to get there.

THE SELF AS CHILD

IDENTITY IN THE FAMILY OF ORIGIN

There is beauty, poetry, and joy in achieving true intimacy with one person. However, we often short-circuit the flow that connects pebble to grenade to jewel. We could loop endlessly between pebble and grenade and back to pebble. If we just blame our mate for our grenades, we will stay stuck in the world of pebbles, never mining the rich jewels within us. We will not have not done our soul work. Our soul will sense rejection and isolation. She will probably knock harder next time and increase the intensity of our pain. If we simply intensify our blaming or our distancing, we will not grow in soul wisdom stature.

One rich source of grenades and jewels is the family of origin— present and past. Our early childhood experiences live presently in our conscious and unconscious, even when they are memories about the past. Our relationships with the living members of our family also provide opportunities for mining jewels. We now turn to those arenas.

MOSES AND THE TABLETS: An Apocryphal Tale

I once heard a tall tale about Moses, a piece of highly embellished fiction. When Moses came down from Mt. Horeb with the first set of tablets upon which God wrote the commandments, he saw that the people were worshipping false gods. He said to himself, "These people are so dense, they will never understand these commandments." Moses thought the original set contained too many items and were too long for the people to understand. So he threw the tablets toward the crowd and decided to go back up the mountain to ask for an abbreviated version. God listened to the pleading of his son. And so we now have just Ten Commandments, all of them written out in very concise statements.

In the "shortened version" of these commandments, so the story goes, the third commandment suffered a loss of clarity in the transition. According to this "legend," the original version of the commandment read: "Honor thy father and thy mother, *even if they are fools.*" The moral of this tale is that our parents deserve our respect even if they are not everything we hoped they would be.

Coming to Terms with Our Parents

There is something profound behind the humor of this fable. All of us face the day when we are disappointed in our parents, when we realize that they are not quite the people we want them to be. Part of the maturing process is coming to terms with who they are and accepting them in their state of being and becoming. The day we stop expecting our parents to be different is the day we take a mighty leap in maturity. We also hope that our parents can accept us for who we are. It would give us a great boost of emotional support in our search for belonging and individuality. But that is not in our control. Only changing our part is within our control. That is our task.

FAMILY OF ORIGIN: The Womb of the Self

Our family of origin is the womb of the self. It was the setting in which, for better or for worse, our self-image was originally and most profoundly developed. Our belonging and individuality were first nurtured and tortured in that environment. In that setting, our soul jewels were revealed through events that affirmed or violated our soul qualities. In those events, we need to see the hand of destiny giving us opportunities for self-direction and self-discovery, despite the ugliness of some events.

We came into this world in a state of innocence and creative expectation. We trusted that the family (our world) would nurture and protect us as we navigated the territories beyond the womb. We believed that our parents, our all-loving caretakers, would guard and cherish our inner jewels.

Along the way, we were clothed, hugged, fed, ignored, entertained, scolded, encouraged, punished, and rewarded. We felt loved, rejected, supported, abandoned, protected, and attacked. We learned to adapt to "our system": the family that destiny found for us. We became part of the dance that involved people quite significant to us. Their dance changed when we joined the group. Why we found ourselves in a particular group at a specific point in time and space is a mystery. The circumstances are things we must deal with, even if we do not understand the reason. That is why we include the facts and the events of our life under the concept of destiny.

When we are commanded to honor father and mother, we are being guided wisely. We cannot escape the parents that live in us—the internal models of self and others. To honor our parents means to know them, to love them, and to deal with them skillfully and lovingly. How we do this without cutoff or capitulation is an important psychological foundation of spirituality. Without loving our families, we cannot possibly understand the commandment to love God and to love our neighbor as ourselves.

As seekers of self-mastery, we need to understand and practice the art of honoring our parents. A spiritual path without this foundation is bound to flounder. Such a path will present too many puzzling contradictions for the seeker to find peace and joy. Getting caught in a triangle without seeing our part in the dance is confusing and discouraging. Like a victim, we will be a reed blown around by the wind.

THE PSYCHOLOGICAL FOUNDATION OF SPIRITUALITY

To honor our parents means to know them, to love them,
and to deal with them skillfully and lovingly. How one does this without
emotional cutoff, either by aggression or capitulation of the self, is a
psychological foundation of spirituality.

A STORY

Not long ago, I received a telephone call from Carol. She sensed that George, her nineteen-year-old nephew, was feeling agitated. Would I talk to him? Gladly, I said. George was a recent addition to Carol's family. She and her husband, Norman, had agreed to have George come live with them for at least a year. George had not done well during his first few weeks in college. Trouble with his peers and a girlfriend led to fist fights. He received some threats of violence. George had difficulty concentrating on his studies. He also showed "obsessive" tendencies toward a girlfriend, who experienced his behaviors as harassing and controlling. His inability to focus on his studies and several drunken episodes led his parents to pull him out of school.

George's mother asked her sister, Carol, to consider having George live with them for a year. He could work in Norman's company and take a few courses at a junior college when he was ready to do so. Agreement was reached and the move had been made two weeks before the phone call. George and his parents came to our clinic to formalize the agreement with Carol and Norman, as well as to set up a counseling relationship with our therapy team. Two therapists worked with him while I led a team of therapists behind a one-way mirror. The "handoff" went well. George's parents, Larry and Heather, offered him to his uncle and aunt and asked him if he was willing to accept them as parental representatives. George agreed.

During that administrative session, the therapy team learned that George's temper was the main reason his parents wanted counseling for him. The two other issues they wanted the therapists to address were his drinking and his lack of concentration. The team also found out that George's father, Larry, had been depressed in the last year. When George started showing signs of trouble, Larry snapped out of his depression and was able to attend to his son's concerns. Although George accepted his situation graciously, he showed much sadness about leaving his family. His father was especially tearful during the ritual of turning his son over to his aunt and uncle.

The following session, George came with his uncle and aunt. He had started working in Norman's corporation and was doing quite well. George was well liked by his three cousins who were much younger. The oldest cousin, a male, was a sophomore in high school, who always looked up to Cousin George. The first signs of adjustment were all positive. The phone call came two days after that session.

After George picked up the phone, he said that he was worried and feeling rather mad that morning. "What are you worried and mad about, George?" I asked.

> George: I'm wondering if I made the right decision about coming here. I'm also mad at those guys in my hometown. Because of them, I left my family and my life has changed so much.
>
> Ramon: So, you're doubting the rightness of your decision. Is that right, George?
>
> George: Yes. I don't know if I should be here. I miss my family and my friends. I'm so mad at those guys that threatened me. They changed my life.

Ramon: You are angry about the fact that those guys in college did things to change your life. Does it feel like you don't have a choice about this—that you were just pushed into it?

George: Yes. That's what makes me so mad. I don't know if I should be here at all. You know, I couldn't sleep last night. I just kept on thinking about this.

Ramon: George, I want you to listen to your feelings. I think your mind is telling you something very important. I believe that your mind is saying, "George, you let those guys have control over you and, because of that, your life has changed." What do you think?

George: I think that's right.

Ramon: I also think that your mind is giving you that REALLY, REALLY MAD FEELING so that you can say to yourself: "I WILL NEVER, NEVER LET ANYONE RUN MY LIFE AGAIN. From here on, I WILL RUN MY OWN LIFE." Does that ring true for you, George?

George: That's exactly right.

Ramon: George, I want you to write these down: (1) *I am mad at me for letting others run my life.* (2) *I will never, never let anyone run my life again. From here on, I will run my own life.* Meanwhile, do not make any decision about leaving or staying. Bring your thoughts with you to the therapy session next week and ask your therapists to help you think this through.

George: Okay, thanks a lot.

THE CONCEPT OF TRIANGLE IN THE FAMILY OF ORIGIN

It is helpful to think this through at two levels: the personal level (atomic) and the relationship level (molecular). Recall the difference between the atomic and molecular levels of analysis. Hydrogen and oxygen, apart from each other, are gases. When these two atoms are combined as H_2O, the molecule (water) shows different qualities from either of the component atoms. Atomic analysis focuses on what is happening inside a person. Molecular analysis looks at the interactional dance between two or more people.

At the personal level, George doubts his decision to stay with his relatives. That doubt shakes his position. George's agitation is not just about mixed thoughts and mixed feelings. He had mixed feelings from the beginning. Now, he doubts the decision itself. This is a matter of will, not simply a comment on his thoughts and feelings. The confusion of position, by itself, is a problem. It is important to understand it. The vacillation between leaving and staying can trigger intense anxiety.

I offered George a temporary solution to this problem by asking him to delay the decision until he had a chance to talk to his therapists about it. If he follows my advice, he would stop vacillating. There will be temporary peace or wholeness "within" him. In other words, his thoughts and feelings, despite being mixed, would be under the leadership of one position. The self would be undivided. That is congruence at the atomic level.

At the relationship level, the dance among people gives us another view of the terrain. One way of analyzing the relationship system (molecule) is to think in terms of twos and threes. As we learned in a previous chapter, one kind of three-way analysis is the concept of triangle. A brief recap may be helpful. A triangle is a coalition of two against one. The triangle can consist of three people in which two are banded together against a third person.

276

George is probably beginning to feel the emergence of a triangle: (1) George, (2) his parents, and (3) his uncle and aunt are the three "points" of the triangle. If he does well while living with his relatives, it could possibly "look bad" for his parents. Since George developed his problems while he was living with his parents, the question arises as to their role in the development of George's problems. If George does well while in his relatives' care, his parents could feel that either they (parents) are the problem or they failed to help George solve his problem. People could conclude that his previous environment was the problem.

George could find himself in a "loyalty bind," thinking, "Should I make my parents look bad and my uncle and aunt look good?" Before there is any kind of definite trend to reveal this, George begins to make noises about going home. One way out of this loyalty bind is to continue having problems even while he is with Carol and Norman. If he had problems even while living with them, it would "prove" that George's problems are his own, not a matter of parental ineptness. Although this move would avert a loyalty bind, there would be no true resolution of his issues. He would still have problems.

Let us look at some other examples. For instance, George could be emotionally allied with his father against his mother. This coalition would presuppose that his parents, Larry and Heather, are probably not dealing effectively with their own marital issues. A marital rift, as we saw, makes parents vulnerable to the development of triangles. George, for example, may have been in conflict with his mother about his lack of responsibility. At that point, Larry could covertly support George in his battles with Heather. Heather would feel like the "outsider" in that threesome. Larry and George would be the "insiders," forming a cross-generational alliance against the mother in the family. This triangle would give Larry the strength of an ally in his covert fight with his wife.

We will keep George in mind as we look at some principles relevant to family-of-origin issues. Mission and meaning issues often emerge in the process of interacting with members of our family of origin.

PRINCIPLES AND GUIDELINES FOR SELF-MASTERY IN THE FAMILY OF ORIGIN

PRINCIPLE I

BLAMING THE PRESENT FOR UNRESOLVED ISSUES IN THE PAST.

Blaming someone or a situation for our unhappiness is usually a sign that we have unresolved issues in the past, particularly in the family of origin. George, for example, did not deal adequately with his growing-up issues at home. Now, he is blaming his friends for his problems. He is also blaming being separated from his parents as the "cause" of his unhappiness, the implication being that if he could be returned home, his problems would be over. This illusion is sometimes called the *geographic cure*.

The reason why George is an interesting example for our study of the family of origin is that we are seeing, in a relatively short time span, the relationship between past patterns and present behavior. This principle helps us to understand the impact of the family of origin on our present ways of functioning.

Imagine George twenty-one years from now. He is married and has two children. When his self-esteem is threatened, he will become intensely anxious. He will either run or become aggressive and obsessive in a dysfunctional manner. Unless he changes the way he behaves now, he will keep on returning to this pattern under stress. The difficulty is that, twenty-one years from now, no one, George least of all, is likely to "see" the pattern in his family of origin and how the forty-year-old is still doing the nineteen-year-old dance. It takes some skill on the part of the therapist and a lot of courage from the client to resolve issues with a distant drumbeat.

PRINCIPLE 2

THE SEQUENCE OF BEHAVIORS REVEALS THE RELATIONSHIP DANCE.

In this kind of "systemic analysis," it is important to look at the sequence of events and responses in order to see the relationship dance. The relationship dance through time will reveal the "molecular structure" of the marriage and the family.

The following is a "molecular" description of how George got involved in the parental triangle. If he were in therapy at age forty, he would benefit from a systemic analysis of his role in the parental dance in the past. It would be useful to see the relationship between his past role and his present behavioral sequences in his family. Here is a "fast forward" description of the parental dance.

George's parents had problems in their marriage. These problems manifested as a sequence of fighting, distancing, warming, and back to fighting. At times in this dance, one spouse occasionally used divorce as a threat. At some point, Larry, the father, started showing signs of depression. The appearance of depression stopped the marital battles and changed the dynamics of the relationship. Heather became attentive toward Larry. The depression became the enemy around which husband and wife temporarily united.

The depression was the third point of a triangle. Note that a triangle can involve two people and an issue, instead of a third person. Let us highlight this matter so that we will remember to spot this dance if we see it around us. As a master-in-training, we are wisely advised always to include ourselves in the analysis of the dance. It requires a holistic view to spot the pattern in a series of apparently independent moves. It would be like seeing the movement of hydrogen in the water molecule without realizing that it was part of a larger movement.

HIGHLIGHT

Family therapists have observed this phenomenon frequently.
An emotional symptom, like depression, becomes a personal manifestation of a relational problem. The symptom can be seen as an "attempted solution" to the pain in the relationship. The triangle provides some closeness to the couple in the form of help from one spouse to the other. However, part of the price is that one spouse has to be down in order for the other to provide support. Many a "relationship on the rocks" has found healing around a crisis. Such "solutions" rarely lead to true resolutions.

The marital closeness around the depression (the common enemy) became a great boost for Larry. As he conquered the depression, the marital fights emerged again. The new dance expanded into a sequence alternating between marital fighting and uniting around Larry's depression. Once the couple realized that their relationship repertoire was quite limited, a feeling of pessimism and hopelessness permeated their lives. This particular "solution" became inadequate.

In the course of all this, mother's unhappiness may have made her more reactive towards her son's lack of responsibility. Mother and son developed a series of fighting and distancing moves in their relationship. When the conflict between mother and son got heated enough, father came out of his depression and began to support Heather in her battles with George. At this point, the marriage united around

George's problems, instead of Larry's depression. It is as if the system "offered" the players options as to where the problem would emerge: in father, in the marriage, or in George.

It is almost impossible to see this dance if we keep our eye focused only on the dancers. The molecular pattern will not emerge in the field of observation. Observing the dance sequences through time is invaluable in detecting the patterns. The atomic view can take you only so far in understanding the human experience. It offers participants fewer options for effective solutions.

This particular pattern of interaction developed when George was in high school. During his high school years, parental involvement would alternate between enmeshing and distancing. When George was doing well, the parents became distant from George and from each other. When stress was high, George would dysfunction in some way, and then the parents would become intrusively enmeshed by taking charge of George's life in ways that enabled his dependency.

So when George left for college, his problems escalated to the point where Larry and Heather had to become involved in more drastic ways. However, the parents' solution took the form of "distancing" George from them in a structured manner. This is when Heather called her sister, Carol.

This stage of the story evokes the roles that distancing and enmeshing play in handling anxiety in relationships. When the anxiety becomes too high, our general moves are fight or fight. Flight involves distance or avoidance/denial in some way. Fight, on the other hand, is a way of enmeshing into the problem through overinvolvement. These are the classic ways of attempting anxiety-driven solutions. Like the Atman project, they become failed substitutes for the resolution. Neither fight nor flight addresses the real self, and, therefore, there is no real encounter with loved ones. Soul needs are not adequately met.

PRINCIPLE 3

THE LOWER THE LEVEL OF SELF-MASTERY, THE GREATER THE EMOTIONAL DISTANCING OR ENMESHMENT IN THE FAMILY.

When we hear the phrase "emotional cutoff," emphasis needs to be placed on the word *emotional*. Otherwise, only the image of distancing will emerge. Most of us will think only of people who rarely see their original family members. Emotional cutoff, however, also includes the enmeshing pattern in which people either capitulate to avoid conflict or fight frequently without much resolution. In either manifestation of the enmeshing pattern, true dialogue is at a minimum and is therefore a form of cutoff.

In the distancing pattern, individuality is not expressed adequately. Conversely, in the enmeshing patterns, belonging is not experienced significantly. They are ineffective substitutes for genuine individuality and belonging.

A good way to grasp emotional cutoff is to understand its polar opposite: a genuine person-to-person relationship, as described in earlier chapters. In the effective dyad, two people have a wide range of flexibility to be themselves and to establish empathy with one another. Family therapists tell us that there is a strong correlation between emotional cutoff and personal reactivity.

The greater the emotional cutoff (distancing or intruding),
the greater the level of emotional grenades triggered in the relationships
of that person. Blunting intimacy by distancing or enmeshing is a way to
"cope" with emotional grenades. Fight or flight are the classic
manifestations of emotional cutoff.

Emotional cutoff may be aggravated by geographical distance. However, physical distance, by itself, is not a true measure of cutoff. The essence of cutoff is lack of emotional contact between people. We can maintain good emotional rapport with our loved ones who are far away, even across continents. It is important to maintain this contact for the robustness of our individuality and our belonging.

The lure of cutoff is that it may temporarily relieve the anxiety about our present issues. Heather and Larry experienced some relief in the knowledge that George was going to be the responsibility of Carol and Norman. It was also a relief for George, at least until his own inadequacies and fears emerged in the new setting.

It is important to spot the different faces of cutoff. Cutoff from our family of origin will manifest itself in our marriage, our parenting, our work, and various aspects of our personal life, sometimes including physical symptoms. Let's listen to what two experts say about the manifestations of emotional cutoff:

When spouses are pressuring one another for more "loyalty," they are doing the same thing to each other that they criticize the extended family for doing. If one or both spouses give in to the pressure to cut off more from families of origin, they take half the problem with them. Cutoff may relieve immediate pressure and lower anxiety, but the person's basic vulnerabilities to intense relationships remain unchanged. The more complete the cutoff with the past, the more likely it is that a more intense version of the past (or its mirror image) will be repeated in the present.

–Michael Kerr and Murray Bowen[1]

PRINCIPLE 4

TO GAIN SELF-MASTERY AND EMOTIONAL CONTACT IN OUR FAMILY OF ORIGIN, WE NEED TO SEE OUR PART IN THE MOLECULAR DANCE.

We cannot escape our past. We need to understand that the past lives in us in the form of stories. Events are done. It is in this sense that we hear people say that "the past is past." However, the past lives in the maps, meanings, or interpretations of the ways the "world out there" works. These deeply held assumptions about life are fashioned as events interact with the jewels of our soul. The patterns in our early childhood and adolescence are especially rich in material for rewriting of stories.

These maps or stories about our past experiences significantly influence our automatic responses to events, especially our emotional grenades. We can reauthor our lives by rewriting the stories about our past. This kind of rewriting will also color the way the future looks to us.

In order to reauthor our past effectively, it is essential to see our part in the dance. Although we have made this point before, it is worth emphasizing it here. Let me turn once more to Kerr and Bowen to highlight this principle:

> If one does not see himself as part of the system, his only options are either to try to get others to change or to withdraw. If one sees himself as part of the system, he has a new option: to stay in contact

with others and change self ... Seeing oneself as part of the system in one's original family enhances one's ability to see oneself as part of the system in one's nuclear family. The same dilemma exists in the nuclear family that exists in the family of origin: If one does not see oneself as part of the system (one is blaming self or blaming others), the only options when problems arise are to attempt to change others or to withdraw. In contrast, if one can see self as part of one's nuclear family system (and the problems in it), it becomes possible to be more of an individual without disrupting any relationships. This results in a calmer system, one in which people are better able to stay in comfortable emotional contact, even during difficult times.

–Michael Kerr and Murray Bowen[2]

The principle of seeing oneself as part of the dance is part of the reason for putting a great deal of emphasis on the way we view cause and effect. The metaphor of pebbles and grenades allows us to view the events and yet see our part of the dance. We view our responses as our contribution to the dance. In the early chapters, we learned to keep an eye on the atom of self while also watching the molecular dance among selves.

We are responsible for the pebbles we throw, yet we cannot control the way people ripple. That is a comment on their nature and on how they have authored their experiences. People are magical ponds with the ability to trigger ripples in each other. Some of these pebbles trigger grenades. It is in the mutual dance of pebbles and grenades that we find the greatest opportunity to grow. We must not use cutoff as a solution. Rather, we need the strength and the humility to see our role so that we can change our part of the dance based on our own beliefs and values.

The ability to see our part in the dance takes love and compassion. This is where our spiritual values can help support our journey of self-mastery. Valuing and respecting others are necessary underpinnings for staying connected with our loved ones even when the scales of justice are unbalanced against us.

PRINCIPLE 5

IT IS IMPORTANT TO FULFILL OUR OBLIGATIONS TO OUR FAMILY OF ORIGIN WHETHER OR NOT THEY RECIPROCATE IN KIND.

Our parents gave birth to us, held us, suffered with us, worried about us, got exasperated in their dealings with us, and much more. We owe them a great emotional debt. We need to pay them back, if we are to be free of this debt. The idea behind fulfilling our obligations to our family of origin is based partly on the notion of emotional indebtedness. It also stems from the great commandment to love our neighbor as we would love ourselves. Our family is the closest neighborhood.

One of the lessons I learned from Ivan Boszormenyi-Nagy,[3] a Hungarian-born family therapist in Philadelphia, was to realize that we all carry an emotional ledger of accounts. This is especially true in relation to our families of origin. It is important to keep this ledger in balance so that we do not avoid or overmanage our significant relationships. One way to do this is to be clear about the nature of our obligations to our extended family.

Most of our parents tell us that we do not owe them anything. They will attest to the fact that they freely chose to bring us into the world and accepted the responsibility of raising us into adulthood. Most parents who say this mean exactly what they say. Still, these words do not erase the reality that, emotionally, we carry this debt. The intent of our parents is good. They may wish to lower the burden of expectations. And that is good. But the task still remains.

The journey of self-mastery requires balancing this emotional ledger. If we do not keep it balanced with our extended family, we will find this ledger unbalanced in other relationships as well, particularly in our intimate world.

We start this balancing process by honoring them as our parents, brothers, sisters, grandparents, grandchildren, uncles, aunts, nieces, and nephews. Although it is impossible to repay our parents dollar for dollar or sweat for sweat, it is important to pay them back some way. Gratitude is the grand way to this place of balance.

Gratitude is the great equalizer.

Expressing our thanks to our loved ones goes a long way toward balancing our accounts. Such a show of gratitude also comes in the form of meeting obligations to our extended family. Each of us needs to determine what our *minimum obligations* are. We need to be quite clear what *minimum* means and that our minimum obligations reflect our beliefs, not those of our parents. They certainly will have different ideas about what minimum means.

IF WE DO NOT MEET OUR MINIMUM OBLIGATIONS

Our minimum obligations reflect our inner sense of justice and fairness. If we fail to meet these obligations, we are vulnerable to feelings of guilt and shame. Guilt and shame weaken our position in relationships and will contribute to our being reactive. We will be inclined to succumb to pressure or to defend our posture aggressively.

It is important to take a proactive attitude in meeting our obligations to our family. For couples, each one needs to determine a different set of obligations. Each spouse needs to take responsibility for making sure these obligations are fulfilled in an acceptable manner. One way to detect emotional cutoff is to see if there is imbalance in the quality of contact between a husband and his family and the wife and her family. A husband who distances from his family of origin becomes emotionally distant or enmeshed in his nuclear family. The same is true for the wife.

PRINCIPLE 6

IT IS HELPFUL TO SEE OUR FAMILY OF ORIGIN AS A RESOURCE FOR SELF-DEFINITION AND AS A SOURCE OF SIGNIFICANT SUPPORT.

There is a tremendous advantage in visiting "home" as an adult. We are no longer dependent on our family financially and legally. This independence gives us more of an opportunity to stay in an emotionally neutral position while we are observing ourselves in contact with our family members. We see all over again the patterns that influenced us as a child. We will likely experience the same old childish feelings. Familiar grenades will probably explode within us. So, we may need to mine those jewels periodically in order to remain a viable participant-observer.

The family of origin then can be a potent resource for self-discovery and self-definition. If we can remain real while in contact with our loved ones, we will grow in our capacity to experience belonging and individuality. As this happens, we will feel the kind of support that is difficult to experience in any other relationship. However, we need to be willing to give of ourselves without placating or capitulating.

This capacity to be a real self with our loved ones is part of self-mastery.

PRINCIPLE 7

THE PRIMARY GOAL OF WORKING WITH OUR FAMILY OF ORIGIN IS TO CHANGE OURSELVES, NOT OUR FAMILY MEMBERS.

In my therapy work, one of the biggest objections I get from clients has to do with why I have them contact their family of origin. I often hear statements like this: "Why should I give them the pleasure of a visit when they haven't done anything for me in a long time!" The other common objection goes more like this: "Every time I go home, I just get worse. I do much better if I stay away from them." Emotional pain or comfort is the criterion often used to evaluate the experience of going home.

Among the best reasons to do our part include the following:

- The main reason to stay in contact with our extended family and to fulfill our obligations is for our own well-being. Since the family of origin is one of the best places to discover important things about us, it is useful to renew our contacts now and then. That is a spiritually grounded reason, and not a selfish one.

- Another reason to do it is for the sake of love. These are surely some of the people we should serve as part of our personal mission, as we shall see in the next chapter. Why not serve those whose destinies are intertwined with ours?

- This work is among the best things we can do for our marriage and for our children. It is good for the next generation. Even if we don't have children, our personal work in self-mastery benefits our relationships, including our social and occupational life.

289

PRINCIPLE 8

MAINTAIN CLEAR BOUNDARIES BETWEEN OURSELVES AND OUR FAMILY OF ORIGIN WHILE MAKING CONTACT.

As adults, we have our own life to live and our own mission to fulfill. As parents, we need to let our children make a life for themselves in the way they see fit. As adult children, we need to live our own life. It is actually freeing for parents to know that they cannot drive us anymore, even when they try. If we have a family of our own, clarity of boundaries means that our identity as a nuclear family is clear and secure. It also means that our loved ones are freer to enter those boundaries, knowing that they are welcome by choice, not by pressure or obligation.

The journey toward maturity means that we and our parents have become co-equals as adults in society. This bridging of the hierarchical gap takes many years of loving, honest contact between the generations. It is a gradual process that leads to an acceptance of each other's right to be who we are. We hope to experience the freedom to pursue a lifestyle based on our own social, religious, and political values and beliefs.

One of the clearest signs of true personal freedom is our capacity to accept our family of origin and give up the project of trying to change them. When we are overresponsible in relation to family members, we tend to cross boundaries of responsibility and become anxious about their actions. Not being responsible for what they do does not mean that we do not care about them. Far from it.

Caring and responsibility are different dimensions of a relationship. When we love someone, we experience joy and pain along with them, precisely because we care. Caring is a position of goodwill in relation to another human being. We wish them well. We often ebb

and flow with them precisely because we have an emotional investment in their well-being. This is the fruit of empathy.

Responsibility is a position. It answers the question of who is
responsible for a certain task. The difference is important. When
boundaries of responsibility are clear, our self-esteem does not depend
on other people's actions. The way we evaluate ourselves depends
much more on our actions than on their evaluation of us. That
razor's-edge difference makes a big difference in the relational dance.

When a loved one is in pain, I feel the pain. But, hopefully, that
loved one does not have the additional weight of wondering whether
that pain is derailing me from my life's mission or meaning. That task
is my responsibility.

IN A NUTSHELL

The ability to be a genuine individual with someone you know
well and live with on a daily basis is among the most rewarding
accomplishments in life. It takes a high level of self-mastery. This is
another way of saying that developing and maintaining an intimate
relationship with a mate is a challenging endeavor. It is well worth the
rewards. The keys to success in this matter revolve around three
major qualities: (1) a commitment of will strong enough to stay put
when grenades are exploding within us, (2) the courage to mine the
jewels within those grenades, and (3) the love and empathy to negotiate actions on the basis of jewels, not on the heat of grenades.

Our interactions with mate and friends provide some of the viable
relationships that can strengthen us along the path of self-mastery.
The quality of those ties depends partly on the way we relate to our
family of origin. As we saw, the family is the ultimate manifestation of
the "neighbor," whom we are commanded to love. Therefore, it is
worthwhile to give careful thought to the ways that we relate to our
extended family.

With that thought in mind, we are well advised to put emotional cutoff from our family of origin on the shelf of last resort. I make this statement with due compassion for those who have extremely difficult relationships with parents and siblings. These are the situations when we need to think carefully about why we would even consider fulfilling our minimum obligations to the original family.

We may elect to work with a family therapist about ways of making useful contact with our family. We may have to plan the calls and visits carefully, making them relatively short. We may need to have a specific strategy in mind as we make contact. Progressive steps might be the only way to make any kind of useful contact. If it has to be that way, that is what we need to do. And we do it for our own sake, for our marriage, and for our children. We do it simply because destiny has ordained that these are some of the people we need to love and with whom we need to define who we are.

If we use *justice* as the standard for contacting and fulfilling our obligations to our family origin, we will often retreat from those opportunities. *Love* is the only standard that will work: love of our own soul, love of God, and our fellow human beings. This is the proactive position: acting on the basis of our beliefs, regardless of what the others do. We do unto others as we would have them do unto us, *even if they don't do unto us.*

When we can live by this principle of self-mastery in our family of origin, we will be able to do so with others. We need to be patient with ourselves and with the efforts that others make toward us. Life is developmental, progressive, complex, mysterious, and wonderfully rich.

---

[1] Kerr, M. and Bowen, M. (1988). *Family Evaluation.* New York: W. W. Norton, p. 272.

[2] Ibid., pp. 272-273.

[3] Boszormenyi-Nagy, I. and Sparks, G. (1973). *Invisible Loyalties.* New York: Harper and Row.

Epilogue

Mystics often compare our relationship to God with the relationship between parent and child. There is a special bond between progenitor and offspring even in the biological sphere. Imagine how much more personal and intimate this bond must be between us and God, out of whose image and likeness we were fashioned. We came as a "spark of light" from the very essence of God. To start the journey of self-mastery, let us commit to making union with God our primary goal in life.

Theologians and mystics tell us that we have existed in God's mind from eternity. This is one of those mysteries that we can only vaguely fathom from the profound depths of our being. It takes faith. It takes contemplation. However, our faith can make that mystery real and vital in our daily lives. To realize that God loves us and knows us uniquely and personally is a deeply healing awareness. This feeling of belonging and being known uniquely is much like the feeling of belonging and acceptance we may experience in our families.

Destiny is not set at the moment of birth, even if some important givens are in effect: the family, the country, the race, and the social class into which we are born. Every significant decision we make puts us into a new set of circumstances. If we go to a certain school, start a business, or accept a new job, we will be involved with people and social structures that we didn't fully engineer. If we marry someone, we marry into a whole new destiny of facts and patterns with which we must learn to dance.

From the start, we are confronted with mystery: our personal relationship with God, the discovery of our soul blueprint-our contract with God-and the facts and events meted out to us by the hand of destiny. Yet the self is there at every moment, responding and participating as a co-creator with God in the unfolding of these realities. You and I are responsible for our response, yet we are not in control of the pebbles thrown into our lives. Do we need faith? Is there an alternative to faith?

EXERCISE: COMMITING TO THE PATH OF SELF-MASTERY

A PRAYER

Take a comfortable posture and a few deep breaths. As you breathe in, deepen your realization that God is in you. As you breathe out, deepen your realization that God is everywhere around you and beyond you. Through God, you are one with the entire universe. Say the following prayer:

"Dear God, I consciously and willingly offer my life to you and to your purposes. I submit my body, my thoughts, my feelings, my wishes, my relationships, my possessions, and my circumstances to you. I choose to discover, daily, the unfolding of your will in my life. I know that your will represents my highest good and that of the universe. I know that the deepest yearning in my being is to be united with you. I accept my soul blueprint, my mission in life, as the surest path towards oneness with you. I accept your grace in my life. And this blessing I wish also for all beings in this earth and in the entire universe. Amen. So be it. Let it be done according to your will."

We carry a unique "light signature" in our spirit/soul. Our soul jewels have unique reflections of the divine that only we can shine. When we pray, we are radiating these individual sparks throughout the universe, enriching it in a way that no one else can. We are truly blessing the world. Prayer, contemplation, and service are ways of participating with God in lifting creation to reflect its divine blueprint.

The path of self-mastery is an act of will. Our willing participation is a prerequisite.

INDEX

About the Author

Ramon G. Corrales, Ph.D., is an author, organizational consultant, family therapist, and seminar leader in self-development and organizational teambuilding. He has over 27 years of experience as an organizational consultant and as a family therapist in private practice. Dr. Corrales' strategic wisdom as a consultant and therapist is encompassed in his masterful approach as a trainer of professionals and a leader in self-development workshops. The self-mastery approach to therapy, developed Dr. Corrales, views the whole person (physical, emotional, mental, spiritual) in a relational context.

Dr. Corrales is founder and director of the Self-Mastery Center, a personal and organizational development center with a consulting, training, and research focus based in Kansas City, Missouri. He is also the author of *Marriage Foundations: Getting the Right Start* (Marriage Foundations for Newlyweds, 1999).

Dr. Corrales received his doctorate from the University of Minnesota in sociology with specialization in family therapy. He is an approved supervisor and a clinical member of the American Association for Marriage and Family Therapy and is a trained practitioner in Neuro-Linguistic Programming (NLP) and a certified Kolbe™ Consultant.

Dr. Corrales may be contacted at the Self-Mastery Center, 9201

St   1e:
81   **CORPORATE MASTERY USA**
9001 W. 110th St., Se. 260, Overland Park, KS 66210
PH: (913) 906-9330 **E-mail:** info@masterycenter.com

SELF-MASTERY

Mission and Meaning in Modern Life

RAMON G. CORRALES, Ph.D.

To order your copy fill out this order form and send to the address below.

Name

Company

Address

City/State/Zip

Phone Number

SELF-MASTERY

Mission and Meaning in Modern Life

RAMON G. CORRALES, Ph.D.

Price per copy	**$18.95**
Quantity ordered	
Subtotal	
Sales tax*	
Shipping and handling**	
Total	

*Please add Missouri sales tax of 7.1% for books shipped to Missouri addresses.
**Please add $3 per book for shipping and handling.
Allow 30 days for delivery.
Full payment must accompany your order.
Prices subject to change without notice.

Quantity orders invited. Please write for bulk account prices.

Checks payable to:

CORPORATE MASTERY USA
9001 W. 110th St., Se. 260, Overland Park, KS 66210
PH: (913) 906-9330 **E-mail:** info@masterycenter.com